The St

Jesus'

Soul Evolution

by Charles Fillmore

Editor and Compiler: Rev. Toni G. Boehm, Ph. D.
Dean (Retired)
Unity School for Religious Studies

Charles Fillmore, author; compiler, Rev. Toni G. Boehm

The Story of Jesus' Soul Evolution

Inner Visioning Press
430 N. Winnebago Dr.
Greenwood, MO 64034
816-304-3044

The image is meant to depict the Unified Field of Consciousness and
the waves of Possibility that surround us, at all times!

Publisher Inner Visioning Press
Published by Lightning Source
Printed in the United States of America

ISBN: **9798427098373**

1. Body, Mind & Spirit
2. Self-help
Title: The Story of Jesus' Soul Evolution

Charles Fillmore, author; compiler, Rev. Toni G. Boehm

Charles Fillmore, author; compiler, Rev. Toni G. Boehm

Table of Contents

Prelude

Acknowledgment

Introduction

Birth

Baptism

Wilderness

Demonstration

Gethsemane

Crucifixion/Tomb

Resurrection/Ascension

About the Editor

Note: This document was created as part of an on-going project through, Awakening Awareness Ministries; Rev. Toni G. Boehm, founder. It is intentionally dedicated to both the sharing of the metaphysical and mystical works of Charles Fillmore, and the birthing of the soul's remembrance.

Charles Fillmore, author; compiler, Rev. Toni G. Boehm

Charles Fillmore, author; compiler, Rev. Toni G. Boehm

The Story of Jesus'
Soul Evolution
by Charles Fillmore
August 8, 1947
Permission for use granted by Unity ®

This is the last major work that Charles Fillmore, co-founder of Unity, completed prior to his transition in 1948. Unity Library received the manuscript on August 8, 1947. The manuscript was placed into an unpublished Fillmore file, where it remained until 1995 for a very brief surfacing; then it was "hidden" again, until it was truly discovered, in 2006. This 1947 work is a metaphysical and mystical masterpiece that vibrates and sizzles with spiritual energy that feels like it is coming to you directly from Mr. Fillmore's lips.

The original manuscript is over 600 pages of metaphysical interpretation of the soul's evolution as experienced by the master teacher Jesus, and as described in the Gospels; as he consciously awakened his I AM Template, per Mr. Fillmore. Fillmore presents his interpretation, as if the Synoptic Gospels were woven together into one tapestry. A tapestry that creates a complete and continuing story of the evolutionary events and initiations in the life of Jesus as he fully awakens the inherent, universal, I AM blueprint that resides in all of us.

Mr. Fillmore states in talks entitled *Regeneration* (1930) and *4th Dimension and Its Work in Man* (1932); *"If one wants to know the journey of the soul as it evolves and grows through regeneration, look at the life of Jesus through his seven major initiations."* I have taken the liberty to divide the original manuscript according to those seven major initiation events.

Please note that this material should come with a warning label: *"Be prepared to experience deep changes within the confines of the subconscious mind as you delve into the depth of this material!"*

In a consciousness of sacred service,

Toni G. Boehm

Rev. Toni G. Boehm, Ph.D.
Awakening Awareness Ministry
Dean, Unity School for Religious Studies (Retired)

Acknowledgments

When I was first introduced to the original manuscript in the Unity Archives, it profoundly touched my soul. In prayer, I received guidance that this valuable information was to be shared with Unity ministers, Licensed Unity Teachers and others interested in studying the works of this great American mystic. That it was to be taken; *"out of the Archives and into our lives."* Thus, the original manuscript was scanned as a .pdf document and offered to those in the Unity movement. There was a great response to the offer. After receiving the material, many wrote back to say – *"This is wonderful material but how can I get it in electronic form so I can use for Sunday lessons, classes, newsletters, articles, etc.?"*

Thus, was born, by and through Spirit, an idea to gather a small group of interested people to type and proof a segment of the original document. The invitation to participate received a resounding, Yes!

Our team transcribed the manuscript word for word from the original, proofed and edited it. It is the fruit of the labor of love and sacred service of these special folks that I acknowledge. Some of those mentioned below had support from others, so to all the unsung heroes not mentioned, thank you for your sacred service.

Rev. David Ridge	(document designer, conversion coordinator, verifier, typist)
Rev. Sam Bowman	(reader, typist)
Priscilla Richards	(Director [retired] of Unity Archives & Library, typist)
Rev. Steve Maynard	(creator of original index)
Rev. Toni G. Boehm	(project coordinator, typist)

And thank you to the Archives staff for their continued care of the Fillmore materials.

NOTE:

1. The numbers on the right-hand side of the page (e.g., 1-2.) correspond to Charles Fillmore's original manuscript pages.

    a. These page numbers were retained to support the reader in case they would like to refer to the original manuscript.

    b. Editorial liberty was taken, however, to create series of page numbers that match the source manuscript. They are grouped to identify the entire segment of either an interpretation or scripture. This allows electronic phrase searches while still preserving the embedded page references.

2. Bullets were utilized instead of paragraph indentations in the Interpretation section to make this document easier to read and use.

3. The headings Birth, Baptism, Wilderness, Demonstration thru Ministry/Transfiguration, Gethsemane, Crucifixion, and

Resurrection/Ascension are the seven major life events/initiations experienced by Jesus; as identified by Charles Fillmore. These initiations were presented in a series of lessons, entitled *Regeneration,* May 1930 and again in 1933. They are not, however, part of the original document; they are an editorial addition meant to provide clarity and understanding of the soul's evolution and spiritual maturation and mastery process.

Charles Fillmore, author; compiler, Rev. Toni G. Boehm

Introduction

Rev. Toni G. Boehm, Ph.D.

Have you ever experienced one of those moments in life, when something unexpected and extraordinary happened? Something that you were totally unprepared for, yet through its happening, your life was altered or changed, perhaps, forever?

This is what I call, Synchro-divinity, at work! Synchronicity, or the vibrational upgrade, Synchro-divinity, is one of those moments when something awesome is up in the universe and you have been "elected" to play a part in it, or to be the star of it. Have you experienced; an "out of the blue moment" where a book drops at your feet? Did you take a turn on street that you were not intentionally headed for; and you "accidentally bump" into someone that changed your life dramatically? Or, did the phone ring and an invitation was extended that ended up changing your life as you know it?

Synchro-divinity is a soul attraction. People, places, books, events, and more are attracted into your life by a invisible higher soul influence and they are brought in to support you and/or to provide emphasis to something going on in your life ~ that is preparing you for the next movement in your souls evolution. Synchro-divinities come to us because we are "energetically" aligned with an invisible force, through the quantum field energetic connection of all is One. This invisible force that arises out of the quantum unified field of consciousness, contains all possibility and potential, and has the capacity to effortlessly move you in order that you might be at the right place, at the right time, and ready for the lesson or idea that is ripe to be emphasized, and/or experienced. It does this because you are prepared for a next level experience in consciousness.

As the soul evolves, as your energy ascends and attunes with higher levels and dimensions of awareness, life becomes filled with these meaningful synchro-divinities. These are more than coincidences, for they are attracted and/or created through an invisible energy that is working for you in the indivisible realms. The more consciously aware you are of how the soul evolves and creates, the faster these types of soul demonstrations occur within and around you.

I would invite you to take a moment to recall a few of your own personal synchro-divine experiences and the feeling of change for good, that it made in your life. These synchro-divinity experiences have the capacity to change lives forever and this is where my story begins, with two major synchro-divine events.

The first synchro-divine event that occurred happened as I was in the kitchen cooking spaghetti and listening to Pavarotti. The phone rang, and is is customary, I picked it up and said, "hello." On the other end of the line was a dear friend, who as

Charles Fillmore, author; compiler, Rev. Toni G. Boehm

conference speaker coordinator for the Unity South East region, was inviting me to keynote at their annual conference. He mentioned that the topic selected for the conference was, "*Unity: A Healing Revival.*"[i] After a few more exchanges of information, I accepted his invitation. Little did I know how this synchro-divine event that appeared as a keynote invitation, would be a life-transforming event.

As is my custom, when preparing for a Unity talk or workshop, I wanted to see what Charles Fillmore, co-founder with his wife Myrtle of Unity School of Christianity, had to say about the topics of healing and revival. So, my first stop was the Unity Library Archives[ii]. I figured there would be plenty about healing, but, revival, I was not quite as hopeful.

To my joy I found that one of the articles pulled by the Unity Library Archives staff was from *Weekly Unity*[iii] and was written by Mr. Fillmore and was about a current revival occurring in Christianity. This lead to me to review the entire magazine and behold, there was an advertisement about the first-ever, Unity conference. It was going to be held at Unity, in just a few months. The conference was entitled, "*Unity, a Healing Revival*"[iv] and was going to occur July 1-14, 1923. This first-ever Unity conference was going to happen at 10th and Tracy in Kansas City and it was promising to be quite the "Holy Spirit" experience.

As a side note, many Unity students are under the impression that the first Unity conference was the "tent-city" conference of 1928. It was the first conference held on the "Unity farm," which is what is now known as Unity Village. However, as I had just discovered, that was a mis-perception, for here in my hand was proof of Unity's first recorded conference; and it was held at 10th and Tracy. Its topic was – Unity, Healing, and Revival.

I was thrilled to find this material and additionally, to discover, that at the conference Mr. Fillmore, each night gave a talk, thus, there were fourteen talks in total. As a student of Unity this was for me, a rich discovery. I was in awe as read Mr. Fillmore's keynote address, on July 1, 1923 and his sharing with the conference attendees of what Unity is, what Unity isn't, what Unity stands for, and how he and Myrtle created this "work" called Unity.

As a Unity student, I was mesmerized with all of it. His words were rich with ideas about Unity that I had never heard before. He spoke of a "*Beginner's Six-Day Healing and Treatment Pamphlet*"[v] that had been used in Silent Unity successfully for 35 years and was the foundation of their healing process. This material was a part of a work that I personally had not heard of before – the *Unity Correspondence Course (U.C.C.).* U.C.C. was originally written in 1909 and became the primer for all Unity study until approximately 1972, when its use was set aside for something that was less staff intensive. Thus, was the beginning of the use of the *Foundations of Unity.* The original U.C.C., was divided into two sections: the Preparatory Lessons (six in total) and the Advanced Lessons (twelve in total) . The student had to answer twenty questions at the end of each section, which they then sent to Unity for grading. Thus, the desire for a work that was less staff intensive.

Charles Fillmore, author; compiler, Rev. Toni G. Boehm

Returning to the conference keynote address that Mr. Fillmore gave; he mentions over and over, the word regeneration, in such a way, that it was like I was hearing it for the first time. Then I realized, that what I was "hearing" was more of an energetic feeling and that that energy was being exuded from the pages as I read them. I felt the power of Spirit that had been imbued in these talks. I also felt a subtle knowing that something new was awakening in me. Suddenly, I remembered something I had read by Mr. Fillmore, years and years ago. I believe it was written under Mr. Fillmore's' pen name, Leo Virgo, which he used at the beginning of his writing career with Unity. Regardless, which name he used, he described how people were writing in and asking what was it that they were feeling when they opened the Unity material, for they felt something tangible. He said it was the vibration of Spirit that was imbued into the writings and that yes indeed it was a tangible energy.

After reading several articles and feeling the building of the energetic vibrations that were thrilling through my being, I then picked up another one of Mr. Fillmore's 1923 conference talks and as I read it, a line jumped right off the page and actually made me gasp.

"... Both the Genesis allegory & Jesus' great life events [seven initiations] are primarily designed to show the process for the unfoldment of the spiritual consciousness in the individual – they are the story of regeneration – which is the great theme underlying all scripture – seen by those who have eyes to see! [vi]

In that instant I realized that regeneration, as I was now coming to understand it, and Jesus' great life events [his seven initiations] were the process of the soul's evolution as it ascends into higher dimensional awareness and the realization of the I AM as the dominant vibration of being. In other words, in Unity speak, as we "take on" the fullness of the Christ Consciousness/Christ Frequency.

Next, I was also led to the *Unity Correspondence Course,*[vii] [UCC] which having been in Unity for over thirty years at that time ~ I did not consciously remembered ever having been introduced to, previously, by any teacher. And to be sure, I was taught by some of the greats, Eric Butterworth, Sig and Janie Paulson, Martha and Frank Guidici, and Ed Rabel, just to name a few.

The U.C.C., for me, was some of the clearest and most organized writings of Charles Fillmore that I had ever read. It opened my heart and mind to a greater understanding and awareness of what Mr. Fillmore was expressing about the role of regeneration in the souls evolution and how Jesus' life was the blueprint or template for that evolution, through what Mr. Fillmore called the awakening of the I AM Template.

I began to gather bits and pieces from the *Unity Correspondence Course, the Revealing Word, 4th Dimension in Man, Holy Spirit and It's Works in Man,* and many other sources in order to compile an outline of what I thought might be included in the seven great life events or initiations of Jesus; that supported him in the full realization of the I AM Template/Blueprint. After, I had initiated possibilities for how growth occurred through the seven life initiations of Jesus, another synchro-divinity experience occurred.

I was in the Unity Archives again, when I happened upon, a lesson by Mr. Fillmore on *Regeneration*[viii], in which he shared the following: *"Luke is the only evangelist who records all seven of the great events in the life of Jesus."*

I gasped, here I had been working diligently on the creation of these seven initiations, sensing and knowing that somewhere, Mr. Fillmore had articulated them; but that just did not know where to look and viola', the initiations appear.

According to Mr. Fillmore in that article, the seven great life events or initiations include:

> 1. *Birth*
> 2. *Baptism*
> 3. *Wilderness/Temptation*
> 4. *Demonstration thru Ministry & Transfiguration*
> 5. *Gethsemane*
> 6. *Crucifixion/Tomb*
> 7. *Resurrection/Ascension.*

Something in my soul vibrated when I found this information and called me to continue searching and delving deeper into the material. For a year, I continued to plumb the depths of the teachings of the *Unity Correspondence Course*, and this idea of the soul's journey being revealed in the life of Jesus and thus, the Gospels. I read the Gospels, continued my research, meditated, prayed, and created what I thought was a good metaphysical rendering of soul's evolution as presented in the Gospels and Jesus' life.

Little did I realize that this idea would send me forth on a journey of discovery that would open new vistas beyond my wildest imagination and that it would imbue my mind with ideas, that would ultimately shift, forever, my soul and its evolutionary path.

All of this was such a powerful experience and now I know that it was just preparing me for the next synchro-divine event that would occur within a year or so. For more than just finding the material needed for a keynote message, I was being prepared for an initiation to a new level of awareness of my own personal ascension of *Soul Evolution* and *Soul Mastery.*

As need would have it, I went to research something in the Unity Archives again, when yet another synchro-divinity occurrence happened. I met a friend there who asked me if I would like to see a copy of a work by Fillmore that had just been pulled by the Archives staff, it was from 1947. In my hands I found a 600 page document, entitled, *The Story of Jesus' Soul Evolution.* The moment I picked it up an energy "thrilled" throughout my being and I knew that I was holding – destiny – my own.

A knowing flooded my being and I realized that this manuscript in my hands was the last major piece of metaphysical interpretation work Charles Fillmore left the world – as part of his legacy. AND – that for the most part it had not seen the light of day since 1947. In that moment, I heard the interior voice say, *"The time is now."* I knew it was referring to the manuscript.

The Archivist shared with me that this manuscript had been rejected for publication by Unity Editorial Staff in 1947, and thus Mr. Fillmore at the age of 92, on August, 7, 1947 brought the manuscript to the library to be placed in an archival file for safe keeping ~ until the world was ready. Holding that manuscript, I began to cry for I had been working several years on piecing a puzzle together – the relationship of the Creative Mind Process of Genesis and Jesus' seven great life events in the Gospels, and how they worked in tandem, metaphysically and literally, to evolve the soul through regeneration – and here Fillmore had already created a prototype.

I opened the manuscript and began to read. Each word, was like a healing balm to my soul. New presentations of ideas by Mr. Fillmore were jumping off the page, I was in awe. My soul knew the world was ready now, for this material, the "world-heart" had been sufficiently opened that these words would not go unheeded by Unity Truth students. In that moment, I knew what was mine to do – to bring this work back to life.

The work presented here is as Mr. Fillmore wrote it; however, editorial license has been taken to divide the sections of the manuscript into the seven great life events of Jesus soul evolution. This was done in hopes that the reader might better identify with journey in the context of their own life.

Therefore, as you read each life event and its metaphysical interpretation, consider how each event has unfolded in your life experience. Remember, the evolutionary process is a spiral and you experience each event or initiation over and over, as reach new rungs on the spiral. I have even come to see that you can have an life-changing experience and that experience will take through all the events or initiation. So, this idea of initiations is multi-layered, multi-dimensional and repeated over and over; for you must deactivate old patterns and clear the systems of your being on multi-levels of being: eco-bio-neuro-psyhic-chemical-physical-mental-emotional-karmic-spiritual-etheric.

As you enter each initiation as revealed through the life of the Master Teacher, Jesus; I invite you to ask yourself questions regarding the elements and characters that are revealed. Charles Fillmore said, as shared per Ed Rabel, "*Honest self-observation is the prelude to Christ Consciousness.*" Meaning you cannot fully awaken and realize the inherent I AM template, without being honest with yourself about who you and how you are showing up, in every moment.

Using the Birth Initiation as an example, you can ask of self, questions such as: What was my birth story? What is my lineage? Where am I in the family line-up? Do we carry a family prophecy? How is it that lineage and prophecy still influencing me today? Do I believe the family story or legacy, such as, "all our men die young"? Or, do I believe that because I am of a certain ethnicity, so people do not respect me. Or, I believe I am a victim of my heritage? Have I really made peace with my religious past?

After you ask yourself these questions, journal your answers, this will support you in keeping a conscious time-line of your growth and expansion. Additionally, I invite you to ask yourself, "*Am I ready to be the energetic placeholder for something new to be birthed through me that will shift me in consciousness, and be a new legacy for my family?*" If your answer is "*yes*" then what are you willing to do to take one sweet, small step forward in consciousness, to make that happen?

I am willing to:

_____

With each initiation/life event ask yourself questions such as these. The intention for participating with this material is *conscious* soul evolution. Conscious soul evolution can only come about as we are awake to *what is,* so practice true self-honesty and self-observation when you answer these questions. In other words, do not try to paint a pretty picture or pretend what happened, didn't happen. Also, as you experience the drama and trauma of life, be willing to let go of the negative energy that you hold around them, as you are willing it's energetic charge will deactivate and dissolve. It's all energy, and your work is not to deny it, hide it, run from it, or … The work is to be present to the energy, in whatever form it has taken in your life ~ horrible mother, overbearing father, abandonment, rape ~ what ever form ~ and shift it into something more interesting ~ soul growth and expansion of awareness.

I have found that the Birth Initiation isn't just about the birth experience, it is a holographic experience, and each segment contains the whole of all the initiations. The birth event has the potential to contain elements of all the life events; meaning that the birth might have an inherent baptism or wilderness experience associated or reflected in it. Thus, we have the capacity for seven times seven in the terms of experiences; rather than one birth, one baptism, one crucifixion, etc.

One last thought. Mr. Fillmore shares that The Story of Jesus' Soul Evolution, is the story of regeneration, the story of how we can consciously awaken the I AM Template that lies dormant in our cellular memories, until awakened and consciously lived into. That is the work, to be so lifted in consciousness, that the I AM Presence in us, becomes the dominant vibration of our being. We BE the Christ Presence in Expression!

References mentioned above:
1 Unity South East Region Annual Conference. October, 2009.
2 Unity Library Archives is located in the old Education building on grounds at Unity Village, MO.
3 Weekly Unity. 4 Unity healing revival 5 Beginners Healing Pamphlet. 6 1923 conference talk.
7 UCC. 8 Regeneration, March 29, 1931 & 1933

Charles Fillmore, author; compiler, Rev. Toni G. Boehm

THE STORY OF JESUS' SOUL EVOLUTION

CHAPTER 1

BIRTH

1-2.

Luke 1:1-7

Forasmuch as many have taken in hand to draw up a narrative concerning those matters which have been fulfilled among us, even as they delivered them unto us, who from the beginning were eyewitnesses and ministers of the word, it seemed good to me also, having traced the course of all things accurately from the first, to write unto thee in order, most excellent Theophilus; that thou mightest know the certainty concerning the things wherein thou wast instructed.

There was in the days of Herod, king of Judaea, a certain priest named Zacharias, of the course of Abijah; and he had a wife of the daughters of Aaron, and her name was Elisabeth. And they were both righteous before God, walking in all the commandments and ordinances of the Lord blameless. And they had no child, because that Elisabeth was barren, and they both were now well stricken in years.

3-5.

Interpretation

• This scripture is most profitable to the student by revealing its spiritual import, especially as it bears upon the growth of the soul in every individual.

• The body of man is a vast kingdom in which many factors have place. In its natural estate this kingdom is ruled by the sense consciousness Herod. There is a higher influence than sense at work in the body. This influence is the spiritual consciousness, whose office it is to transmute the finer essences of the body into spiritual substance. The name Zacharias means "remembered of Jehovah," and represents spiritual consciousness. He is wedded to Elisabeth, who may be compared with the soul in the exalted state that it attains through living an entirely blameless, devoted life. Such a soul is inevitably united in an indissoluble union with Spirit.

• The literal meaning of the name Elisabeth is "my God is oath", or "a worshipper of God". The soul, in its adoration of God, is without consciousness of sin or condemnation. It is blameless, and its world is a world of innocence and peace.

• It is through the higher self in man represented by Zacharias that the promise of his regeneration in mind, soul, and body is made to him. We read that Elisabeth and Zacharias were "stricken in years and had no child". This means the falling into the belief in years, and failure to bring forth the fruits of mature spirituality, which is a certain consciousness of spiritual substance, life, and intelligence.

6.

Luke 1:8-10

Now it came to pass, while he executed the priest's office before God in the order of his course, according to the custom of the priest's office, his lot was to enter into the temple of the Lord and burn incense. And the whole multitude of the people were praying without at the hour of incense.

7-8.

Interpretation

• The priest's entering into the temple represents spiritual meditation-- metaphysically called "going into the silence." All extraneous thoughts, interests, and aspirations collect by degrees around the transmuting process "the whole multitude of the people were praying at the hour of incense".
• The burning of the incense signifies the transmutation of the finer essences of the body. These essences are transmuted to what may be termed the fourth or radiant dimension, and a foundation is laid for an organism of permanent character. Paul calls it the "celestial body." This process takes place whenever the I AM makes union in the body with the Lord, or Higher Self.

9-10.

Luke 1:11-17

And there appeared unto him an angel of the Lord standing on the right side of the altar of incense. And Zacharias was troubled when he saw him, and fear fell upon him. But the angel said unto him, Fear not Zacharias: because thy supplication is heard, and thy wife Elisabeth shall bear thee a son, and thou shalt call his name John. And thou shalt have joy and gladness; and many shall rejoice at his birth. For he shall be great in the sight of the Lord, and he shall drink no wine nor strong drink; and he shall be filled with the Holy Spirit, even from his mother's womb.

And many of the children of Israel shall be turn unto the Lord their God. And he shall go before his face in the spirit and power of Elijah, to turn the hearts of the fathers to the children, and the disobedient to walk in the wisdom of the just; to make ready for the Lord a people prepared for him.

11-15.

Interpretation

• In deep concentration on the desired Truth of one's being, one becomes aware of the thought of the Lord the angel, Gabriel. The thought that we as spiritual beings can control our destinies, and that we are even now making our lives what they are, at first instills fear. Zacharias was afraid of the angel. Humility of spirit hesitates to take to itself power that hitherto has been conceded to God only. Also we fear at first, even in moments of exaltation, to cast off all reliance on previously accepts props and to launch out into the deeps of a new experience.

• We are sometimes afraid, too, of our own thoughts; afraid of leaving the beaten track and getting off onto unknown trails; afraid of seeming "queer," or religious cranks. However, the thought of God persistently held brings us the assurance that we are on the right road. The angel of the Lord stood "on the right side of the altar of incense."

• Prophecy is the pioneering instinct of the mind. When uplifted and inspired by an exalted ideal, the mind gains the understanding that desire brings its own fulfillment. Once the divine concept of life has entered the soul, that concept must, in the spiritual course of events, come to birth.

• The law of mind action is that interest attaches to the point of concentration. Concentration, which is the putting of the entire mind on the idea of the Divine Being, in other words concentration on God, brings many of our instinct permanently under the dominion of the law that we have grasped with new understanding. "And many of the children of Israel shall he turn unto the Lord their God."

• A desire is a natural inward impulse. It may have been formed by the long-continued thought habit of previous incarnations.

• Our religious ideals and instincts are already prepared for the new way of life to be ushered in by the better understanding of the law. We are simply "to make ready for the Lord a people prepared for him," by denying all lessor rules of action and turning wholeheartedly toward the light whose unfailing rays show the path that we must follow.

• John represents the crystallization in the soul of spiritual thoughts joined with regenerated substance. This union brings forth an ego that opens the way for a still greater ego, the Christ of God, the highest expression of Divine Mind in man.

• "And he shall go before his face in the spirit and the power of Elijah" means that force, energy, fire, power, simplicity and naturalness are the characteristics of the ego developed under these devotions of man with God.

16-17.

Luke 1:18-25

And Zacharias said unto the angel, whereby shall I know this? for I am an old man, and any wife well stricken in years. And the angel answering said unto him, I am Gabriel, that stand in the presence of God; and I was sent to speak   unto thee and to bring thee these good tidings. And behold, thou shalt be silent and not able to speak, until the day that these things shall came to pass, because thou believed not my words, which shall be fulfilled in their season.

And the people were waiting for Zacharias, and they marveled while he tarried in the temple, And when he came out, he could not speak unto them, and they perceived that he had seen a vision in the temple: and he continued making signs unto them, and remained dumb. And it came to pass, when the days of his ministrations were fulfilled, he departed unto his house. And after these days Elisabeth his wife conceived; and she hid herself five months, saying, Thus hath the Lord done unto me in the days wherein he looked upon me, to take away my reproach among men.

18-20.

Interpretation

• These soul processes being unusual, even the spiritually minded do not understand what is taking place, and what the result will be, although assured by the messengers of the Lord a propitious outcome. Where no explanation can be offered, the natural attitude of the individual is one of silence. Zacharias was made silent.

• Elisabeth represents the soul, which, after many apparently fruitless experiences and a long-continued search for the way of life, conceives the idea of divine grace John as the law of man's being. In order to receive the blessing of a son something positive was required of Zacharias; namely the establishment of his faith in the invisible good as being present and active, instead of a negative faith or acceptance of appearances. Thus the promise of God to Zacharias of a son was not alone a promise to gratify his personal desires; it was a promise that, with a spiritual background to his life, the impossibilities confronting the natural man no longer exist. The activity of faith in mind and body breaks up crystallized cells formed by states of mind not in accord with spiritual law. Zacharias' mind by faith in the all-potent Spirit. Thus the soul Elisabeth that seems barren of fruit is by faith in Spirit made to bring forth a son John.

21-23.

Luke 1:26-35

Now in the sixth month the ange1 Gabriel was sent from God into a city of Galilee, named Nazareth, to a virgin betrothed to a man whose name was Joseph, of the house of David; and the virgin's name was Mary. And he came in onto her, and said, Hail, thou that art highly favored, the Lord is with thee. But she was greatly troubled at the saying, and cast in her mind what manner of salutation this might be. And the angel said unto her. Fear not, Mary; for thou hast found favor with God.

And behold, thou shall conceive in thy womb and bring forth a son, and shalt call his name JESUS. He shall be great, and shall be called the Son of the Most High: and the Lord God shall give him the throne of his father David; and he shall reign over the house of Jacob forever; and of his kingdom there shall be no end. And Mary said unto the angel, How shall this be, seeing I know not a man? And the angel answered and said unto her, The Holy Spirit shall come unto thee, and the power of begotten shall be called the Son of God.

Interpretation

• As explained by the angel to Mary, we should not overlook the fact that this coming into the activity of the Christ body is the result of an exalted idea sown in the mind and brought forth in the soul. Therefore, Mary, the soul, becomes devout and expectant and believes in the so-called miraculous as a possibility. Mary expected the birth of the Messiah as the Holy Spirit had promised. She was overshadowed by that high idea and it formed in her mind the seed that quickened into the cell and in due season there were aggregations of cells strong enough in their activity to attract the attention of the consciousness, and what is called the birth of Jesus took place.

26.

Luke 1:36-38

And behold, Elisabeth thy kinswoman, she also hath conceived a son in her old age; and this was the sixth month with her that was called barren. For no word from God shall be void of power. And Mary said, Behold, the handmaid of the Lord; be it unto me according to thy word. And the angel departed from her.

27.

Interpretation

• The word of God is all-powerful, all-potential, as is proved by the experience of Elisabeth in bringing forth John, and Mary is bringing forth Jesus.

28-31.

Luke 1:39-86

And Mary arose in those days and went into the hill country with haste, into a city of Judah; and entered into the house of Zacharias, and saluted Elisabeth. And it came to pass, when Elisabeth heard the salutation of Mary, the babe leaped in her womb; and Elisabeth, was filled with the Holy Spirit; and she lifted up her voice with a loud cry, and said, Blessed art thou among women, and blessed is the fruit of thy womb. And whence is this to me, that the mother of my Lord should come unto me? to me, that the mother of my Lord should come unto me? For behold, when the voice of thy salutation came into mine ears, the babe leaped in my womb for joy. And blessed is she that believed; for there shall be a fulfillment of the things which have been spoken to her from the Lord. And Mary said,
> My soul doth magnify the Lord, And my spirit hath rejoiced in God my savior.
> For he hath looked upon the low estate of his handmaid:
> For behold, from henceforth all generations shall call me blessed.

For he that is mighty hath done to me great things; And holy is his name.

And his mercy is unto generations and generations on them that fear him.

He hath showed strength with his arm:

He hath scattered the proud in the imagination of their heart.

He hath put down princes from their thrones, and hath exalted them of low degree.

The hungry he hath filled with good things; and the rich he hath sent empty away.

He hath given help to Israel his servant, that he might remember mercy

As he spoke unto our fathers toward Abraham and his seed forever.

And Mary abode with her about three months, and returned unto her house.

32-33.

Interpretation

• This Scripture no doubt has an esoteric meaning; yet it is also historical. The power represented by Elisabeth on the intellectual plane corresponds to that represented by Mary on the spiritual plane. These thought forces are closely related. In truth Elisabeth represents the intellectual soul and Mary the spiritual soul. Being closely related, they are naturally drawn to each other. "And Mary arose in those days and went into the hill country with haste into a city of Judah; and entered into the house of Zacharias and saluted Elisabeth.

• When Mary saluted her cousin, the babe leaped in Elisabeth's womb. This reveals a close soul sympathy between the two reincarnating souls, John and Jesus. The song of Mary is the expression of a soul that is convinced that it is working according to law, and that the blessings of the Most High are being poured out upon it.

34.

Luke 1:57-58

Now Elisabeth's time was fulfilled that she should be delivered; and she brought forth a son. And her neighbors and her kinsfolk heard that the Lord had magnified his mercy toward her; and they rejoiced with her.

35-36.

Interpretation

• The fruit of spiritual consciousness in the innocent soul is a new idea, or outward expression of grace and mercy. The soul, imbued with knowledge of the higher law, has brought forth a new idea of grace, to open the way to freedom for the entire man and to the unification of all his powers. This is an occasion for rejoicing. When we gain the first inkling of the Truth that we can free ourselves from the grip of undesirable thought and life habits, we are filled with joy that knows no bounds.

•   This freeing thought has come from our own mind; it is our son. All our neighbors and kinsfolk the related thoughts or ideas in consciousness rejoice with us. Our environment takes on new meaning; our life has new significance; our experiences, even these that have been negative in character, are illumined in our mind as instances of the outworking of a law that insures our ultimate good.

37.

Luke 1:59-64

And it came to pass on the eighth day, that they came to circumcise the child; and they would have called him Zacharias, after the name of his father. And his mother answered and said, Not so; but he shall be called John. And they said unto her, There is none of thy kindred that is called by this name. And they made signs to his father what he would have him called. And he asked for a writing tablet, and wrote saying, His name is John, And they marveled all. And his mouth was opened immediately, and his tongue loosed, and he spoke again.

38-39.

Interpretation

•   After we have had time to assemble our impressions, to take stock of the meaning of the new idea incur mind, and to measure its import in our lives, we are at first inclined to think of it as the spiritual consciousness opening up broader avenues of expression in and through us. "They would have called him Zacharias, after the name of his father."

•   But deep in the soul is the conviction that a special function of Spirit performs the work of preparing man to free himself from the clutch of sense. As long as he labors under a burden of condemnation, either that of his own conscience or the external censure of others, the way to achieve freedom is not open to him. Only when he perceives the truth that grace and mercy are included in the divine law as a very integral part of it does he find the voice of praise and blessing in his own heart. So the forerunner of freedom is the knowledge that grace and mercy are inalienable from the divine law. "His name is John."

40.

Luke 1:65-66

And fear came on all that dwelt round about them: and all these sayings were noised abroad throughout all the hill country of Judaea. And all that heard them laid them up in their heart saying, What then shall this child be? For the hand of the Lord was with him.

Interpretation

•   "And fear came on all that dwelt round about them" does not necessarily mean a state of dread or anxiety in the mind. It means rather a consciousness of an idea not fully understood, but so all-pervading and so tenacious as to be instinctive.

•   The understanding that grace and mercy are inseparable from the redeeming action of the higher law opens up a realm of boundless expectation. "What then shall this child be?"

42-45.

Luke 1:67-80

And his father Zacharias was filled with the Holy Spirit, and prophesied, saying, Blessed be the Lord, the God of Israel; for he hath visited and wrought redemption for his people, and hath raised up a horn of salvation for us in the house of his servant David {as he spoke by the mouth of his holy prophets that have been from of old}, salvation from our enemies, and from the hand of all that hate us; to show mercy towards our fathers, and to remember his holy covenant; the oath which he sware unto Abraham our Father, to grant unto us that we being delivered out of the hand of our enemies Should serve him without fear, in holiness and righteousness before him all our days.

Yea and thou, child, shalt be called the prophet of the Most High; for thou shalt go before the face of the Lord to make ready his ways; to give knowledge of salvation unto his people in the remission of their sins, Because of the tender mercy of our God, Whereby the dayspring from on high shall visit us, to shine upon them that sit in darkness and the shadow of death: to guide our feet into the way of peace. And the child grew, and waxed strong in spirit, and was in the deserts till the day of his showing unto Israel.

46.

Interpretation

•   Zacharias, symbolizing a prophetic state of consciousness has here received the inspiration of Spirit according to his understanding of law and is here imparting that prophecy to all responding thoughts in consciousness.

47-48.

Mat. 1:18-21

Now the birth of Jesus Christ was on this wise: When his mother Mary had been betrothed to Joseph; before they came together she was found with Child of the Holy Spirit. And Joseph her husband, being a righteous man, and not willing to make her a public example, was minded to put her away privately. But when he thought on these things, behold, an angel of the Lord, appeared unto him in a dream, saying, Joseph, thou son of David, fear not to take unto thee Mary thy wife: for that which is conceived in her is of the Holy Spirit. And she shall bring forth a son; and thou shalt call his name JESUS; for it is he that shall save his people from their sins.

49-53.

Interpretation

• Everything first takes place in the mind. In truth it is in mind where real demonstrations find their impetus. Joseph and Mary's betrothal was to them such a sacred and holy thing that it stirred into activity the most spiritual forces of their souls, which forces perhaps had never been set into expression before, and their spiritual union was consummated. There followed such an outpouring of the Holy Spirit which is God's Word in action that Mary, through Joseph, was over-shadowed by this heavenly power, and though she did not "know man" in a physical way, the initial germ seed was thereby projected, and she conceived and brought forth the child, Jesus.

• Metaphysically interpreted within the soul, Mary, the Virgin mother, represents a pure state of mind that ponders spiritual things in her heart and believes in revelations from angels and messengers from God. Her imagination is so intense that she vitalizes the ultra-microscopic germs of life and they multiply in her body without external contact.

• Joseph represents the outer mind that practices obedience to the Lord, gained in dreams and external symbols. Nazareth, their home, represents the commonplace if not unpopular environment in which the spiritually-minded are usually found.

• Mary was "found with child of the Holy Spirit" means the miraculous conception by which the Virgin Mary is held to have conceived without original sin. Joseph, not fully understanding the prophecy, "was minded to put her away privately," meaning that we do not in the first stages of the birth of Christ in us understand the process, and sometimes are moved to put it away from us. Joseph's soul the name Joseph meaning "from perfection to perfection" is so heavily charged with divine life that it cannot express itself intelligently, because no union has yet taken place between it and the understanding, which union -- when it is consummated -- always equalizes and adjusts.

• An angel is a messenger of the Lord. Metaphysically, our angels are our spiritual perceptive faculties, which ever dwell in the presence of the Father.

54.

Mat. 1:22-25

Now all this is come to pass, that it might be fulfilled which was spoken by the Lord through the prophet, saying Behold, the virgin shall be with child, and shall bring forth a son, And they shall call his name Immanuel;

which is, being interpreted, God with us. And Joseph arose from his sleep, and did as the angel of the Lord commanded him, and took unto him his wife; and knew her not till she had brought forth a son: and he called his name JESUS.

55-57.

Interpretation

• A prophet is one who can tell what the mind is going to bring forth by the nature and activity of its thoughts. A prophecy is the foreshadowing of events which are to take place, "For unto us a child is born, unto us a son is given; and the government shall be upon his shoulder: and his name shall be called Wonderful, Counselor, Mighty God, Everlasting Father, Prince of Peace."

• Mary was a virgin. The word virgin means "pure," "undefiled," "unsullied," "undisturbed" "fresh," "unadulterated." Metaphysically, the son Immanuel who was brought forth means the consciousness that God is with us and we are one with Him; the understanding of how the "Word became flesh" in Jesus Christ and is now being made flesh in us even, as it was in Him. Joseph represents the natural man, Jesus, progressing toward the Christ man, who willingly follows the leadings of Spirit.

58-59.

Luke 2:1-7

Now it came to pass in those days, there went out a decree from Caesar Augustus, that all the world should be enrolled. This was the first enrolment made when Quirinius was governor of Syria. And all went to enroll themselves, everyone to his own city. And Joseph also went up from Galilee, out of the city of Nazareth, Into Judaea to the city of David, which is called Bethlehem, because he was of the house and family of David; to enroll himself with Mary, who was betrothed to him, being great with child. And it came to pass, while they were there, the days were fulfilled that she should be delivered. And she brought forth her firstborn son; and she wrapped him in swaddling clothes, and laid him in a manger, because there was no room for them in the inn.

60-61.

Interpretation

• Joseph and Mary represent wisdom and love, which have been ideas in mind, but are now to bring forth a manifestation , in substance. Going up to Jerusalem Bethlehem? to be enrolled, as was the custom in that day, illustrates the conformity to man-made law. "Render unto Caesar the things that are Caesar's."

• Swaddling clothes were bands of cloth in which it was customary to wrap young children. These swaddling clothes represent the confinement to the limitations of the physical nature "manger" of this first emanation of Divine Life, "there being no room for them in the inn" outer consciousness.

62-65.

Luke 2:8-20

And there were shepherds in the same country abiding in the field, and keeping watch by night over their flock. And an angel of the Lord stood by them, and the glory of the Lord shone round about them: and they wore sore afraid. And the angel said unto them, Be not afraid; for behold, bring you good tidings of great joy which Shall be to all the people: for there is born to you this day in the city of David a Savior, who is Christ the Lord. And this is the sign unto you: Ye shall find a babe wrapped in swaddling clothes, and lying in a manger.

And suddenly there was with the angel a multitude of the heavenly host praising God, and saying, Glory to God in the highest, and on earth peace among men in whom he is well pleased.

And it came to pass, when the angels went away from them into heaven, the shepherds said one to another, Let us now go even unto Bethlehem, and see this thing is come to pass, which the Lord hath made known unto us. And they came with haste, and found both Mary and Joseph, and the babe lying in the manger. And when they saw it, they made known concerning the saying which was spoken to them about this child. And all that heard it wondered at the things which were spoken unto them by the shepherds.

But Mary kept all these sayings, pondering them in her heart. And the shepherds returned, glorifying and praising God for all the things that they had heard and seen, even as it was spoken unto them.

66-71.

Interpretation

• Vigilance in watching our flocks thoughts makes us receptive to the spiritual aide of existence. As the shepherds in Oriental countries have a name for every sheep, which is trained to come and go at command, so we should be familiar with our thoughts, and discipline them so thoroughly that they will be obedient to us when we send forth our desire. This familiarity with our mental realm leads to an acquaintance with the character, and gives one an opportunity to strengthen the weak points and transform the undesirable tendencies. It thus clears up and harmonizes the soul so that it is receptive to divine ideas.

• A thought realm in constant turmoil and mortal confusion cannot possibly receive a message from the spiritual realms of consciousness. The birth of Christ in the individual is a great mystery. It cannot be explained in words. It is veiled in darkness even to those who are on its vary verge; this is typified by the shepherds who were watching their flocks by night. Those to whom the mystery is revealed have to be vigilant in keeping their thoughts, or flocks, secure from the invasion of ideas that would destroy their purity, their faith, their very life.

• The life of a Christian's mind is faith in the power of God to reveal himself to man. The true believers have always expected and looked for superhuman events. Yet, as explained in Scripture, when the "glory of the Lord shone round about them the shepherds... they were sore afraid." This fear is of the human in us, and we can overcome it gradually. When the light and its accompanying vibratory forces reach a certain point, there is always a trembling of the mortal part. This, however, grows less and less as the development of the Christ in us proceeds.

• The proclamation of peace on earth by the heavenly host symbolizes the calling together of a great multitude of angelic thoughts praising God and giving thanks for the great demonstration. The higher or heavenly realms of consciousness praise God for this evidence in the body.

• The proclamation of peace on earth by the heavenly host symbolizes the calling together of a great multitude of angelic thoughts praising God and giving thanks for the great demonstration. The higher or heavenly realms of consciousness praise God for this evidence in the body or earth of a force that will restore peace and harmony.

• "But Mary kept all these sayings, pondering than in her heart." There should be outer affirmations of the new life, but the substantial growth is attained through quiet communion within the soul.

• The message of the angels to the shepherds are those periodical outbursts of divine illumination which come to us, and we, for the time, know that something unusual is going on within, but we have our duties in life to fulfill, and we return to our flocks duties, and glorify and praise God for all the things we have heard and seen.

72-73.

Luke 2:21.24

And when eight days were fulfilled for circumcising him, his name was called JESUS, which was so called by the angel before he was conceived in the womb. And when the days of their purification according to the law of Moses were fulfilled, they brought him to Jerusalem, to present him to the Lord as it is written in the law of the Lord, Every male that openeth the womb shall be called holy to the Lord, and to offer a sacrifice according to that which is said in the law of the Lord, a pair of turtledoves, or two young pigeons.

74-75.

Interpretation

• Circumcision is symbolical of the cutting off of mortal tendencies, and is indicative of purification and cleanliness. Under the law of Jesus Christ, circumcision is fulfilled in its spiritual meaning -- the purification of the individual from the law of sin and death. One is circumcised in the true inner significance of the word only by being thoroughly purified in soul. Then the glory of the inner soul cleansing and purifying works out into the outer consciousness and the body and sets one free from all sensual, corruptible thoughts and activities. Thus man manifests wholeness and perfection throughout his being.

• He who keeps the precepts of divine law, and seeks to embody the principles of Truth in mind, body, and affairs, is circumcised unto the Lord, which is the essential purification.

76-77.

Luke 2:25-32

And behold, there was a man in Jerusalem, whose name was Simeon; and this man was righteous and devout, looking for the consolation of Israel: and the Holy Spirit was upon him. And it had been revealed unto him by the Holy Spirits that he should not see death, before he had seen the Lord's Christ. And he came in the Spirit into the temple: and when the parents brought in the child Jesus, that they might do concerning him after the custom of the law, Then he received him into his arms, and blessed God, and said, Now lettest thou thy servant depart, Lords according to thy word, in peace; for mine eyes have seen thy salvation, which thou hast prepared before the face of all peoples; a light for revelation to the Gentiles, and the glory of thy people Israel.

78-79.

Interpretation

• Simeon means one who listens and obeys. The listening faculty of mind shows itself in the devout Christian as the mental state that looks for and expects spiritual guidance and instruction direct from God. It may be summed up in the word "obedience."

• One who believes that God communes with man, and opens the way to such communion by being obedient to every hint received in vision, dream, or "still small voice," is guided by the Holy Spirit.

• Immortal life must be demonstrated by each individual. Those who are devout, receptive, obedient, are shown that they are on the way to immortal life. They find in the Temple body the Lord's Christ: that is, the Lord's anointed.

• The new consciousness of indwelling immortal life takes the place of hope, expectancy, obedience Simeon, and the old consciousness is allowed to depart in peace.

80-81.

Luke 2:33-39

And his father and his mother were marveling at the things which were spoken concerning him; and Simeon blessed them, and said unto Mary his mother, Behold, this child is set for the falling and the rising of many in Israel; and for a sign which is spoken against; yea and a sword shall pierce through thine own soul; that thoughts out of many hearts may be revealed. And there was one Anna, a prophetess, the daughter of Phanuel, of the tribe of Asher she was of a great age, having lived with a husband seven years from her virginity, and she had been a widow even unto fourscore and four years, who departed not from the temple, worshipping with fasting and supplications night and day. And coming up at that very hour she gave thanks unto God, and spoke of him to all them that were looking for the redemption of Jerusalem. And when they had accomplished all things that were according to the law of the Lord, they returned into Galilee, to their own city Nazareth.

82-83.

Interpretation

•   In this scripture Simeon, symbolizing one who listens spiritually and obeys by listening to the inner voice, is able to prophesy the greatness of the coming of Him who is to prove Himself to be the fulfillment of the promise of the Messiah.

•   Anna, the prophetess, who had long been a vestal virgin in the temple, represents a certain conservation of spiritual life which has been built up by devotion and faithfulness.

•   This spiritual life is transmitted through many incarnations as an inheritance of the soul and is of great importance and is of importance in forming the Christ body. Nothing is lost in the evolution or the soul. Grace is apparent in the impersonal, sharing of the just perceived truth with others who have been seeking the same truth, but who have not yet reached the clearness of vision required to gain perfect perception of the law.

84-85.

Mat. 2:1-6

Now when Jesus was born in Bethlehem of Judaea in the days of Herod the king, behold, Wise men from the east came to Jerusalem, saying, Where is he that is born King of the Jews? for we saw his star in the east, and are come to worship him, And when Herod the king heard it, he was troubled and all Jerusalem with him. And gathering together all the chief priests and scribes of the people he inquired of them where the Christ should be born. And they said unto him, In Bethlehem of Judaea: for thus it is written through the prophet, And thou Bethlehem, land of Judah, Art in no wise least among the princes of Judah: For out of thee shall come forth a governor, Who shall be shepherd of my people Israel."

Interpretation

• The new man is called ".Jesus" whose name means the same as the name "Jehovah," the I AM, the supreme will.

• Jesus was born in Bethlehem of Judaea. Bethlehem means "house of bread," or the abiding-place of substance, and Judaea means "praise," or spiritual recognition. The tribe of Judah is symbolical of the aggregation of thoughts that acknowledges spiritual things as the one and only reality; thus the substance of which the Jesus man is born in us must be spiritual in its character.

• When sense consciousness Herod rules, it dominates all intellectual, as well as ecclesiastical thoughts. These thoughts symbolize the chief priests and scribes of the peoples all of which on this plane go to make up the intellectual man.

• The Wise Men from the East symbolize the stored-up resources of the soul which rise to the surface when the soul is stirred by a great spiritual revelation. In scriptural symbology, East always means the within. The coming of the Wise Men signifies that from the regions of the interior wisdom come thoughts of reverence for the holy life that has begun its growth in the consciousness.

• When the Jesus ego first appears in the subconsciousness *(subconscious – Ed.)* it is a mere speck of light, a "Star in the east." The star symbolizes intuition; the wise men were guided by intuition. Stars represent subjective and not fully understood guiding lights. They represent the inner realms of consciousness that, like books of life, have kept the records of past lives and held them in reserve for the great day when the soul would receive the supreme ego, Jesus. The star that pointed the way for the wise men was also in the East; and it typifies man's inner conviction of his divine son ship.

Mat. 2:7-11

Then Herod privately called the Wise-men, and learned of them exactly what time the star appeared. And he sent them to Bethlehem, and said, Go and search out exactly concerning the young child; and when ye have found him bring me word, that I also may come and worship him. And they, having heard the king, went their way; and lo, the star, which they saw in the east, went before them, till it came and stood over where the young child was. And when they saw the star, they rejoiced with exceeding great joy.

And they came into the house and saw the young child with Mary his mother; and they fell down and worshipped him; and opening their treasures they offered unto him gifts, gold and frankincense and myrrh.

Interpretation

• Herod, the sense ego, seeks to destroy the one who he feels will eventually dethrone him, but the Lord keeps him in ignorance of what is going on in his domain. So it is found that those in regeneration are, like Herod, seldom conscious of the new ego that is building up a kingdom in substance Bethlehem, within the very center of the body. Herod, the man of flesh, feels that something is going on and seeks occult wisdom Wise men, but does not seek under the divine law. He would have wisdom's aid in destroying that which in the end is the salvation of the whole consciousness.

• Herod with sense consciousness as his stronghold controls temporal government, but he cannot stop the growth of the new life within us, if we are obedient to Spirit, if we, like Joseph, watch for the guidance of the Lord.

• When the soul makes a spiritual demonstration there is great rejoicing. When one begins to have faith that he is destined to do the will of God, all the riches of his experience -- gifts of gold riches of Spirit; frankincense, the beauty of Spirit; and myrrh the eternity of Spirit -- are bestowed upon the young child. When the wise thoughts from within bring their presents, there is great rejoicing and satisfaction in consciousness. The presents which the wise men bring are symbolical of the inner resources open to the Christ Child.

95.

Mat 2:12

And being warned of God in a dream that they should not return to Herod, they departed into their own country another way.

96.

Interpretation

• In this instance as in all others, the Lord is continually seeking to guide man into the higher way of life, which always lead into the "country" of peace, wisdom and good will.

97.

Mat. 2:13

Now when they were departed, behold, an angel of the Lord appeareth to Joseph in a dream, saying, Arise and take the young child and his mother, and flee into Egypt, and be thou there until I tell thee: for Herod will seek the young child to destroy him.

Interpretation

• When in the silence and in dreams we see a little child, we may know that the Christ body Jesus has begun to form in our subconscious minds. Then we should be watchful to see that the subtle desires of sense Herod do not rob the young child of its vitality and thus kill it out of consciousness. The young child must be cared for and fed daily with spiritual thoughts; otherwise it will pine away and we shall find ourselves back in the old sense state, with Herod, sense consciousness in supreme control.

100.

Mat. 2:14-15

And he arose and took the young child and his mother by night, and departed into Egypt; and was there until the death of Herod: that it might be fulfilled which was spoken by the Lord through the prophet, saying, Out of Egypt did I call my son.

101-102.

Interpretation

• The name "Joseph" means from "perfection unto perfection". The Lord often speaks to this state of consciousness through what is commonly known as dreams and visions. Both the Wise-men and Joseph were guided by dreams. The message is thrown on the screen of the mind in the form of thought pictures, which the quickened soul readily interprets.

• It is wise to protect the new born spiritual consciousness from coming into contact with the personal ego, Herod. Under the guidance of Spirit no harm comes to it; it is taken down into the protected places of the subconsciousness *(subconscious – Ed.)* Egypt until the personal ego destroys itself.

103-104.

Mat. 2:16-18

Then Herod, when he saw that he was mocked of the Wisemen, was exceeding wroth, and went forth, and slew all the male children that were in Bethlehem, and in all the borders thereof, from two years old and under, according to the time which he had exactly learned of the Wise-men. Then was fulfilled that which was spoken through Jeremiah, the prophet, saying, A voice was heard in Ramah weeping and great mourning, Rachel weeping for her children; And she would not be comforted, because they are not.

Interpretation

• When the human self does not have its way it loses its temper, flies into a rage, is destructive, and kills out many potentially good forces.

Mat. 2:19-21

But when Herod was dead, behold, an angel of the Lord appeareth in a dream to Joseph in Egypt, saying, Arise and take the young child and his mother, and go into the land of Israel: for they are dead that sought the young child's life. And he arose and took the young child and his mother, and came into the land of Israel.

Interpretation

• Joseph represents the natural man with a higher spiritual principle in the course of development. He represents that in one that knows what is going on spiritually and would preserve the new spiritual development that is taking place in the subconsciousness *(subconscious – Ed.)* Egypt. Sense consciousness Herod is dead; therefore the new spiritual consciousness the Christ child is no longer in danger. It is free to express openly that which is real Israel.

Mat. 2:22-23

But when he heard that Archelaus was reigning over Judaea in the room of his father Herod, he was afraid to go thither; and being warned of God in a dream, he withdrew into the parts of Galilee, and came and dwelt In a city called Nazareth; that it might be fulfilled which was spoken through the prophets, that he should be called a Nazarene.

Interpretation

• Archelaus represents a phase of the sense will son of Herod the Great, or ruling rower, in sense consciousness which was still dominant.
• Galilee represents the life activity or soul energy of man acting In conjunction with substance. Nazareth, a city of Galilee, means a sprout, a small thing held of slight significance, hence a term of reproach. It typifies the commonplace mind of man: but it is in the commonplace mind that the Great Ideal takes root and grows up in consciousness. Much as the water lily, whose leaves and blossoms are very beautiful, is rooted deep in the mud of the lake bottom, so is the Christ idea rooted deep in primal substance.

- It grows up in and through the commonplace mind of the everyday man as the long stem of the lily extends through the wavering medium of intervening water to reach the free air upon the surface. Both mud and water are necessary to the full flowering of the water lily. In like manner, the subconscious mind, under laid by pure substance and overlaid by the superconscious mind of Spirit as sunshine and air rest upon the surface of the water, forms silently but surely the precious flower of God-like character.

- Throughout the gospel story of Jesus there runs continually a thread of fulfilled prophecy. To the casual reader who sees nothing beyond the literal narrative, it would seem sometimes that the parallelism is far-fetched. The statement that Jesus was taken as an infant to live in Nazareth that it might be fulfilled which was spoken through the prophets, that he should be called Nazarene", is one of these statements. The prophecy itself, in the words given, is not found in the Scriptures.

- So it is seen that the fulfillment of prophecy takes place because prophecy is a foreknowledge of Truth to be demonstrated. The I AM has knowledge of all Truth, but to the natural man this knowledge comes dimly, -- as a vague presentiment, a foreknowledge or prophecy of Truth to come. With the Christ man comes Truth — fulfillment.

113-115.

Luke 2:40-52

And the child grew, and waxed strong, filled with wisdom; and the grace of God was upon him. And his parents went every year to Jerusalem at the feast of the Passover. And when he was twelve years old, they went up after the custom of the feast; and when they had fulfilled the days, as they were returning, the boy Jesus tarried behind in Jerusalem; and his parents knew it not; but supposing him to be in the company, they went a day's journey; and they sought for him among their kinfolk and acquaintance: and when they found him not, they returned to Jerusalem, seeking for him.

And It came to pass, after three days they found him in the temple, sitting in the midst of the teachers, both hearing them, and asking them questions: and all that heard him were amazed at his understanding and his answers. And when they saw him, they were astonished; and his mother said unto him, Son, why hast thou thus dealt with us? Behold, thy father and I sought thee sorrowing. And he said unto them, How is it that ye sought me? Knew ye not that I must be in my Father's house? And they understood not the saying which he spoke unto them. And he went down with them, and came to Nazareth; and he was subject unto them: and his mother kept all these sayings in her heart. And Jesus advanced in wisdom and stature, and in favor with God and men.

Interpretation

• Jesus represents our growing inner consciousness that we are sons of God. Joseph represents the Son of man—the conscious mind. Mary represents divine motherhood---the subconscious mind. Both of these ideas have place in individual consciousness, and they unite to bring forth a complete expression of God -- the perfect manifest man Jesus. The growth of strength and wisdom in consciousness is not always plain to the outer man. The grace of God upon him brings about an inner spiritual strength that remains hidden until it reaches a given development in all parts of mind and body. First the person realizes a change in thought; next, a distinct freedom in body.

• When the growth is regular, there is a spiritualization of the centers of the mind and the body, until the whole twelve centers or powers have been raised to a higher rate of activity and there comes a clearer perception of Truth.

• Joseph and Mary, in their hurry to return home, forgot the young child Jesus, or take it for granted that he is in their company. But He is not found, and they return to seek Him. This means that we are to be specific in bringing forth from the invisible side of our being all the factors that enter into consciousness. If we do not bring forth these factors, we shall have to return sorrowing, after "three days". This return symbolizes an entering into spirit, soul, and body, where we find the Son of God "in the temple, sitting in the midst of the teachers". The thoughts in the organism that preside over and regulate the various functions are here referred to as "teachers". The wisdom of God individualized Jesus, gives these teachers a new understanding of divine law, and all are amazed at the revelation.

• The work of Jesus in the "Father's house" is essential to the development of health of mind and body. The outer consciousness may not understand verse 50 why the all-powerful Son of the Most High should spend so much time in inner communion. Experience proves that this communion is necessary. Those who give due attention to it find that harmony is established and that harmony may be brought to the outer realms Nazareth and made to serve and to be subject, in the common walks of life.

• The balancing of the within and the without brings about the harmonious evolution in soul and body that is described in verse 52: "And Jesus advanced in wisdom and stature, and in favor with God and men."

Luke 3:1-2

Now in the fifteenth year of the reign of Tiberias Caesar, Pontius Pilate, being governor of Judaea, and Herod being tetrarch of Galilee, and his brother Philip tetrarch of the region of Ituraea and Trachonitis, and Lysanias tetrarch of Abilene, in the high-priesthood of Annas and Caiaphas, the word of God came into John the son of Zacharias in the wilderness.

Interpretation

The name John, in Hebrew, means "Jehovah is gracious". It is that attitude of mind in which we are zealous for the rule of Spirit. It is not the Spirit, but a perception of spiritual possibilities, and an activity in making conditions in which the Spirit may rule.

Annas and Caiaphas have much the same meaning. Caiaphas was high priest at the time of the ministry and the crucifixion of Jesus and during the persecution of the disciples a little later. Annas held a high position among the Jews, and was a leading factor in these persecutions.

Metaphysically, Annas and Calaphas represent very influential religious thoughts of the intellect, that are given over to rites and ceremonies — the outer letter of the word, without the inner spiritual Truth. The Bible history of these men shows how a merely formal religion will persecute and attempt to kill the inner Christ Spirit and all that pertains to it. A purely intellectual understanding and practice of religion cannot comprehend the deep inspirations of the heart and the loving, forgiving informality and non-resistance of the inner Spirit of Truth. There is nothing truly satisfying to the soul in formal religion.

(Editorial Note: In the original manuscript the linage was placed at 174 a-k by Mr. Fillmore. In order to keep the integrity of the seven initiation-events intact, the lineage, as an important aspect of the Birth Initiation, has been moved to the end of this Birth segment. Rev. Toni G. Boehm, compiler)

174a-b-c-d-e-f-g-h-i-j-k.

Mat. 1:1-14

The book of the generation of Jesus Christ, the son of David, the son of Abraham.

Abraham begat Isaac; and Isaac begat Jacob; and Jacob begat Judah and his brethren; and Judah begat Perez and Zerah of Tamar; and Perez begat Hezron; and Hezron begat Ram; and Ram begat Amminadab; and Amminadab begat Nahshon; and Nahshon begat Salmon; and Salmon begat Boaz of Rahab; and Boaz begat Obed of Ruth; and Obed begat Jesse; and Jesse begat David the king.

And David begat Solomon of her that had been the wife of Uriah; and Solomon begat Rehoboam; and Rehoboam begat Abijah; and Abijah begat Asa; and Asa begat Jehoshaphat; and Jehoshaphat begat Joram; and Joram begat Uzziah; and Uzziah begat Jotham; and Jotham begat Ahaz; and Ahaz begat Hezekiah, and Hezekiah begat Manasseh; and Manasseh begat Amon; and Amon begat Josiah; and Josiah begat Jechoniah and his brethren, at the time of the carrying away to Babylon.

And after the carrying away to Babylon, Jecheniah begat Shealtiel; and Shealtiel begat Zerubbabel; and Zerubbabel begat Abiud; and Abiud begat Eliakim; and Eliakim begat Azor; and Azor begat Sadoc; and Sadoc begat Achim; and Achim begat Eliud; and Eliud begat Eleazar; and Eleazar begat Matthan; and Matthan begat Jacob; and Jacob begat Joseph the husband of Mary, of whom was born Jesus, who is called Christ.

So all the generations from Abraham unto David are fourteen generations; and from David unto the carrying away to Babylon fourteen generations; and from the carrying away to Babylon unto the Christ fourteen generations.

Interpretation

• Abraham, father source, founder of a multitude. Metaphysically, Abraham represents the power of the mind to reproduce its ideas in unlimited expression. This ability of the mind to make substance out of ideas is called faith.

• Isaac, He God laughs; joy; singing; leaping. Metaphysically, Isaac represents divine son ship. He signifies the joy of the new birth and the new life in Christ.

• Jacob, heel catcher. Metaphysically, Jacob represents the mental consciousness within each of us. He also represents an idea of the I AM identity.

• Judah, praise Jehovah: confession of Jah. Metaphysically, Judah represents the spiritual faculty that corresponds to accumulation or increase in the mental; this is prayer and praise.

• Perez, broken through; demolished. Metaphysically, Perez represents victory through praise, or making a way out of apparent limitation and error and predominating over them by means of prayer and praise.

• Zerah, rising of light, sunrise, birth of a child, germination of a seed; beginning of light; brightness; splendor. Metaphysically, Zerah represents the first conscious awakening to the presence of this new inner light, or understanding the sun rises in the east, and the east signifies the within.

• Tamar, standing forth; upright; palm tree; phoenix. Tamar represents victory and conquest palm tree through uprightness upright. This victory or overcoming power is of the soul in the individual.

• Hezron, inclosed; verdant fields. Metaphysically, Hezron represents single thoughts, and a group of thoughts that are not yet free in their expression in the consciousness and organism.

• Ram, lifted up. Metaphysically, Ram means exalted spiritual understanding in consciousness.

• Amminadab, people of liberality. Metaphysically, Amminidab represents the broad-mindedness and generosity of true spiritual thoughts in man.

• Nahshon, hisser; whisperer. Metaphysically, Nahshon represents the reception of divine wisdom and knowledge into individual consciousness.

- Salmon, covered. Metaphysically, Salmon represents the idea of peace and perfection's becoming established in individual consciousness.
- Boaz, alacrity; in strength. Metaphysically, Boaz represents the cheerful willingness, promptness, and quickness of action, also richness and power of thought, and strength of character, that when established in substance Bethlehem, house of bread and allied with the love of the natural man Ruth open the way for the birth of the Christ into consciousness. David, the great-grandson of Boaz, is a type of the Christ.
- Rahab, large, freedom, unrestraint. Metaphysically, Rahab represents the natural love in man, which when centered on spiritual things opens the way for man to enter into spiritual consciousness.
- Obed, serving; worshipping. Metaphysically, Obed represents an active thought, in the spiritual consciousness of man, that pertains to service and worship. "God is Spirit; and they that worship him must worship in spirit and truth."
- Ruth, sympathetic companion; friendship; pleasing; beautiful. Metaphysically, Ruth represents the love of the natural soul for God and for the things of Spirit.
- Jesse, strong; upright. Metaphysically, Jesse represents the eternal existence of I AM, and when man is firm and strong in this realization, he is in the state of mind from which will come God's idea of man, Christ.
- David, beloved. Metaphysically, David represents divine love individualized in human consciousness.
- Solomon, entire; peace. Metaphysically, Solomon represents the state of mind that is established in consciousness when the soul is unified with wisdom and love.
- Uriah, the lord is my light; fire of Jehovah; flame of Jehovah.

CHAPTER 2

BAPTISM

125-126.

Luke 3:3-6

And he came into all the region round about the Jordan reaching the baptism of repentance unto remission of sins; as it is written in the book of the words of Isaiah the prophet, the voice of one crying in the wilderness, Make ye ready the way of the Lord, make his paths straight, every valley shall be filled, and every mountain and hill shall be brought low; and the crooked shall become straight, and the rough ways smooth; and all flesh shall see the salvation of God.

127-129.

Interpretation

• The work of John the Baptist is of interest to us because it deals with the transformation of the inner life of the individual. John is typical of the innate principle in man that ever seeks to do right. John the Baptist dealt with the uprooting of negation, rather than with the actual constructive work of the Christ consciousness.

• There is to be a descent into the consciousness of a higher principle, called in Scripture, the Lord. There must be preparation for this more heavenly order of being. "Prepare ye the way of the Lord, make his paths straight." Luke 3:4 The mental department of man is a tangible reality. Thoughts occupy space and have form and shape. They make the "valley", and "every mountain and hill" which are to be evened up before "all flesh shall see the salvation of God". All your flesh shall see the salvation of God when you have made your "crooked" thoughts straight.

• If your flesh is not saved from the ills that mortal flesh is heir to, it is because you have not opened the way for the saving Christ principle by purifying and harmonizing your thoughts.

130.

Mark 1:4

John came, who baptized in the wilderness and preached the baptism of repentance unto remission of sins.

Matt 3:4-6

Now John himself had raiment of camel's hair, and leathern girdle about his loins; and his food was locusts and wild honey. Then went out unto him Jerusalem, and all Judaea, and all the region round about the Jordan; And they were baptized of him in the river Jordan, confessing their sins.

Interpretation

•   The consciousness represented by John the Baptist is greater than any state of mind centered in selfish gratification of sense desires. The change it brings about is accomplished by means of baptism; by pouring into the mind the dissolving power of the word, which breaks up and washes away all ideas of materiality. This is the word in the form of denial -- a negative force.

•   Spiritual baptism is positive -- an affirmation. The slightest positive affirmation of Spirit has more power to form a thought habit than has the most emphatic denial. The smallest gleam of spiritual thought in man is greater than the mightiest reasoning of the intellect, and the intellectual concept of life must give way before the understanding that comes through the Holy Spirit.

•   The habit of right thinking is a straight path for the entrance of Spirit into the conscious mind. Like all worthwhile habits, it requires for its formation constant, devoted effort. It requires denial of the claims of sense. John's clothing was of camel's hair, with a leathern girdle; the garb of the ascetic, chosen for service, not for its appeal to the love of luxury as does the "soft raiment" of those who "are in Kings houses". His food was whatever the wilderness offered, close at hand. Neither time nor thought was spent in considering the desires of the flesh man.

135-136.

Mat. 3:7-9

But when he saw many of the Pharisees and Sadducees coming to his baptism, he said unto them, Ye offspring of vipers, who warned you to flee from the wrath to come?

Bring forth therefore fruit worthy of repentance: and think not to say within yourselves, We have Abraham to our Father: for I say unto you, that God is able of these stones, to raise up children unto Abraham.

And even now the axe also lieth at the root of the trees: every tree therefore that bringeth not forth good fruit is hewn down, and cast into the fire.

137-143.

Interpretation

•   Who warned us "to flee from the wrath to come" is immaterial. It is sufficient for us to realize that by changing our habitual state of mind from the negative to the positive pole of thought we can avoid the continuation of undesirable effects. We can "bring forth therefore fruits worthy of repentance", or make the results of our effort worth the pains that we must take to effect a change of mind on our part.

- Those of us who were not reared from birth in the way of Truth find the work of denial and the breaking up of fixed thought habits very necessary to the clearing of the mind or "the way of the Lord", or the self-controlled habit of thought. We see in our own experience the effects of past unrighteous thinking. Hatred, envy, intolerance, dishonesty of motive, insincerity -- these and other negative traits are the vipers whose offspring we, through ignorance of the law, have allowed ourselves to become. The first viper to be destroyed is the hydra-headed theory of heredity and tradition. Don't fall back on our father Abraham, which is heredity in the Adam line of descent, but bring forth in yourself the fruits of our Father God. Negative tendencies are not simply fruits of our past thinking; they have became great "trees" of habit in the inner life, which bring forth after their kind every season that our thinking makes favorable to their harvest.

- Under the evolutionary law of nature, which Abraham represents, "God is able of these stones to raise up children unto Abraham". John here infers that those who count themselves subject to the law under which Abraham lived and died are mortal instead of spiritual. Lay the axe at the very "root of the tree"; deny all mortal ancestry. Affirm God to be your father and your mother and that you are subject to His law only; then deny the thought of selfishness, or desiring more than you have daily use for. Be just in thought. Do not extort, but silently affirm, "I am willing to abide by the exact law of justice: that which is mine shall come to me, and no more". Let no violent thoughts go from you. Breathe peace and love and harmony through your mind, and baptize the whole world daily in its refreshing sweetness. Then when you have made the proper conditions in your mind there will descend into it a fuller life, a purer love and a greater power than you have ever had; you will be baptized with the Holy Ghost.

- We are to deny place in mind to any thought whose effects are seen to be undesirable. By giving the vitality of our faith to negative beliefs we have encouraged the growth in ourselves of tendencies to sickness, disease, melancholy, doubt, suspicion, uncharitable judgment, and countless other evil "fruits". We are to rid ourselves absolutely of all negative mental growths that keep our consciousness in shadow; to make in the wilderness of the subconsciousness *(subconscious – Ed.)* a clearing into which the "light of the world" may shine.

144.

Luke 3:10, 11

And the multitudes asked him, saying, What then must we do? And he answered and said unto them, He that hath two coats, let him impart to him that hath none; and he that hath food, let him do likewise.

Interpretation

•   Selfishness is the second "viper". Learning the lesson of unselfishness is a necessary step in the reformation of our working principles. We must learn to share our good. Whatever we have realized of divine goodness we must pass on to others. The law of life is not a static principle; to prove its nature, it must keep in motion.

•   The vast majority of our thoughts "the multitude" have no special motive or objective; yet one must share with others whatever good may be in these thoughts. We are concerned largely with material needs – clothing, food, shelter. We are not to hold as all together our own what our thoughts draw to us of these things. When we have attracted substance in the form of material blessings, we are to share those blessings, and thereby attract to ourselves love.

Luke 3:12-13

And there came also publicans to be baptized, and they said unto him, Teacher, what must we do? And he said unto them, Extort no more than that which is appointed you.

Interpretation

•   Another step in mental training is the acquisition of honest thinking. He who becomes aware of the power of the mind to achieve visible and tangible results may feel the temptation to use that power in unworthy ways, the third viper. He may wish to go further than the impersonal nature of Truth justifies, for his own enjoyment and gratification he may try to attract from others more love, more friendship and esteem than they would voluntarily give him.

•   He can do this by fixing his thoughts on them in a personal way, but such thinking is a dishonest use of the law. Those who naturally attract others, who mentally cause others to give them either material substance or immaterial thought with its very real accompaniments, must keep this power to "tax" within bounds. It is appointed to us to attract a moderate amount of the attention of other souls and of their substance. Under the new regime we must "extort no more than that which is appointed you".

Luke 3:14-17

And soldiers also asked him, saying, And we, what must we do: And he said unto them, Extort from no man by violence, neither accuse any one wrongfully; and be content with your wages. And as the people were in expectation, and all men reasoned in their hearts concerning John, whether haply he were the Christ; John answered, saying unto them all, I indeed baptize you with water; but there cometh he that is mightier than I, the latchet of whose shoes I am unworthy to unloose: he shall baptize you in the Holy Spirit and in fire: whose fan is in his hand, thoroughly to cleanse his threshing-floor, and to gather the wheat into his garner; but the chaff he will burn up with unquenchable fire.

152-154.

Interpretation

• Soldiers are indicative of the faculties in man that carry out the behest of the ruling power. The natural man is ruled by an unstable combination of personal desire and will. The truly enlightened man is amenable only to the spiritual I AM, or divine indwelling purpose.

• When all has been done toward the unmaking of negative mental habits, the good work still remains to be undertaken. This work is the establishing of oneself in the Christ consciousness. John taught that we are to do honestly and conscientiously the work in which we are already engaged. He went little further. Dedication of the life to the inner law, and concentration on the underlying Spirit back of every appearance, kindle in the soul the fire or enthusiasm for the divine ideal. The mighty sweep of true understanding winnows the wheat from the chaff — reveals the vital issues of life stripped of all trivial and superficial interests. This goal is set before the eyes of everyone who prepares his mind for the incoming of the Holy Spirit.

155-156.

Mat. 3:13-15

Then cometh Jesus from Galilee to the Jordan unto John, to be baptized of him. But John would have hindered him, saying, I have need to be baptized of thee, and comest thou to me? But Jesus answering said unto him, Suffer it now; for thus it becometh us to fulfill all righteousness. Then he suffereth him.

156.

Luke 3:18-22

With many other exhortations therefore preached he good tidings unto the people; but Herod the tetrarch, being reproved by him for Herodias his brother's wife, and for all the evil things which Herod had done, added this also, to them all that he shut up John in prison.

Now it came to pass, when all the people were baptized, that, Jesus also having been baptized, and praying, the heaven was opened. And the Holy Spirit descended in a bodily form, as a dove, upon him, and a voice came out of heaven, Thou art my beloved Son: in thee I am well pleased.

Interpretation

• The baptism of John the Baptist represents the cleansing of the mind that must precede the receiving of the higher or spiritual consciousness. After Jesus had received this cleansing of consciousness, the Holy Spirit descended upon him with its peace dove, and acknowledged him as Son; in other words, he received the second or spiritual baptism. This means that the illumined intellect John the Baptist prepares the consciousness for the "peace that passes understanding. The old life must be left behind before the new life with Christ can begin. But the sense man, feeling the result of law, tries to do away with the progressive, up building Spirit. Herod would have John imprisoned.

• All Christian workers recognize the necessity for preparing the mind for the descent of the Son of God consciousness that follows the spiritual baptism. In every church revival this law is exemplified over and over; the necessity of letting go of the old life is proclaimed as part of the price of the new grace in Christ Jesus. The great joy that comes to those who comply with this condition is evidence of the efficacy of the process. To receive new ideas one must willingly give up old ones. Some people are slow of spiritual growth because they are tenacious in holding to mortal thoughts. The thoughts and the ways of the mortal man are dear to them -- they do not go with Jesus to be baptized of John.

• Events portend a Holy Spirit baptism the world over. There is a great influx of spiritual power into the world. Those who accept Truth and put away the evils of the carnal mind find soul happiness and bodily health far beyond anything ever before experienced in human history. Truly, the heavens are now opened, and the proclamation is being made to all who are genuinely repentant: "Thou art my beloved son: in thee I am well pleased."

CHAPTER 3

WILDERNESS (AND TEMPTATIONS)

161-163.

Mark 1:12-13a

And straightway the Spirit driveth him forth into the wilderness. And he was in the wilderness forty days.

Mat. 4:3-11

And the tempter came and said unto him, If thou art the Son of God, command that these stones became bread. But he answered and said, It is written, Man shall not live by bread alone, but by every word that proceedeth out of the mouth of God. Then the devil taketh him into the holy city; and he set him on the pinnacle of the temple. And said unto him, if thou are the Son of God, cast thyself down: for it is written, He shall give his angels charge concerning thee: and, on their hands they shall bear thee up, lest haply thou dash thy foot against a stone. Jesus said unto him, again it is written, Thou shalt not make trial of the Lord thy God.

Again, the devil taketh him unto an exceeding high mountain, and showed him all the kingdoms of the world, and the glory of them; And he said unto him, All these things will I give thee, if thou wilt fall down and worship me. Then saith Jesus unto him, Get thee hence, Satan: for it is written, Thou shalt worship the Lord thy God, and him only shalt thou serve.

Mark 1:13b

And he was with the wild beasts; and the angels ministered unto him.

Luke 4:13

And when the devil had completed every temptation, he departed from him for a season.

Mat. 4:2

And when he had fasted forty days and forty nights, he afterward hungered.

164-174.

Interpretation

• In the development of the Christ Mind, an entirely new and wider set of ideas and situations must be met; the allegories of Jesus are meant to show us how to deal with the thoughts and desires of the soul, and how to place them under proper discipline. Spiritual discernment and unselfish devotion to the highest form of Truth are demanded of those who would meet and overcome the temptations of personal consciousness. Thousands are baptized by Spirit, but when led into the wilderness of their own subjective natures they fail to avail themselves of the guidance of Spirit.

• They use their God-given power for selfish ends and fall short of the Jesus Christ man. He "hath been in all points tempted like as we are, yet without sin."

• In the wilderness of the subconscious mind are both angels and wild beasts. Among the multitude of undisciplined and uncultivated thoughts that compose this realm below the surface of consciousness lurk various selfish ambitions. Over these in authority rule the angels our spiritual perceptive faculties through whose ministrations we are enabled to conquer the demands of the natural self.

• Few of those persons who live on the surface of life feel inclined to probe the depths of their own subconsciousness *(subconscious – Ed.)*, in order to learn who and what they are. After Jesus Christ was baptized of the Holy Spirit, He immediately felt impelled to sound these inner depths in the determination to find Himself and thus to make sure of His mission. He knew that man must be disciplined and tested before he can be sure that the individual spiritual consciousness or "Christ in you," is master of his thoughts. The Spirit of Truth is the universal power that connects man with God, and like an enthusiastic teacher helping a bright pupil, it pushes us forward to the lessons that will most quickly prove our ability. "Straightway the Spirit driveth him forth into the Wilderness."

• Spiritually discerned, the temptation of Jesus teaches a quickening of the whole man when the Holy Spirit descends into the consciousness.

• The Devil is the mass of thoughts that have been built up in consciousness through many generations of earthly experiences, and crystallized into what may be termed human personality, or carnal mind. Acquisitiveness, vanity and ambition rise up and ask for recognition. Many have been quickened by the Christ Spirit only to fall under the subtle spell of this mortal world along some of these lines. Making money out of spiritual powers is especially common in this day. This is the first temptation turning stones into bread. For us to yield would be to affirm material things to be sufficient to satisfy our hunger, and to depend on them, instead of looking for the bread that comes down from heaven -- the word of God. Hereafter we are to feed our souls with new truths daily, in order that we may grow in spiritual ways.

• The second temptation means that we are challenged to go suddenly from a high state of spiritual illumination down into body consciousness, personality devil assuring us of/safety. We must not make a display of our spiritual power. To do so puts us at the mercy of the personal consciousness.

• Bragging about one's healing ability, or any other spiritual acquirements, is vanity, heady egotism, the "pinnacle of the temples".

• The third temptation comes when we have attained mastery over such material thoughts, so that we can control even outer events. To exercise this control for personal ends is to exalt personality worship the devil.

- The difference between the Son of God and the son of man is brought out in Jesus' answer to the tempter, "get thee hence, Satan: for it is written, Thou shalt worship the Lord thy God, and him only shalt thou serve." When this temptation arises in our experience we should know that under divine law there is but One worthy of our worship and service, the. Lord our God.
- "The exceeding high mountain" is the exalting of material things end the ambition to rule over people and earthly organizations.
- The one who would attain Christ-hood, become the "image and likeness of God" in both soul and body, must meet each of these various tendencies of the mortal consciousness with a firm No!
- When the quickening of Spirit takes place in consciousness to the extent that the Christ within us is realized, felt, and known, we rise above the demands of the flesh-and-sense world. We depend on the inspiration of Spirit rather than on the reasoning's of the intellectual man. The enticements of sense and of pride of the intellect fall away. Even the first faint dawn of Spirit in man's conscious mind becomes a treasure, worth more to him than all intellectual gifts.
- The temptation of Jesus took place within Himself. The place of overcoming is within the consciousness of man.
- The forty-day fast is a complete denial of sense demands. When we keep such a fast we are living, in thought, above material needs. We are "led up" in Spirit and our appetites and our passions are for a season so subdued that we think they will never again trouble us. "And when the devil had completed every temptation, he departed from him for a season." But "he afterward hungered." There is a return to sense consciousness.

174 a-b-c-d-e-f-g-h-i-j-k.

(Reminder Editorial Note regarding 174 a-b-c-d-e-f-g-h-i-j-k: Although the linage was placed at this point in manuscript, 174 a-k, the lineage is an important aspect of the Birth Initiation/Event and is referred to in several segments of the Birth Initiation. Thus, it was moved to the Birth section. No other major editorial changes of this nature were made to this document. Rev. Toni G. Boehm)

CHAPTER 4

MINISTRY THROUGH DEMONSTRATION

(AND TRANSFIGURATION)

175-179.

Mat. 4:12a

Now when he heard that John was delivered up,

Luke 4:14-30

And Jesus returned in the power of the Spirit into Galilee: and a fame went out concerning him through all the region round about. And he taught in their synagogues, being glorified of all. And he came to Nazareth, where he had been brought up: and he entered, as his custom was, into the synagogue on the Sabbath day, and stood up to read.

And there was delivered unto him the book of the prophet Isaiah. And he opened the book, and found the place where it was written,
  The Spirit of the Lord is upon me,
Because he anointed me to preach good tidings to the poor:
He hath sent me to proclaim release to the captives,
And recovering of sight to the blind,
To set at liberty them that are bruised,
To proclaim the acceptable year of the Lord.

And he closed the book, and gave it back to the attendant, and sat down: and the eyes of all in the synagogue were fastened on him. And he began to say unto them, To-day hath this scripture been fulfilled in your ears. And all bare him witness, and wondered at the words of grace which proceeded out of his mouth: and they said, Is not this Joseph's son?

And he said unto them, Doubtless ye will say unto me this parable, Physician, heal thyself: whatsoever we have heard done at Capernaum, do also here in thine own country. And he said, Verily I say unto you, No prophet is acceptable in his own country. But of a truth I say unto you, There were many widows in Israel in the days of Elijah, when the heaven was shut up three years and six months, when there came a great famine over all the land; and unto none of them was Elijah sent, but only to Sarephath, in the land of Sidon, unto a woman that was a widow. And there were many lepers in Israel in the time of Elisha the prophet; and none of them was cleansed, but only Naaman the Syrian. And they were all filled with wrath in the synagogue, as they heard these things; and they rose up, and cast him forth out of the city, and led him unto the brow of the hill whereon their city was built, that they might throw him down headlong. But he passing through the midst of them went his way.

Interpretation

• In individual consciousness when the indwelling Christ is set into full action the illuminating power of the word spreads the glad tidings to different states of consciousness and they throw open their doors for a greater inflow of spiritual understanding.

• Truth is presented in such unpretentious garb, in such simple guise, that those who have fostered its growth do not recognize it when it bursts forth. Jesus represents the Spirit of Truth declaring its mission and power in the place of its development—the common, everyday mind (Nazareth). The highest spiritual truth may be flashed into your mind while you are performing the commonest duties of life. Nazareth is a type of inferiority; it was considered a community of commonplace, if not disreputable people. "Can any good thing come out of Nazareth?" Yet here in this scrubby village Jesus was reared—here in your mediocre mind the Christ truth is expressed.

• But we know these trite statements of Truth so well—they are so familiar to us that we cannot conceive that they are the mighty power which we are seeking to relieve us from the bonds of sense. "Is not this Joseph's son?" The power that brings salvation from every ill is within us. In no other place will we find the Truth that sets us free.

• Do you want healing without fulfilling the law of right thinking and doing? Then you are not receiving the Christ Spirit in its right relation. You are seeking the temporal instead of the eternal, and if you let this superficial phase of mind rule, you will reject the Christ Spirit and cast him out of your mind.

• (Do you want healing without fulfilling the law of right thinking and doing? Then you are not receiving the Christ Spirit in its right relation. You are seeking the temporal instead of the eternal, and if you let this superficial phase of mind rule, you will reject the Christ Spirit and cast him out of your mind.)

• All true healing, all true lasting reform of character, is brought about through spiritualizing the mind. When the Christ "comes unto his own," he comes with this thorough process as the foundation of his work in the soul. The transient healing of a leper among thousands or the temporary alleviation of the needs of a widow through the power of God, are not highly prized by those who seek thorough regeneration. These things are possible, but they do not last unless there is a sure foundation—a right relation established between the Creator and the created. Many times it is highly beneficial to an error state of consciousness to have to listen to the unadulterated truth as given forth by the Spirit of Truth. Whether graciously accepted or not, it leaves its impress on this error state of mind, and in one experience or another, filters through and is a great help in casting out error and establishing the truth. Every day your inner ears are filled full of this Truth. You know the right, you know the just, you know the pure. This is the Scripture written upon the heart which is always filling you full. "Today hath this scripture been fulfilled in your ears."

187.

Mat. 4:13-17

And leaving Nazareth, he came and dwelt in Capernaum, which is by the sea, in the borders of Zebulun and Naphtali: that it might be fulfilled which was spoken through Isaiah the prophet, saying,
The land of Zebulun and the land of Naphtali,
Toward the sea, beyond the Jordan,
Galilee of the Gentiles,
The people that sat in darkness
Saw a great light,
And to them that sat in the region and shadow of death,
To them did light spring up.
 From that time began Jesus to preach, and to say, Repent ye; for the kingdom of heaven is at hand.

189-190.

Interpretation

• The Galilean ministry of Jesus has its parallel in the experience of everyone who enters upon the spiritual development for which Jesus stands. This ministry represents the second movement of Truth in the consciousness. First is the perception of Truth, which is typified by John the Baptist. The natural man sets himself right and so opens the way for the higher principle, the Christ light.
• With the coming of the Christ light to his consciousness one begins to realize the good news (gospel) that the Kingdom of god is not afar off, but is at hand. He awakens to the fact that by changing his mind from error to truth, by believing in the good only, he can bring into his present experience all that pertains to the kingdom of heaven—light, peace, harmony, joy, health, spiritual understanding, abundance of every good.
• To repent means to change the mind. It is an admission to God of our shortcomings and a sincere desire to do better in the future.

191-193.

Luke 5:1-11

Now it came to pass, while the multitude pressed upon him and heard the word of God, that he was standing by the lake of Gennesaret; and he saw two boats standing by the lake: but the fishermen had gone out of them, and were washing their nets. And he entered into one of the boats, which was Simon's, and asked him to put out a little from the land. And he sat down and taught the multitudes out of the boat.

And when he had left speaking, he said unto Simon, Put out into the deep, and let down your nets for a draught. And Simon answered and said, Master, we toiled all night, and took nothing: but at thy word I will let down the nets. And when they had done this, they inclosed a great multitude of fishes; and their nets were breaking; and they beckoned unto their partners in the other boat, that they should come and help them. And they came, and filled both the boats, so that they began to sink. But Simon Peter, when he saw it, fell down at Jesus' knees, saying, Depart from me; for I am a sinful man, O Lord. For he was amazed, and all that were with him, at the draught of the fishes which they had taken; and so were also James and John, sons of Zebedee, who were partners with Simon. And Jesus said unto Simon, Fear not; from henceforth thou shalt catch men. And when they had brought their boats to land, they left all, and followed him.

194-195.

Interpretation

•   The boat symbolizes a positive, sustaining state of consciousness that prevents one from sinking into a negative condition (water). When the indwelling Christ is established in this positive state of consciousness it is able to teach to the multitude (of thoughts) the truths of Being that will help them in establishing the firm Christ consciousness.

•   Your thinking faculty is always active, zealous, impulsive, but not always wise. Its nature is to think, and think it will. Its food is ideas,-- symbolized in the Gospels as fishes—that is forever casting its net on the right, or left, for a draught. You alone can direct where its net shall be cast. You are he who says, "Cast the net on the right side." The "right side" is always on the side of Truth, the side of power. Whenever you, the Master, are there, the nets are filled with ideas, because you are in touch with the infinite storehouse of wisdom.

196.

Luke 4:31-34

And he came down to Capernaum, a city of Galilee. And he was teaching them on the Sabbath day: and they were astonished at his teaching; for his word was with authority. And in the synagogue there was a man, that had a spirit of an unclean demon; and he cried out with a loud voice, Ah! what have we to do with thee, Jesus thou Nazarene? art thou come to destroy us? I know thee who thou art, the Holy One of God.

197.

Mark 1:25-28

And Jesus rebuked him, saying, Hold thy peace, and come out of him. And the unclean spirit, tearing him and crying with a loud voice, came out of him. And they were all amazed, insomuch that they questioned among themselves, saying, What is this? a new teaching! with authority he commandeth even the unclean spirits, and they obey him. And the report of him went out straightway everywhere into all the region of Galilee round about.

198-204.

Interpretation

• Capernaum means "village of Nahum," and the name Nahum means "consolation" or "comforter." So Capernaum—village of comfort or consolation—refers to an inner conviction of the abiding compassion and restoring power of Being.

• The synagogue fitly represents the mind of man, or the phase of man's mind, that is given over to religious thought. The synagogues of the Jews can also be said to represent aggregations of religious ideas based on Truth, thoughts that have not yet received the inspiration of the whole Truth. They are what might be called fixed religious states of consciousness, bred in us by tradition, education, and inheritance. It is part of the very tissue of our brain cells, and holds its sway even after we have fully accepted the new revelation.

• In the new birth, or regeneration, the rebuilding of your consciousness begins in this synagogue or religious mentality. The mentality must be taught the truth about God, the one supreme Mind. The true Sabbath day is the inner peace and the assurance of omnipresent good, which come to one as he learns to rest from mortal thought and to abide in the consciousness of Spirit.

• The man with the unclean spirit refers to a fixed state of thought in which impurity is dominant. In other words, it is sense consciousness possessed with the belief that it can find satisfaction in the sensations of the flesh. Man has built within himself a seeming law that is based on mortal thought desire, and this must be put away. In right relation the temple of God (man's organism), is pure, holy, and perfect, but in order that it may manifest as it really is in Spirit, the demon of sensuality must be cast out. The unclean spirit of doubt—doubt of the wisdom of following spiritual leading all the way questions the necessity of unqualified loyalty to the Christ ideal. "What have we to do with thee, Jesus thou Nazarene" art thou come to destroy us?" The doubter fears to identify himself with "the Holy One of God," lest he lose what makes his life dear to him—his personality.

• The undisciplined thoughts are astonished at the teaching of the I AM or higher mind of Spirit. "With authority he commandeth even the unclean spirits, and they obey him."

• Spirit inspires from within. When the inspiration, or inner teaching of Spirit, comes to us we do not feel the need of quoting anyone as authority, since the truth itself is authority and it bows to no human exponent.

• The demon of impure thought and desire recognizes that the one who speaks with the authority of I AM is the "Holy One of God." The rebuke of Jesus, metaphysically interpreted, is a denial of sense power and an affirmation of peace, followed by the command to "come out of him." The "tearing" and the "crying" result from the resistance of sense thought to Truth. To be torn by impure thoughts and desires is an old experience, but the authority of the Christ is always able to command obedience to the highest Truth, the conviction of the true self that loyalty to Spirit works out one's greatest good even in the common round of daily life (in all the region of Galilee round about).

205.

Mark 1:29-31

And straightway, when they were come out of the synagogue, they came into the house of Simon and Andrew, with James and John. Now Simon's wife's mother lay sick of a fever; and straightway they tell him of her: and he came and took her by the hand, and raised her up; and the fever left her, and she ministered unto them.

206-208.

Interpretation

• The name Simon means "hearing," "obeying." Under the dominance of mortal mind one hears—gives heed to unbelieving thoughts that attribute power to evil. Thus fears and anxieties are introduced into the soul.
• The healing of Simon's wife's mother illustrates the authority of the spiritual man over disease. All those who have quickened and made alive the sleeping consciousness of their own souls can speak to the sick and raise them.
• The most potent and powerful factor in the quickened subconsciousness *(subconscious – Ed.)* is love or compassion. When man awakens the soul love and unites it with the Spirit, there is a great sympathy and compassion flowing constantly forth that is life-giving and spiritualizing to everything that it touches. The touching of her hand by Jesus typifies the sympathetic life touching and unifying all life. "Jesus took her by the hand and raised her up." The head and the heart meet and bring poise and harmony in mind and body, which is wholeness.
• The actual work of redemption first begins in this spiritual understanding (or understanding of ideas). The process of redemption does not destroy former ideas, even though they be purely intellectual. It is a sublimation or transmutation of forces, to the end that they may be used in working out greater ideals.

209-210.

Mark 1:40-45

And there cometh to him a leper, beseeching him, and kneeling down to him, and saying unto him, If thou wilt, thou canst make me clean. And being moved with compassion, he stretched forth his hand, and touched him, and saith unto him, I will; be thou made clean. And straightway the leprosy departed from him, and he was made clean. And he strictly charged him, and straightway sent him out, and saith unto him, See thou say nothing to any man: but go show thyself to the priest, and offer for thy cleansing the things which Moses commanded, for a testimony unto them. But he went out, and began to publish it much, and to spread abroad the matter, insomuch that Jesus could no more openly enter into a city, but was without in desert places: and they came to him from every quarter.

211-214.

Interpretation

• This Scripture reveals the work of the I AM, the spiritual consciousness in us, as setting into action new life and energy in the various centers in our organism, redeeming and strengthening all their sick, weak thoughts.

• The healing of the leper symbolizes the cleansing which takes place when we begin to realize that our life is spiritual and not material. As the more abundant life of Spirit finds its way freely into our being, the leprous character of our old ideas of life comes to light, and the ideas are cleansed.

• Whenever leprosy is brought to our attention in the Bible, the idea of uncleanness is attached to it; whenever a leper is mentioned as being healed, we are informed that he was cleansed or made clean. It can be seen readily that this disease belongs to material thoughts about life, and to attachment to the grosser sensations of the flesh. These error ideas must be denied away and the purifying, renewing power of Spirit affirmed and realized.

• Thus the fullness of glad, free, abundant Christ life is awakened in us, and we are resurrected into newness of life, health, and joy.

• In all the work of redemption, the spiritual I AM (symbolized by Jesus) realizes that its powers and its authority depend upon its constant contact with Principle. It therefore withdraws at intervals and makes sure of its relationship with Spirit.

• No press of duties, no insistence on the part of seekers after its attention, can divert spiritual I AM from its habitual recourse to the enabling power of its Source. Long before the time arrives for active work to be done, the power to do that work should be sought and made sure of. After such a period of establishing a closer union with Spirit, the I AM is strengthened and is ready to continue its ministry.

215.

Luke 4:40-41

And when the sun was setting, all they that had any sick with divers diseases brought them unto him; and he laid his hands on every one of them, and healed them. And demons also came out from many, crying out, and saying, Thou art the Son of God. And rebuking them, he suffered them not to speak, because they knew that he was the Christ.

Interpretation

•   In this scripture after pressing desires have received attention and there is time for calm reflection and meditation, the way is opened for weak and anxious thoughts to be brought before the altar of the Lord where many of them are redeemed and transmuted into constructive power.

Mark 1:35

And in the morning, a great while before day, he rose up and went out, and departed into a desert place, and there prayed.

Luke 4:42-44

and the multitudes sought after him, and came unto him, and would have stayed him, that he should not go from them. But he said unto them, I must preach the good tidings of the kingdom of God to the other cities also: for therefore was I sent. And he was preaching in the synagogues of Galilee.

Interpretation

•   "In the morning, a great while before day, he...prayed." Reserves of spiritual strength should never be allowed to run low, regardless of the exigent demands of daily life. Indeed, the more pressing those demands become, the greater is the supply of spiritual strength required to cope with them.
•   As soon as Jesus was renewed and strengthened by contact with Spirit, He went forth again to preach and free. He went to the other cities also, denoting that His outer activity corresponded to His inner quickening.

Mat. 4:23-25

And Jesus went about in all Galilee, teaching in their synagogues, and preaching the gospel of the kingdom, and healing all manner of disease and all manner of sickness among the people. And the report of him went forth into all Syria: and they brought unto him all that were sick, holden with divers diseases and torments, possessed with demons, and epileptic, and palsied; and he healed them. And there followed him great multitudes from Galilee and Decapolis and Jerusalem and Judaea and from beyond the Jordan.

Interpretation

•   The text states definitely and clearly that Jesus went about preaching and healing all manner of diseases among the people. In the 24th verse some diseases are named, and they include those which doctors call organic and which certain practitioners of Christian healing have put aside as beyond the power of God.

222-224.

Luke 5:17-26

And it came to pass on one of those days, that he was teaching; and there were Pharisees and doctors of the law sitting by, who were come out of every village of Galilee and Judaea and Jerusalem: and the power of the Lord was with him to heal. And behold, men bring on a bed a man that was palsied: and they sought to bring him in, and to lay him before him. And not finding by what way they might bring him in because of the multitude, they went up to the housetop, and let him down through the tiles with his couch into the midst before Jesus. And seeing their faith, he said, Man, thy sins are forgiven thee. And the scribes and the Pharisees began to reason, saying, Who is this that speaketh blasphemies? Who can forgive sins, but God alone? But Jesus perceiving their reasonings, answered and said unto them, Why reason ye in your hearts? Which is easier, to say, Thy sins are forgiven thee; or to say, Arise and walk? But that ye may know that the Son of man hath authority on earth to forgive sins (he said unto him that was palsied), I say unto thee, Arise, and take up thy couch, and go unto thy house. And immediately he rose up before them, and took up that whereon he lay, and departed to his house, glorifying God. And amazement took hold on all, and they glorified God; and they were filled with fear, saying, We have seen strange things to-day.

225-231.

Interpretation

• The spiritual nature in man knows that man's birthright is fullness of life and health. The men who carried the palsied man to Jesus signify an innate desire to restore the body to health. The inner urge for a more perfect manifestation of wholeness was so strong that even the multitude could not daunt them. "They went up to the housetop, and let him down through the tiles with his couch." Jesus was moved by their determination and faith, and readily asked forgiveness and healing for the man.

• Letting the sick man down through the roof means that the thoughts of man regarding his life and his body must be raised to a higher state than the mere mortal and physical before they can get the attention of the super-consciousness, or Christ the I AM. One accomplishes this elevating of the thoughts by affirming that one's life, strength, power, and substance are not material but spiritual.

• When one's thoughts are thus lifted to the plane of the Christ consciousness of life and perfection, one is forgiven and healed. True repentance is a definite turning away from error to Truth in thought, word, and deed. Forgiveness is the erasing of the error, and when the cause of disease is removed, manifest health follows quickly.

•   Jesus perceived that the scribes were reasoning among themselves and calling Him a blasphemer. They did not understand that man must conform to the divine standard of mental and soul harmony, so that the discordant effects disappear and the sin is forgiven.

•   Jesus' healing always called forth the censure of the scribes. He taught that it is the prerogative of the Son of man to forgive sin. But the scribes thought it blasphemy for man to claim to do what they construed to be the exclusive privilege of God. So those who today read only the letter of life, and have no understanding of mental action and the metaphysical character of the soul, reason.

•   To one who is helpless in the grip of sin or sickness, affirmation is a sure road back to health and wholeness.

•   When man discerns the law of thought and its effect on the vital energies of the organism, he should begin at once to exercise the dominion of the supreme I AM. He should not only forgive the sin mentally but also speak a word of freedom to the condition, saying to the ignorant thought, "Thy sins are forgiven," and to the thought of lack of power, "Arise, and take up thy couch, and go unto thy house."

•   Jesus shows that forgiveness of sin is followed by a release from those conditions which the sin has brought about.   Peloubet says, "There are in the Bible nine terms for sin—debts, missing the mark, lawlessness, disobedience, transgression, fault (moral aberration), defeat, impiousness, dis-harmony or discord. For all sin we need forgiveness. And there are as many words for forgiveness as for sin—forgive, remit, send away, cover up, blot out, destroy, wash away, cleanse, make them as if they had never been."

•   The crowds that gathered to hear Jesus symbolize the concentration of thoughts that follows the proclamation of truth in the mentality.

232.

Mat. 9:9

And as Jesus passed by from thence, he saw a man, called Matthew, sitting at the place of toll: and he saith unto him, Follow me. And he arose, and followed him.

233-234.

Interpretation

•   Matthew (called Levi in Mark 2: 14 and Luke 5: 27) represents the will faculty in man. He willingly left all and followed Jesus. In the regeneration man must follow Jesus and learn to control, direct and govern the faculties of mind. To do this efficaciously, he must in a measure withdraw his attention from outer or material occupations, and give his thought and time to things of the Spirit.

•   The will always enters into man's decisions. The will makes the final choice to give up all and follow Jesus. The surrendering of the old ideas and conditions that the greater increase of good may come into one's life is based on this faculty. The will has been given over to the thought of accumulation but imposes a tax on all external resources (tax gatherer). In spiritual unfoldment the will is converted and is taught by prayer and meditation how to stabilize the universal substance. Under the spiritual law the will becomes a producer instead of a parasite. When the individual will has become a disciple of the Christ, spiritual I AM, the schooling of man begins.

235-236.

Mat. 9:10-15

And it came to pass, as he sat at meat in the house, behold, many publicans and sinners came and sat down with Jesus and his disciples. And when the Pharisees saw it, they said unto his disciples, Why eateth your Teacher with the publicans and sinners? But when he heard it, he said, They that are whole have no need of a physician, but they that are sick. But go ye and learn what this meaneth, I desire mercy, and not sacrifice, for I came not to call the righteous, but sinners.

Then come to him the disciples of John, saying, Why do we and the Pharisees fast oft, but thy disciples fast not? And Jesus said unto them, Can the sons of the bride chamber mourn, as long as the bridegroom is with them? but the days will come, when the bridegroom shall be taken away from them, and then will they fast.

237-242.

Interpretation

• When men set up a law its observance burdensome, they are slaves of their own creation. The Jews had become burdened with observance of the letter of the law, and had a multitude of ridiculous prohibitions and external formalities, from which Jesus sought to rescue them by His teaching and example. Before man can rise into his natural dominion, he must understand and realize that God's whole plan of creation is to bring forth the perfect man.
• This means that man is the supreme thing in creation and that all laws are for his convenience. The universal tendency of great men to manifest excellency proves that it is natural. Most of them, however, miss the mark by seeking to dominate other men and nations before they have mastered themselves.
• Feasting is symbolical of abundance, and represents a condition in which the individual is appropriating. Jesus is the bridegroom, who is providing generously for His friends. This represents the period in our spiritual growth in which we realize the inexhaustible abundance of the Christ Mind. We attain our highest realizations of truth, when with spiritual perception, we see our birthright.
• All the teachings of Jesus Christ point to increase, to abundant good to be realized and enjoyed here and now. Those who forsake all to follow Him are promised a hundred fold in this present time. His promises of good to

those who keep His sayings, and follow His example, are so magnificent that men have construed them amiss. They have said that these promises will be fulfilled in heaven, after death, and that they are figures pertaining to the soul, and so forth. Jesus, however, stated emphatically that these things are to be fulfilled now; the kingdom of heaven (all the fullness of God) is at hand.

• The old man of the flesh is not overcome in a day, and he will assert his presence now and then, so forcibly that the bridegroom will seem to have been taken away. These are the "days" that will come. Then we may need to "fast"; that is, deny the seeming error. Since the overcoming power of Jesus Christ never leaves those who have faith in Him (Lo, I am with you always), we may be restored quickly to our realization of abundant good, if we will. One gains freedom by keeping the spirit of the law; seeking to observe the letter only, tends to great bondage. Jesus kept the inner spirit of the law though He did not try to abide by all the external rules that the Jews had established.

243.

Mat. 9:16-17

And no man putteth a piece of undressed cloth upon an old garment; for that which should fill it up taketh from the garment, and a worse rent is made. Neither do men put new wine into old wine-skins: else the skins burst, and the wine is spilled, and the skins perish: but they put new wine into fresh wine-skins, and both are preserved.

244-246.

Interpretation

• In order to unfold spiritually it is necessary continually to infuse into soul and body consciousness the newness and the beauty and strength of the Christ nature. In this state of consciousness there can be a constant inflowing of Spirit.

• This scripture teaches us the necessity of cleansing, harmonizing, and renewing our body temples (wine-skins) by knowing the truth of their infinite, abiding nature, that they may be able to contain the constant inflow of new spiritual life and power (the new wine) which is the experience of those who continue in truth.

• Our body temples must be renewed by our speaking to them words of Truth, that they may be made able to receive and hold the abundant, resurrecting Christ life. In mind and body we must be purified and regenerated in order to enter into an abiding life consciousness.

• We do not overcome our errors by covering them in our consciousness and refusing to recognize them in any way. A right adjustment is made by uncovering them, by correcting them through exercise of the forgiving love of the Christ mind, and by feasting upon words of Truth. The intellectual thought forces within man need greater discipline than the spiritual thought forces.

Mat. 12:1-8 (4)

At that season Jesus went on the Sabbath day through the grainfields; and his disciples were hungry and began to pluck ears and to eat. But the Pharisees, when they saw it, said unto him, Behold, thy disciples do that which it is not lawful to do upon the Sabbath. But he said unto them, Have ye not read what David did, when he was hungry, and they that were with him; how he entered into the house of God

Mark 2:26

when Abiathar was high priest

Mat. 12:4b

and ate the showbread, which it was not lawful for him to eat, neither for them that were with him, but only for the priests? Or have ye not read in the law, that on the Sabbath day the priests in the temple profane the Sabbath, and are guiltless? But I say unto you, that one greater than the temple is here. But if ye had known what this meaneth, I desire mercy, and not sacrifice, ye would not have condemned the guiltless. For the Son of man is lord of the Sabbath.

249-256.

Interpretation

•   Jesus was endeavoring to make the people understand that man is lord of the Sabbath and is only exercising his God-given authority when he lets God's will express in him and through him in any form.

•   The true Sabbath day is that state of mind in which we rest from outer work and give ourselves to meditation and to the study of things spiritual.

•   The Sabbath is of real benefit to man, and if he observes it in the right spirit he will come into great spiritual illumination on that day.

•   One who understands the true spirit of the Sabbath does not need to follow certain prescribed rules laid down by men. It is necessary to open the mind to an appreciation of God's rest and peace. On the Sabbath, Jesus' disciples plucked corn and ate, much to the displeasure of the Pharisees, whose lives were governed by definite detailed rules of action concerning this day.

•   When they remonstrated with Jesus, he informed them that the "Sabbath was made for man, and not man for the Sabbath."

•   When we have the spirit of the Sabbath we need no outer rules. Man requires rest and man requires recreation, but the greatest rest is attained by abiding in the spirit of the Sabbath, which is the fruition of all our efforts. The greatest recreation is in the renewing of the mind and body by letting the substance and life of the Christ Mind enter freely into the organism.

- We should remember that after a spiritual affirmation is made there should be a period of rest from making affirmations. During this rest period the mind should be in a quiet attitude of confidence, and should tend to spirituality, to building one up in Truth. We must be certain that results will follow. The farmer plows his ground and plants his seed, but he waits for the seed to grow before he cultivates. In developing his abilities, man should make certain efforts through study and meditation. Then he should have periods of quietness in order to let his ideas unfold. After a certain growth has been made he can again work, and cultivate his growing talents.

- Metaphysicians have found that it is necessary to have periods of relaxation from metaphysical effort. A change of mind from deep seriousness to the consideration of things in lighter vein will sometimes give ideas sown by Spirit opportunity to grow and develop.

- The observance of every seventh day as a day of rest, or Sabbath, has its source deep in the constitution of things.

- "And on the seventh day God finished his work which he had made; and he rested on the seventh day from all his work which he had made. And God blessed the seventh day and hallowed it."

- The quotation from Genesis presents in concrete words a law that pervades the universe. The rock-ribbed earth beneath our feet bears record of six great creative periods, with a seventh in process. Seven movements of the creative law are found at the foundation of the world about us. The seven colors of the spectrum, the seven notes of music, the seven senses of man (Intuition and telepathy being the two not yet universally developed), all point to these degrees, or days of action and rest.

- Among nearly all peoples similar rest days have been instituted, and history shows that Moses was not the originator of the system. The observance of a weekly rest day is now very widely held to prove a natural basis in the needs of man. The persistency with which such an institution has been maintained for many ages among Jews, Christians, Mohammedans, and some of the so-called pagan nations, amply supports this view. It has been found by experience that one day in seven is the right proposition. During the French Revolution, when the decade was substituted for the week, and each tenth day devoted to rest, it was found insufficient. Moses borrowed the usage from the Babylonian civilization, as recently discovered cuneiform tablets record the observances of a seventh day of holy rest.

257-260.

Mat. 12:9-12

And he departed thence, and went into their synagogue: and behold, a man having a withered hand. And they asked him, saying, Is it lawful to heal on the Sabbath day? that they might accuse him.

Mark 3:4a

And he saith unto them, Is it lawful on the Sabbath day to do good, or to do harm? to save a life, or to kill?

Mat. 12:11-12

What man shall there be of you, that shall have one sheep, and if this fall into a pit on the Sabbath day, will he not lay hold on it, and lift it out? How much then is a man of more value than a sheep! Wherefore it is lawful to do good on the Sabbath day.

Mark 3:4b-6

And when he had looked round about on them with anger, being grieved at thehardening of their heart, he saith unto the man, Stretch forth thy hand. And he stretched it forth; and his hand was restored. And the Pharisees went out, and straightway with the Herodians took counsel against him, how they might destroy him.

Mat. 12:15-21

And Jesus perceiving it withdrew from thence: and many followed him; and he healed them all, and charged them that they should not make him known: that it might be fulfilled which was spoken through Isaiah the prophet, saying,

> Behold, my servant whom I have chosen; My beloved in whom my soul is well pleased:
> I will put my Spirit upon him, And he shall declare judgment to the Gentiles.
> He shall not strive, nor cry aloud; Neither shall any one hear his voice in the streets.
> A bruised reed shall he not break, And smoking flax shall he not quench,
> Till he send forth judgment unto victory. And in his name shall the Gentiles hope.

261-263.

Interpretation

• By the power and understanding gained in the inner spiritual worship, we can free the mind from such bondage to inefficiency as is typified by the man with the withered hand, whom Jesus healed. The hand represents executive ability.

• Jesus observed the Sabbath, but it had become burdened with worship of the letter, and had a multitude of ridiculous prohibitions and external formalities, from which he rescued it by His bold freedom and disregard of manmade laws.

• Jesus claimed that it was a very grievous sin or error to allow the mind to be so blinded by manmade laws that it could not use reason and common sense logic.

• It is lawful to do good on the Sabbath, whether it consists in preaching in a pulpit, healing the sick, or in any other way saving men from ignorance and its results.

- Spiritual man does not fight knowing that everything must be adjusted under divine law. When there are those who are hidebound in their ideas it is best to leave them to work out their own salvation. (And Jesus perceiving it withdrew from hence) often the price is paid by many hard experiences. However all roads eventually lead to the light. Those who follow in the footsteps of Jesus always are led into paths of peace and true success and thus escape the rough places along life's highway.

264-265.

Mark 3:7-12

And Jesus with his disciples withdrew to the sea: and a great multitude from Galilee followed; and from Judaea, and from Jerusalem, and from Idumaea, and beyond the Jordan, and about Tyre and Sidon, a great multitude, hearing what great things he did, came unto him. And he spake to his disciples, that a little boat should wait on him because of the crowd, lest they should throng him: for he had healed many; insomuch that as many as had plagues pressed upon him that they might touch him. And the unclean spirits, when-so-ever they beheld him, fell down before him, and cried, saying, Thou art the Son of God. And he charged them much that they should not make him known.

266-271.

Interpretation

- Immediately after healing the man with the withered hand Jesus withdrew to the Sea of Galilee. Here a great multitude came to Him to be taught and healed.
- Galilee means "circle, circuit, to whirl," and symbolizes life activity, soul energy, power, and force acting in conjunction with substance. A flow of nervous energy is continually making the circuit of the nerves that comprise the nervous system of man, and is carrying all kinds of messages from the mind. This is the Sea of Galilee.
- The "great multitude" that came to Jesus signifies the legion of thoughts that swarm the mind, seeking harmony. The different places whence the multitude came for healing bespeak the varying characteristics of the thoughts that throng to the place of great realization of vitality and energy in consciousness, to be renewed and uplifted.
- Judea means "praise," "confession," and signifies the mental attitude in which the Christ consciousness shall be opened to us—while we are praising the Lord and confessing God. But the Jews who lived in Judea in Jesus' time did not understand the truth. Neither do our thoughts understand it; they must be taught to praise the good and to confess God aright. Jerusalem signifies the heart center of consciousness. Eventually it will be the abode of love and peace, but we are told in the Bible that out of the heart proceed evil thoughts. The thoughts of our hearts come to the Christ or spiritual I AM in us to be cleansed, and established in righteousness. Idumaea is the Greek

name for Edom. It means "red," "bloody," "earth," and signifies the mortal phase of man's consciousness, under material thought. Jordan means "the descender," also "river of judgment." It represents the great stream of thought that is constantly flowing through the subconsciousness *(subconscious – Ed.)*, and is made up of thoughts good, bad, and indifferent. In other words, it is the descending life flow of thoughts through the organism from head to feet. In man's ignorant and unredeemed state, it is muddy with sense concepts and turbulent with materiality, hence it must be taught the Christ truth and restored to its innate purity and perfection. Tyre (meaning "rock," "strength," "siege," "binding") and Sidon (meaning "a fishery," "fortified," "hunting," "venison") signify a great increase of ideas in the animal phase of consciousness in the individual: also a tendency to establish and strengthen these thoughts in consciousness. So an uplifting and transmuting must be accomplished in this realm of the mind.

• The "unclean spirits" knew Jesus to be the Son of God: "And he charged them much that they should not make him known." This teaches us that we shall discern and confess the truth of our Christ sonship, through the Spirit of truth only. Error and impure thoughts must be cast out by the word of power.

272-280.

Luke 6:12-19

And it came to pass in these days, that he went out into the mountain to pray; and he continued all night in prayer to God. And when it was day, he called his disciples; and he chose from them twelve, whom also he named apostles: Simon, whom he also named Peter, and Andrew his brother, and James and John, and Philip and Bartholomew, and Matthew and Thomas, and James the son of Alphaeus, and Simon who was called the Zealot, and Judas the son of James, and Judas Iscariot, who became a traitor; and he came down with them, and stood on a level place, and a great multitude of his disciples, and a great number of the people from all Judaea and Jerusalem, and the sea coast of Tyre and Sidon, who came to hear him, and to be healed of their diseases; and they that were troubled with unclean spirits were healed. And all the multitude sought to touch him; for power came forth from him, and healed them all.

Interpretation

• The disciples of Jesus represent, in mind analysis, the faculties. The twelve powers of the mind to be educated and established with authority to cast out all discordant thoughts, are: faith (Simon Peter); strength (Andrew); Judgment (James); Love (John); power (Phillip); imagination (Bartholomew); will (Matthew, called Levi in Mark 2: 14 and Luke 5: 27); understanding (Thomas); order (James, son of Alphaeus), zeal (Simon, the Canaanite); renunciation (Judas, the son of James, also called Thaddaeus in Matthew 10: 3); and life (Judas, the betrayer).

- When one determines to exercise the Christ, or I AM, dominion in consciousness, one seeks to express his faculties and powers in harmony with the divine law (Jesus began to call his disciples).
- Most of the disciples of Jesus are represented as fisherman, which implies the striving to catch living ideas (fish) in the waters (thoughts) of this mortal world. The I AM, Jesus, now sees the futility of this struggle with temporal things and sets energies at work upon things eternal. The scattered faculties are drawn together and brought to a recognition of the Master, I AM.
- When the mind of man is focused on materiality, its objects and aims, the faculties are not developed along permanent lines. Each faculty must be developed by use in order to fulfill the Divine-Man Idea.
- The mind in its unregenerate state is without discipline. It follows the law of least resistance and a great spiritual energy frequently finds outlet through some human weakness, and those who should be giants are pigmies in the world. But all this is changed when Truth is revealed.
- It is not enough that man should awaken to a knowledge of his spiritual forces, powers, and possibilities. These forces or primal ideas must become living factors in his daily life. They must be definitely applied in bringing forth the spiritual man.
- It is by closer association with people that we learn to know them; it is also through closer association with ideas and their activities that we come to know them intimately and convert them into vital agencies in our attainment. We learn the spiritual aspect of our forces as we begin to associate with them in their spiritual relationship.
- Truth reveals to us that every faculty must be used to spiritual ends in order to fulfill the Law of Being. None of the faculties are to be despised or condemned, but used aright. Acquisitiveness, (Judas Iscariot) is a good faculty, but turned to things material it becomes a great hindrance to soul development. Exercised in its native realm, the free essences of Being, it draws to us the supplies of the universe and through it we enter into permanent possessions. In giving His Son, the Christ, spiritual man, or Jehovah to be the true inner self or spiritual I AM of each individual, God gave His whole gift to man. In the Son is all possibility; there, in embryo, is all that the Father is and has. Through these twelve faculties man enters into possession of his divine inheritance the great gift of the Christ, and, what is all important, he learns to bestow upon others the same gift that he has received.

281.

Mat. 5:1-1

And seeing the multitudes, he went up into the mountain: and when he had sat down, his disciples came unto him.

Interpretation

• "He went up into the mountain" means that the I AM ascends into the higher regions of consciousness, or into a state of elevated spirituality. The I AM becomes the open door through which spiritual truths are reflected into the common thoughts.

Mat. 5:2-3

And he opened his mouth and taught them, saying, Blessed are the poor in spirit: for theirs is the kingdom of heaven.

Interpretation

• To be poor in spirit is to make oneself a mental vacuum that we may be filled with Spirit. If those who think they have great spiritual acquirements give them up and become "poor" in spiritual pride, the real Kingdom with all its enduring riches shall be theirs.

Mat. 5:4

Blessed are they that mourn: for they shall be comforted.

Interpretation

We get a blessing out of mourning by taking all our grief's to God. Then the Holy Spirit, "the comforter," will take away the desolation and deepen our souls in sympathy and love. Those who cry and yearn for Spirit shall receive its consolation.

Mat. 5:5

Blessed are the meek: for they shall inherit the earth.

Interpretation

• The meek inherit the earth. The "earth" represents the body. Those who are meek without are usually meditative within, and through introspection and concentration become unified with the body substance in its

Principle. Also, thoughts receptive to spiritual realities, take hold of that invisible substance, and it becomes theirs—they possess it.

289.

Mat. 5:6

Blessed are they that hunger and thirst after righteousness: for they shall be filled.

290.

Interpretation

- The sincere desire to do right—the longing for the pure, the just, the true, shall meet with fulfillment.

291.

Mat. 5:7

Blessed are the merciful: for they shall obtain mercy.

292.

Interpretation

- Charity begets charity; mercy begets mercy; love begets love. Forgive yourself, everybody, and the consciousness that there is "no condemnation in Christ Jesus" shall be yours.
- The quality of mercy is not strain'd; It droppeth as the gentle rain from heaven upon the place beneath; it is twice bless'd, It blesseth him that gives, and him that takes."

293.

Mat. 5:8

Blessed are the pure in heart: for they shall see God.

294.

Interpretation

The pure in heart see God. The God-Spirit is absolutely pure and undefiled. Those who put away all thoughts of evil and dwell consciously in the realization that all is good, come face to face with the Original Mind of Being. God is love, and they that love without the adulteration of selfishness, or the lust of sense, come into the very presence of the Good—they actually see God.

295.

Mat. 5:9

Blessed are the peacemakers: For they shall be called the sons of God.

Interpretation

• A peace-maker is one who reduces to peace and harmony all the thoughts of strife, anger, and retaliation in his own mind. The ability to say "peace" to thoughts, and have them obey, entitles man to son-ship of the Most High.

Mat. 5:10

Blessed are they that have been persecuted for righteousness sake: for theirs is the kingdom of heaven.

Interpretation

• Jesus pours out blessings on the persecuted. Those who meet with opposition to spiritual development, both within and without, are true to the highest, grow strong through the combat. Thus persecutions are often blessings in disguise. "The blood of the martyrs is the seed of the church." The disciples, to whom these blessings are addressed, represent the primal faculties of the mind. Those who have withstood and overcome in Truth's righteous way, the persecutions of sense thought shall have harmony within— the kingdom of heaven.

Mat. 5:11-12

Blessed are ye when men shall reproach you, and persecute you, and say all manner of evil against you falsely, for my sake. Rejoice, and be exceeding glad: for great is your reward in heaven: for so persecuted they the prophets that were before you.

Interpretation

When the shafts of ridicule and censure come thick and fast because of your steadfastness to Principle, ward them off by words and thoughts of rejoicing, because it is evidence of the power of your thought and word. You are developing the Kingdom of Power within, which is the acme of all spiritual attainment. Do not resent the stirred up thoughts, but in the dominion of your own harmony quietly be glad.

Mat. 5:13

Ye are the salt of the earth: but if the salt have lost its savor, wherewith shall it be salted? It is thenceforth good for nothing, but to be cast out and trodden under foot of men.

Interpretation

• In its inner meaning, the church consists of the spiritual consciousness in every individual. It consists of those thoughts that understand, love, and obey the truth as it was taught and demonstrated by Jesus Christ. Those thoughts in the individual are the salt of his earth (the seemingly more material and manifest part of his being).

• Salt is a preservative. The inner powers of man preserve the integrity of His manhood through many experiences and incarnations. If they are ignored generation after generation, and the external life fills the measure of development they lose their vitality and are finally accounted of no value.

• The truth about life, light, love, substance, faith, strength, and all that God is, becomes the power that lifts one from error and its results into eternal life, wholeness, peace, and joy—the kingdom of heaven on earth. Then to the extent that truth reigns in the minds and the lives of individuals, they become a preservative power in the outer world.

Mat. 5:14-16

Ye are the light of the world. A city set on a hill cannot be hid. Neither do men light a lamp, and put it under the bushel, but on the stand; and it shineth unto all that are in the house. Even so let your light shine before men; that they may see your good works, and glorify your Father who is in heaven.

Interpretation

• Light is a symbol of understanding. Your world is your consciousness. When understanding is developed it illuminates the head, and the halo of the saint becomes a literal fact. This shines unto every part of the body-temple, especially it shines through the eyes.

• When Jesus declared, "I am the light of the world" (John 8: 12), He referred to the Christ within Himself. When He told His followers, "Ye are the light of the world,"

Mat. 5:17-20

Think not that I came to destroy the law or the prophets: I came not to destroy, but to fulfill. For verily I say unto you, Till heaven and earth pass away, one jot or one tittle shall in no wise pass away from the law, till all things be accomplished. Whosoever therefore shall break one of these least commandments, and shall teach men so, shall be called least in the kingdom of heaven: but whosoever shall do and teach them, he shall be called great in the kingdom of heaven. For I say unto you, that except your righteousness shall exceed the righteousness of the scribes and Pharisees, ye shall in no wise enter into the kingdom of heaven.

Interpretation

• The scribes and Pharisees cut off their spiritual vision by criticism and condemnation. Righteousness must exceed the righteousness of the scribes and Pharisees before the Kingdom of Heaven can be gained. Men exclude themselves from the Kingdom of Heaven by forming a character which unfits them for even seeing its possibilities.

• As Jesus fulfilled the law by founding the kingdom which the prophets longed for, so the indwelling Christ forms a realm where the best is seen to be a possibility and all seems worthwhile. To teach others the way must become a sense of privilege in service, greater than both rights and duties. We teach by actions as plainly as by precepts.

• We must become fulfillers. The full blown flower does not destroy but fulfills the bud. Christ, in founding the Kingdom of peace and joy, fulfills all the desire and aspirations of men.

Mat. 5:21-24

Ye have heard that it was said to them of old time, Thou shalt not kill; and whosoever shall kill shall be in danger of the judgment: but I say unto you, that ever one who is angry with his brother shall be in danger of the judgment; and whosoever shall say to his brother, Raca, shall be in danger of the council; and whosoever shall say, Thou fool, shall be in danger of the hell of fire. If therefore thou art offering thy gift at the altar, and there rememberest that thy brother hath aught against thee, leave there thy gift before the altar, and go thy way, first be reconciled to thy brother, and then come and offer thy gift.

Interpretation

• These verses give the cause of all the fiery conditions of mind and body—anger. Whoever gets angry will be in danger of the "hell of fire," as translated in the Revised Version. The old translation gives "hell fire," and the inference has been that a place called hell was meant, where punishment was meted out by burning the soul after death; Jesus did not mean anything of the kind. He knew that anger set up a fiery condition in the mind which was reflected into the body as a destroying force. All fevers, hot flashes, consuming cankers, in fact every symptom that shows fever can be traced to anger. The remedy is also here given—reconciliation, forgiveness.

Mat. 5:25-26

Agree with thine adversary quickly, while thou art with him in the way; lest haply the adversary deliver thee to the judge, and the judge deliver thee to the officer, and thou be cast into prison. Verily I say unto thee, Thou shalt by no means come out thence, till thou have paid the last farthing.

Interpretation

• The adversary means the deceiving phase of mind in man that has fixed ideas in opposition to Truth. The adversary is a liar-in-wait, the accuser, the opposer, the hater, the enemy.

• It is a state of mind formed by man's personal idea of his power and completeness apart from God. The word adversary represents puffed up personality, which, after having tempted one to do evil, turns about, and discourages the soul by accusing it of sin. To agree with this adversary means to assume a non-resistant state of mind, yet with a positive knowledge that every "jot and tittle" must come under the law, and that error destroys itself. We do not openly disagree with our adversary, knowing that the fulfillment of the divine law of love adjusts all such conditions.

Mat. 5:27-28

Ye have heard that it was said, Thou shalt not commit adultery; But I say unto you, that every one that looketh on a woman to lust after her hath commited adultery with her already in his heart.

Interpretation

• One commits adultery in his own consciousness when he allows himself to be guided by the emotions and desires of the human soul, thus inviting the activity of certain error habits, which the power of the Christ Word alone can dissolve. Adultery also means faithlessness to the marriage vow. Adultery, which is the only reason for divorce according to Jesus is faithlessness, or infidelity.

Mat. 5:29

And if thy right eye causeth thee to stumble, pluck it out, and cast it from thee: for it is profitable for thee that one of thy members should perish, and not thy whole body be cast into hell.

Interpretation

• The eye is the seeing power of the mind. When one is functioning in an opaque state of consciousness, the seeing power of the mind is not functioning on Truth ideas, but usually on darkened, malformed thoughts which cause us to stumble. These false perceptions always result in one's making the wrong move, and therefore should be cast out. If one continues it will bring about a state of sorrow and pain called hell.

Mat. 5:30

And if thy right hand causeth thee to stumble, cut it off, and cast it from thee: for it is profitable for thee that one of thy members should perish, and not thy whole body go into hell.

Interpretation

• The right hand represents the power of the mind to grasp complex situations and straighten them out. If one feels that he has not the ability to exert this power to handle the affair, one should cast out the thought of weakness and inability and affirm he has the power to handle every situation. Then the Spirit will give one what he affirms or decrees. "Thou shalt also decree a thing, and it shall be established unto thee."

Mat. 5:31-32

It was said also, Whosoever shall put away his wife, let him give her a writing of divorcement: but I say unto you, that everyone that putteth away his wife, saving for the cause of fornication, maketh her an adulteress: and whosoever shall marry her when she is put away committeth adultery.

326-329.

Interpretation

• We are often asked what we believe in regard to divorce. We usually suggest, in answer to such questions, that unless there is some very vital reason why two persons who are married cannot or should not stay together, a separation will not solve their problem. Persons who do not find so much happiness as they expect in married life should not be in a hurry to think that they have made a mistake that can be rectified only by a divorce.

• There is always more or less adjusting to be done by those living in personal consciousness. If both the man and woman who have married are willing to engage in this work of adjustment, they will soon discern the cause of their seeming differences and will grow more and more unselfish, thereby finding true happiness, as they learn to give up to each other.

• Not every couple that has gone through a marriage ceremony, even one performed by a minister, is really joined by God. There must be an inner, soul, or spiritual union before this is true. We must bear in mind, too, that the male and female as created by God in the beginning are the qualities of divine love and divine wisdom in each individual. True marriage in its highest sense is a union of these qualities in consciousness. The outer marriage of two persons is but a symbol of this inner marriage. Each soul has within itself all the elements of completeness. The person who enters the outer form of marriage does so because he thinks that he sees in another some soul quality that he lacks in himself. As each one comes into an understanding of the truth of his being and enters into the marriage of the Lamb (union of Wisdom and Love within his own soul), he will find himself in a resurrected state of those whom Jesus said: "They neither marry nor are given in marriage, but are as the angels in heaven."

330.

Mat. 5:33-37

Again, ye have heard that it was said to them of old time, Thou shalt not forswear thyself, but shalt perform unto the Lord thine oaths: but I say unto you, swear not at all; neither by the heaven, for it is the throne of God; nor by the earth, for it is the footstool of his feet; nor by Jerusalem, for it is the city of the great King. Neither shalt thou swear by thy head, for thou canst not make one hair white or black. But let your speech be, Yea, yea; Nay, nay: and whatsoever is more than these is of the evil one.

Interpretation

• We should exercise care in the use of the names of Deity because the name of a thing represents its character. If we use the name of God in a vehement, angry state of mind, we throw the force and power which that name represent into our words, and they produce far-reaching effects. It is said that "curses like chickens come home to roost." So they do, and whoever uses the name of Deity in his cursings must eventually suffer the violent reaction which is sure to follow. A simple "yes" and "no" meets all the requirements of a refined mind.

332-334.

Mat. 5: 38-42

Ye have heard that it was said, An eye for an eye, and a tooth for a tooth: but I say unto you, resist not him that is evil: but whosoever smiteth thee on thy right cheek, turn to him the other also. And if any man would go to law with thee, and take away thy coat, let him have thy cloak also. And whosoever shall compel thee to go one mile, go with him two. Give to him that asketh thee, and from him that would borrow of thee turn not thou away.

335.

Interpretation

• The law of non-resistance as taught by Jesus is demonstrated only by erasing from the individual consciousness every thought of personal rights. So long as we believe that we are entitled to certain considerations and possessions we cannot demonstrate perfect non-resistance.
• We return good for evil by realizing that there is but one Mind and one Good, and that the mind that thinks evil has no real power, therefore it is not to be taken into account.
• If a man took your coat, you could give him your cloak and yet be clothed, if you were in the God consciousness, where "the earth is the Lord's, and the fullness thereof." One who is demonstrating according to the law which Jesus proclaimed never tries to force the return of his goods, though he may know that they were taken without his permission. One who is heeding the teaching of his own indwelling Christ does not spend his time trying to find error within himself, or in trying to freedom from all thought of loss. Those who believe in, or fear loss and evil, are the ones who experience loss and evil.

336.

Mat. 5:43-48

Ye have heard that it was said, Thou shalt love thy neighbor, and hate thine enemy: but I say unto you, love your enemies, and pray for them that persecute you; that ye may be sons of your Father who is in heaven: for he maketh his sun to rise on the evil and the good, and sendeth rain on the just and the unjust. For if ye love them that love you, what reward have ye? do not the publicans the same? And if ye salute your brethren only, what do ye more than others? do not even the Gentiles the same? Ye therefore shall be perfect, as your heavenly Father is perfect.

337-339.

Interpretation

• After a certain restoring work has been done in the individual, his mentality must be taught the truth. We find the higher self impressing upon the consciousness the law of love, which embraces non-resistance and living up to the ideals which one would hold for other persons.

• It is possible to be perfect even as God is perfect. In the higher spiritual consciousness we are all perfect, and that being the standard of our humanity, we must all sooner or later attain to it and demonstrate it in our minds and bodies.

• Universal love is the remedy for all ills given by Jesus, and he insists that it shall be just as far-reaching in man as it is in God. It is not a fulfillment of the Divine law to love only those who love us, or are friendly to us or our work, but we must love our enemies and do good to them that do evil to us. To carry out this we shall need more than human love and fortitude—the love of God must fill the heart.

• We love our enemies by realizing that God is love and that all persons are God in manifestation. In the silence of our own souls we quicken the consciousness of divine love and realize it throughout our beings; then we pour out love upon all the world, especially upon anyone or anything that seems to be at cross purposes with us. In this way the seemingly angry, rebellious tendencies in both the conscious and subconscious realms of mind become kind and loving; we also manifest a love which causes all enmity in the outer to disappear quickly.

340.

Mat. 6:1-4

Take heed that ye do not your righteousness before men, to be seen of them: else ye have no reward with your Father who is in heaven. When therefore thou doest alms, sound not a trumpet before thee, as the hypocrites do in the synagogues and in the streets, that they may have glory of men. Verily I say unto you, They have received their reward. But when thou doest alms, let not thy left hand know what thy right hand doeth: that thine alms may be in secret: and thy Father who seeth in secret shall recompense thee.

Interpretation

•   Hypocrite, in classic Greek means an actor in a theater: so the word came to mean anyone who pretended to be one thing while really he was something far different. Appearing to be lovingly thoughtful for others, while thinking only of self and reputation is to deserve only the reward of a hypocrite. No wise man would seek the reward of an empty applause, which might satisfy the boastful giver. Modest truth asks the approval of Spirit only.

•   The one who eliminates personality from good works, and does good from the standpoint of love, instead of duty or his reputation, does not look for the approval of men because the approval of Spirit is known. Personal praise does not satisfy the individual who has eliminated pride from the mind.

•   Jesus had a good reason for saying that alms should be given in secret. In the first place it may be more kind to the receiver of the gift, that it be given secretly. We are not even to let ourselves know about giving alms. It is to be done so naturally that it is done, as it were, subconsciously with no question as to the recipient being worthy, and without doubt as to whether or not it can be afforded. God being with us dispenses with all anxiety about recompense.

•   There is a law of giving and receiving which regulates all accounts of debit and credit. Do not try to keep balances equal by giving alms and taking self-respect. Give to fulfill your need to give, and not another's need to receive. Your need to give may be the greater.

Mat. 6:5-8

And when ye pray, ye shall not be as the hypocrites: for they love to stand and pray in the synagogues and in the corners of the streets, that they may be seen of men. Verily I say unto you, They have received their reward. But thou, when thou prayest, enter into thine inner chamber, and having shut thy door, pray to thy Father who is in secret, and thy Father who seeth in secret shall recompense thee. And in praying use not vain repetitions, as the Gentiles do: for they think that they shall be heard for their much speaking. Be not therefore like unto them: for your Father knoweth what things ye have need of, before ye ask him.

Interpretation

•   The subject of prayer is of vital importance to the Christian overcomer; yet one that has been greatly misunderstood and misapplied by the majority of people throughout the ages.

•   Prayer has been defined as "the taking hold of God's willingness." When man prays as he should, he will get what he prays for; his prayer will heal sickness, sorrow, lack, and in harmony of every kind. He will become a perfect instrument for the transmission of divine power.

• Pretenders alone failed to call forth the sympathy and compassion of Jesus. He saw that sincerity of purpose, singleness of mind and heart, are absolute prerequisites to entry into the kingdom. Peace of mind, clearness of vision, sureness of intuition, and soundly balanced judgment come only to those whose minds and hearts are single in the desire to do right, who are willing to see right done regardless of its immediate consequences to themselves. The Scribes and Pharisees—the conventional ideas which the world seeks to impose upon all who live according to its standards—are far from right. They are founded not on Truth, but on the accepted and crystallized ideas of the natural man. Their only weight comes from the great mass of persons who lend credit to the natural man's ideas.

349.

Mat. 6:9-15

After this manner therefore pray ye. Our Father who art in heaven, Hallowed be thy name. Thy kingdom come. Thy will be done, as in heaven, so on earth. Give us this day our daily bread. And forgive us our debts, as we also have forgiven our debtors. And bring us not into temptation, but deliver us from the evil one. For if ye forgive men their trespasses, your heavenly Father will also forgive you. But if ye forgive not men their trespasses, neither will your Father forgive your trespasses. For thine is the kingdom, and the power, and the glory forever.

350-356.

Interpretation

• It is in prayer that the natural man first gives way completely. Jesus saw that man, even in his worship of God, is bound by tradition and custom, by man-made laws. He taught His disciples the greatest prayer that has ever been uttered—the greatest because the simplest. First, acknowledgment of Spirit as the true, the only, reality; recognition of the higher realm of mind and soul as constantly operative in life; the upward, unselfish outlook. Thy name, Thy kingdom, Thy will. These come first, are all-important. Afterward, our daily bread, forgiveness of our debts, sustaining strength in our temptation, deliverance of ourselves from evil. Then, again, thy kingdom, thy power, thy glory. Man's daily needs, placed between two absolute acknowledgments of spiritual immanence and spiritual power, must of necessity be met and permeated by that immanence and spiritual power, until man transcends all needs and becomes aware of his true nature—Spirit.

• Affirm spiritual harmony manifesting in every earthly condition. Self-will and the blindness of ignorant doing without knowing will soon be straightened out if we affirm the will of God being done in the substance as it is in the Spirit.

- The focal point of individuality is the will. The will is the center in mind and body around which revolve all the activities that constitute consciousness. The will is the creation of I AM. Without will man would be a ghost, a shadow, a claim of stability without the substance at the center. Will is the projection of I AM. It is man's very self, and to give it up seems like destroying the man. And it is self-destruction to give up the will to any except its source, God. The I AM is the metaphysical name of the spiritual self, as distinguished from the mortal self. One is governed by God, the other by self. Christ is the Scriptural name for spiritual I AM. Jesus called it the Father. It is the Father of the personal will, and a conscious unity between the two must be made to preserve the oneness of creation. That is what is meant by "he that doeth the will of my Father." We must do the very will of God in our wills, which is virtually surrendering the whole man to God.

- A mighty antidote for avarice is the asking that our supply be given to us day by day. What oceans of misery would be dried up if we could all cease to lay up stores for a possible day of want in a problematical future. Be not anxious about tomorrow; tomorrow will take care of itself.

- We cannot reasonably ask forgiveness unless we ourselves have forgiven. This is a fair proposition. Then we should at once set about forgiving everybody who has sinned against us, or whom we think has wrong us in any way. God, the supreme law of love, cannot hold a grudge against any one, and we cannot have the companionship of this sweet, pure mind until we make our minds as near like it as possible.

- Those who cultivate the presence of God find that they have times of great upliftment spiritually, mentally, and physically. There is a quickening of the whole man. The abundant life has been poured out to us, and every faculty is quickened. When the Spirit descended upon Jesus, he was driven into the wilderness, and there tempted by the adversary to do certain things for His own aggrandizement.

- The whole man is not purified at a single descent of the Spirit, but certain mortal selfish tendencies remain in consciousness. These are stimulated by the spiritual energy which is given out to us from the Father, and we have to be on guard against these ambitions of the personality, or adversary. Hence the prayer, "Bring us not into temptation, but deliver us from evil."

357.

Mat. 6:16-18

Moreover when ye fast, be not, as the hypocrites, of a sad countenance: for they disfigure their faces, that they may be seen of men to fast. Verily I say unto you, They have received their reward. But thou, when thou fastest, anoint thy head, and wash thy face; that thou be not seen of men to fast, but of thy Father who is in secret: and thy Father, who seeth in secret, shall recompense thee.

Interpretation

- Evidently Jesus expected His followers to fast.
- It is a fact that fasting renders the mind more acute, keener of apprehension and more powerful in its activity.
- Fasting from untrue and unprofitable thoughts would unburden the mind and release its energy for higher uses. "Starve out the sin, and not the bib—that is thy fast." When the mind no longer transmits its partial knowledge, its unreliable information, then from the Silence there leaps forth the flame of actual knowledge.

359-361.

Mat. 6:19-23

Lay not up for yourselves treasures upon the earth, where moth and rust consume, and where thieves break through and steal: but lay up for yourselves treasures in heaven, where neither moth nor rust doth consume, and where thieves do not break through nor steal: for where thy treasure is, there will thy heart be also. The lamp of the body is the eye: if therefore thine eye be single, thy whole body shall be full of light. But if thine eye be evil, thy whole body shall be full of darkness. If therefore the light that is in thee be darkness, how great is the darkness!

362.

Interpretation

- One lays hold of the treasures of heaven by dwelling in mind on the idea of substantial abidingness of Being and the eternal reality of all true substance. Men have not recognized the treasures of heaven because they have centered their minds upon the manifestation of matter instead of on the idea back of the manifestation. We should spend our energies in unfolding the spiritual consciousness rather than in accumulating material possessions.
- The most elusive thing in existence is matter, and those who think it what it appears, have such a slight hold upon it that it is continually disappearing out of their hands. This has been repeated so far in their experience that they are in constant dread of losing their possessions, and an anxious fear hangs over them like a pall. It is this state of mind Jesus seeks to heal in this treatment against anxiety. Do not be anxious about your life, your food, your body, but change the base of your thought by realizing how all creation is cared for by the Father.

Mat. 6: 24

No man can serve two masters: for either he will hate the one, and love the other; or else he will hold to one, and despise the other. Ye cannot serve God and mammon.

Interpretation

• The two masters refer to the inner spiritual reality—God—and to the material things of the manifest world. If we live altogether in the outer or material consciousness, believing that outer possessions and appearances are the real and true substance of life and the source of happiness and contentment, we shall have little love for or thought of the heavenly Father; the inner things of Spirit that are the true substance under and back of all manifestations will not appeal to us or even be known by us.

Mat. 6:25-34

Therefore I say unto you, be not anxious for your life, what ye shall eat, or what ye shall drink; nor yet for your body, what ye shall put on. Is not the life more than the food, and the body than the raiment? Behold the birds of the heaven, that they sow not, neither do they reap, nor gather into barns; and your heavenly Father feedeth them. Are not ye of much more value then they? And which of you by being anxious can add one cubit unto the measure of his life? And why are ye anxious concerning raiment?

Consider the lilies of the field, how they grow; they toil not, neither do they spin: yet I say unto you, that even Solomon in all his glory was not arrayed like one of these. But if God doth so clothe the grass of the field, which to-day is, and to-morrow is cast into the oven, shall he not much more clothe you, O ye of little faith? Be not therefore anxious, saying, What shall we eat? or, What shall we drink? or, Wherewithal shall we be clothed? For after all these things do the Gentiles seek; for your heavenly Father knoweth that ye have need of all these things. But seek ye first his kingdom, and his righteousness; and all these things shall be added unto you. Be not therefore anxious for the morrow: for the morrow will be anxious for itself. Sufficient unto the day is the evil thereof.

Interpretation

• Outer "things" come and go; if we put our trust in them, dread and fear as regards the future is sure to be our portion. Jesus is seeking to heal the state of mind that dwells in outer seeming. Instead of being anxious about our life, our food, our body, our temporal supply, we must change the basis of our thought by knowing the truth about our heavenly Father and by realizing how all creation is cared for by Him.

• When man is anxious and fearful, he is not so well cared for as are the birds and flowers, because by the prohibitory power of his own thoughts he interferes with God's provision for his needs. If men lived as close to nature as the birds and flowers live, a thought atmosphere would be created that would contact the whole human family with the Over soul, and intuition would become universal. Man then would not observe the wild animals to ascertain the character of the coming winter, but he would be informed direct in a far more comprehensive way about all the processes of nature. He would understand how to overcome or adjust that in nature which seems to be inharmonious and destructive, such as great storms, and the like.

• An understanding of Truth, an understanding of God the Father and of our relation to Him, a conscious knowledge and laying hold of the spiritual ideas that exist in the one Mind—God, our Father—and that have in them unlimited possibilities; these constitute the kingdom of heaven and true riches. From them comes forth abundant, unfailing supply to meet our every need.

371.

Mat. 7:1-5

Judge not, that ye be not judged. For with what judgment ye judge, ye shall be judged: and with what measure ye mete, it shall be measured unto you. And why beholdest thou the mote that is in thy brother's eye, but considerest not the beam that is in thine own eye? Or how wilt thou say to thy brother, Let me cast out the mote out of thine eye; and lo, the beam is in thine own eye? Thou hypocrite, cast out first the beam out of thine own eye; and then shalt thou see clearly to cast out the mote out of thy brother's eye.

372-373.

Interpretation

• The consciousness of judgment in the natural man tends toward criticism instead of toward impartiality. Therefore it is wise to refrain from letting one's thoughts form any definite opinion along the line of changing the acts of another or the judgment to be meted out to that one for any seeming offense.

• When the soul is established in a keen, conscious integrity, it unfolds a penetrating insight into Spirit, which reveals that eventually the outworking of divine law stamps any situation with the judgment of God, which is always just. Therefore all responsibility is centered in the Father. But the individual has only to keep the beam out of his own eye and he will go forward steadily in soul unfolment.

Mat. 7:6

Give not that which is holy unto the dogs, neither cast your pearls before the swine, lest haply they trample them under their feet, and turn and rend you.

Interpretation

•	Unless one is spiritually alive one does not appreciate the things of the Spirit. The person in whom the selfish, animal nature predominates does not value spirituality or integrity of character.

Mat. 7:7-12

Ask, and it shall be given you; seek, and ye shall find; knock, and it shall be opened unto you: for every one that asketh receiveth; and he that seeketh findeth; and to him that knocketh it shall be opened. Or what man is there of you, who, if his son shall ask him for a loaf, will give him a stone; or if he shall ask for a fish, will give him a serpent? If ye then, being evil, know how to give good gifts unto your children, how much more shall your Father who is in heaven give good things to them that ask him? All things therefore whatsoever ye would that men should do unto you, even so do ye also unto them: for this is the law and the prophets.

Interpretation

•	The heavenly Father is much more willing to give to His children than the earthly father. We are His children and heir to the kingdom. Every good thing is ours by divine right. It is man's share in the creative process to bring the unmanifest into the manifest. In prayer when we ask of the Father, or seek that which is ours, or knock at the door of the kingdom, we are "taking hold of God's willingness" to answer our petitions and are blessed accordingly. The law is, "Every one that asketh receiveth; and he that seeketh findeth; and to him that knocketh it shall be opened."

Mat. 7:13-14

Enter ye in by the narrow gate: for wide is the gate, and broad is the way, that leadeth to destruction, and many are they that enter in thereby, For narrow is the gate, and straightened the way, that leadeth unto life, and few are they that find it.

Interpretation

• The narrow gate is the spiritual mind that requires absolute conformity to law, before one can enter into the understanding of Truth, which is the objective of all life.

• It requires effort, determination, and work to be able to enter in. The broad gate is the easy, negative way by which we conform to sense consciousness and the pleasures of the world. The majority of people like the easy way of the world which results in their minds' muscles becoming soft and flabby. When trials come they find they are not able to cope with them.

383.

Mat. 7:15

Beware of false prophets, who come to you in sheep's clothing, but inwardly are ravening wolves.

384-385.

Interpretation

• A prophet is one who foretells coming events. Students of metaphysics know that in reality every idea is the prophecy of its own fulfillment. False prophets are those thoughts that have a false foundation.

• These false ideas also have their representatives in individuals. One who gives his mentality over to false ideas and foretells the coming to pass of their false standards is a false prophet. The religious false prophet is the outer representative of deceptive religious thoughts. These thoughts seem innocent and harmless, like sheep, but are, in reality selfish and dangerous. Unless an idea has a foundation in Truth it is a false prophet, and the individual who foretells the working out of ideas not in Divine Mind is a prophet of the false.

386.

Mat. 7:16-20

By their fruits ye shall know them. Do men gather grapes of thorns, or figs of thistles? Even so every good tree bringeth forth good fruit; but the corrupt tree bringeth forth evil fruit. A good tree cannot bring forth evil fruit, neither can a corrupt tree bring forth good fruit. Every tree that bringeth not forth good fruit is hewn down, and cast into the fire. Therefore by their fruits ye shall know them.

387-388.

Interpretation

• Every idea that brings forth in accordance with God is to be fostered in consciousness until it comes to its fruition or fulfillment, but ideas that bring forth fruits out of harmony with the good are to be burned or purified until they conform to its divine standard. It is not necessary to wait for the fulfillment of an idea to tell the character of its fruit.

• We are given spiritual discernment and can feel whether we are in the presence of good or adverse ideas. Adverse ideas are not to be entertained. As soon as they present themselves, we must substitute that divine ideal which spiritual discernment reveals prophecies shall fail; the Word of God shall not pass away but shall fulfill itself in righteousness in all the earth.

• By entertaining only such ideas as move in harmony with Divine Mind, we establish ourselves upon a true and permanent foundation. We also place ourselves within the kingdom of heaven, that it may become established in the earth; being no longer prophets of evil, but harbingers of the Good.

389-390.

Mat. 7:21-27

Not everyone that sayeth unto me, Lord, Lord, shall enter into the kingdom of heaven; but he that doeth the will of my Father who is in heaven. Many will say to me in that day, Lord, Lord, did we not prophesy by thy name, and by thy name cast out demons, and by thy name do many mighty works? And then will I profess unto them, I never knew you: depart from me, ye that work iniquity.

Every one therefore that heareth these words of mind, and doeth them shall be likened unto a wise man, who built his house upon the rock: and the rain descended, and the floods came, and the winds blew, and beat upon that house; and it fell not; for it was founded upon the rock. And every one that heareth these words of mind, and doeth them not, shall be likened unto a foolish man, who built his house upon the sand: and the rain descended, and the floods came, and the winds blew, and smote upon that house: and it fell: and great was the fall thereof.

391-395.

Interpretation

• In order to really work in righteousness one must have the quickening of the Spirit.

• It is possible upon an intellectual plane to do many things, and when so doing it is quite easy to say, "Lord, Lord, see what I have done; I am spiritual." But spirituality consists of more than physical or mental demonstrations. To be spiritual one must receive from the Spirit. No man knows God save him to whom God has revealed Himself, and until we have this revelation one's works are more or less vain.

• It is possible to heal and do good works in the name of the Lord, and claim these works as evidence of the truth of our doctrine, and yet be unrecognized by the Lord in the final summing up. Many honest people are in this day basing their entry into the kingdom on their ability to heal the sick.

Yet Jesus says that unless they are doing God's will in all things they will be declared workers of iniquity. Right along with this healing power is usually the desire for personal recognition on the part of the healer. He is not working wholly in the name of the Lord, but for self also. This is selfishness, which is a barrier at the door of Divine Harmony. Then again, works of a mystical character are performed in the name of the Christ, while the true Christian spirit of modesty and love is lacking. No merit is made in spirit by such methods.

• Some persons work for the erection of temporal churches in which to worship the Lord. They are like the man who built his house upon the sand: their foundation is the shifting substance of human thought, and in the time of trial they will be found wanting.

• We may come very close to the kingdom of heaven by doing good works and surrendering to the Spirit the various faculties of the mind, but we never fully enter into and abide in heaven, or Divine Harmony, without surrendering all that makes up the personality, of which the will is the center. Spiritual character is the rock foundation of Being.

• We may do the "works of the Lord" by making our wills obedient to the will of the Spirit, following the guidance and words of the Lord within. In this way we build ourselves into God, and establish a substantial, faith-giving state of consciousness: our house is built upon a rock.

396.

Mat. 7:28

And it came to pass, when Jesus had finished these words, the multitudes were astonished at his teaching: for he taught them as one having authority, and not as their scribes.

397.

Interpretation

• Words spoken from our own conception need to be backed up by all sorts of external authorities. When we speak weak words we seek to re-enforce them with "the law," what this one says, what that one does, and the like. He who speaks what the Spirit within reveals to him, speaks with authority and his words, having real substance, need no backing.

398-399.

Mat. 8:5-13

And when he was entered into Capernaum, there came unto him a centurion, beseeching him, saying, Lord, my servant lieth in the house sick of the palsy, grievously tormented. And he saith unto him, I will come and heal him. And the centurion answered and said, Lord, I am not worthy that thou shouldest come under my roof; but only say the word, and my servant shall be healed. For I also am a man under authority, having under myself soldiers:

and I say to this one, Go, and he goeth; and to another, Come, and he cometh; and to my servant, Do this, and he doeth it. And when Jesus heard it, he marveled, and said to them that followed, Verily I say unto you, I have not found so great faith, no, not in Israel. And I say unto you, that many shall come from the east and the west, and shall sit down with Abraham, and Isaac, and Jacob, in the kingdom of heaven: but the sons of the kingdom shall be cast forth into the outer darkness: there shall be the weeping and the gnashing of teeth. And Jesus said unto the centurion, Go thy way; as thou hast believed, so be it done unto thee. And the servant was healed in that hour.

400-403.

Interpretation

•	The central truth of the story of the healing of the centurion's servant is spiritual man's dominion over disease and death. The foundation of this dominion is faith. Jesus said, "I have not found so great faith, no, not in Israel."

•	The omnipresence of Mind is another great truth that is illustrated. The "word" of Jesus was evidently intuitively heard by the sick servant, though he was far from the house. Absent healing is done in much the same way today. Where the consciousness of the healer is functioning in the Spirit and the patient, or some very close friend, has faith, there is always a response. The laws that Jesus used are universal, and just as operative today as when He used them.

•	Jesus sent forth His "Word." The Word differs from the centurion's command because the centurion's command proceeded from the intellect while that of Jesus was from the Spirit. One was with material authority and confined to the realm of forms; the other was with spiritual authority, unconditioned, directing and controlling all thoughts.

•	Yet it was the centurion's faith that caused Jesus to send forth His healing Word. The significance of this is that the centurion believed that Jesus could order about disease as he ordered his soldiers—say to fever and palsy, "Go!" and it would go. Thus the intellect may not have faith in its own power to command disease, but its expectancy of power on a higher plane will call it into action.

•	This is one of the peculiar laws of mind action, which is being proven everywhere by those who put it to the test. The "many" here mentioned by Jesus refers to those Pharisees who were steeped in intellectual lore and who looked to the old church fathers, Abraham, Isaac, and Jacob for salvation instead of to the development of their own souls. They will discover for themselves that the thought of heredity does no sustain them, and that the development of their own spiritual faculties is the one and only thing that will bear them up and bring them into the light of the perfect day.

Luke 7:11-17

And it came to pass soon afterwards, that he went to a city called Nain; and his disciples went with him, and a great multitude. Now when he drew near to the gate of the city, behold, there was carried out one that was dead, the only son of his mother, and she was a widow: and much people of the city was with her. And when the Lord saw her, he had compassion on her, and said unto her, Weep not. And he came nigh and touched the bier: and the bearers stood still. And he said, Young man, I say unto thee, Arise. And he that was dead sat up, and began to speak, and he gave him to his mother. And fear took hold on all: and they glorified God, saying, A great prophet is arisen among us: and, God hath visited his people. And this report went forth concerning him in the whole of Judaea, and all the region round about.

Interpretation

• The name Nain means "suitable," "dwelling." Man is the suitable dwelling place for and expression of life, Truth, and substance. When the individual recognizes the abidingness of Truth, and acts on it by means of his I AM (Jesus), an inner quickening takes place and he is awakened to a newness of life and youth throughout his being. This is indicated by Jesus' raising the widow's son to life.

Mat. 11:1-3

And it came to pass when Jesus had finished commanding his twelve disciples, he departed thence to teach and preach in their cities. Now when John heard in the prison the works of the Christ, he sent by his disciples and said unto him, Art thou he that cometh, or look we for another?

Luke 6: 20-23

And when the men were come unto him, they said, John the Baptist hath sent us unto thee, saying, Art thou he that cometh or look we for another? In that hour he cured many of the diseases and plagues and evil spirits; and on many that were blind he bestowed sight.

And he answered and said unto them, Go and tell John the things which ye have seen and heard; the blind receive their sight, the lame walk, the lepers are cleansed, and the deaf hear, the dead are raised up, and the poor have good tidings preached to them. And blessed is he, whosoever shall find no occasion of stumbling in me.

Interpretation

• John the Baptist represents the intellect hemmed in through seeing sin and evil large, and condemning them. If we see the evil as a reality it becomes power so formidable that it paralyzes all our efforts, and we accomplish nothing in the service of Truth. We fight it and it fights back. In the end it imprisons those who stoop to quarrel with it. (John was in prison).

• Sin and evil cannot be met successfully on their own plane of action—which is in material consciousness. The Christ does not strive with sin and evil in its many forms, but asserts absolute Spirit dominion and heals these "plagues and evil spirits." When intellect (John) sends out its thoughts of doubt as to the identity of the miracle-worker, the reply is not one of argument. Jesus did not argue when John and his followers doubted His works—He simply asked them to behold the results, "The blind receive their sight, the lame walk, the lepers are cleansed, and the deaf hear, the dead are raised up, and the poor have good tidings preached to them.

Luke 7:24-27

And when the messengers of John were departed, he began to say unto the multitudes concerning John, What went ye out into the wilderness to behold? A reed shaken with the wind? But what went ye out to see? A man clothed in soft raiment? Behold, they that are gorgeously appareled and live delicately, are in king's courts. But what went ye out to see? A prophet? Yea, I say unto you, and much more than a prophet. This is he of whom it is written, Behold, I send my messenger before thy face, who shall prepare thy way before thee.

Mat. 11:11-19

Verily I say unto you, Among them that are born of women there hath not arisen a greater than John the Baptist: yet he that is but little in the kingdom of heaven is greater than he. And from the days of John the Baptist until now the kingdom of heaven suffereth violence, and men of violence take it by force. For all the prophets and the law prophesied until John. And if ye are willing to receive it, this is Elijah that is to come. He that hath ears to hear, let him hear. But whereunto shall I liken this generation? It is like unto children sitting in the marketplace, who call unto their fellows and say, We piped unto you, and ye did not dance; we wailed, and ye did not mourn. For John came neither eating nor drinking, and they say, he hath a demon. The Son of man came eating and drinking, and they say, Behold, a gluttonous man and a wine-bibber, a friend of publicans and sinners! And wisdom is justified by her works.

Luke 7:29-30

And all the people when they heard, and the publicans, justified God, being baptized with the baptism of John. But the Pharisees and the lawyers rejected for themselves the counsel of God, being not baptized of him.

415-417.

Interpretation

• In this Scripture Jesus was revealing that John the Baptist was the herald making straight the way of the Lord. He signifies a high, intellectual perception of Truth not yet quickened of Spirit. He symbolizes that attitude within us which is zealous for the rule of Spirit. Such an attitude is not in itself spiritual, but a perception of spiritual possibilities and an activity in making conditions in which Spirit may rule.

• Until one is really ready for Truth, the spiritual Word makes very little impress on him. The consciousness is not ready to receive the truth because of our irresponsible way of living. The least of the spiritual thoughts in man is greater than the mightiest reasoning of the intellect. The intellectual concepts of things must give way to the understanding that comes from the Holy Spirit.

• Without doubt John the Baptist was Elijah come again. The cause of God may be championed with such enthusiasm, as in the case of Elijah, that it produces violence and destructiveness. This no doubt was the general state of religious affairs until the coming of the Christ.

418-419.

Mat. 11:20-24

Then began he to upbraid the cities wherein most of his mighty works were done, because they repented not. Woe unto thee, Chorazin! Woe unto thee, Bethsaida! For if the mighty works had been done in Tyre and Sidon which were done in you, they would have repented long ago in sackcloth and ashes. But I say unto you, it shall be more tolerable for Tyre and Sidon in the day of judgment, than for you. And thou, Capernaum, shalt thou be exalted unto heaven? Thou shalt go down unto Hades; for if the mighty works had been done in Sodom which were done in thee, it would have remained until this day. But I say unto you that it shall be more tolerable for the land of Sodom in the day of judgment, than for thee.

420-423.

Interpretation

• Cities in the Scripture are symbols of fixed states of consciousness. As Jesus warned the scribes and Pharisees that harlots and sinners would get into the kingdom of heaven before them, so he rebuked certain states of mind fixed in self-righteousness.

- Chorazin and Bethsaida were doubtless cities of the Holy Land (although neither had been definitely located) and witnessed the mighty works of Jesus, yet were not moved to change their ways and accept the Truth. They are types of minds that are fixed in their ideas of what is religiously proper and do not open to the more interior phases of Truth.

- Bethsaida and Chorazin represent the state of mind that has a limited amount of Truth and believes that portion to be the full measure. This is the self-righteous phase of consciousness. The openly wanton and wicked cities of Tyre and Sidon stand a better change in the day of judgment; that is, those who are wholly wrong will offer no excuse when their sins or shortcomings bring them before the law of adjustment; they will admit their errors and repent. But those who have a limited amount of Truth, which they hover over and declare to be the whole Truth, are in danger of mental and spiritual crystallization.

- Capernaum represents Christian sympathy, which has been exalted unto heaven but shall be brought down to hell, or Hades,--nothingness; that is the sympathy that pours its thought-substance out to error. It is that sympathy that helps the sick along in their delusions by sympathizing with them. It mourns over the dead and joins with those who grieve. Yet the praises of the "sympathetic tear" are sung by poets; orators eulogize it and preachers enjoin it. Thus it is "exalted to heaven." But when Truth is revealed by her works, casting out these demons of sickness and raising these dead, then false sympathy is brought down to hades—nothingness.

424-425.

Mat. 11:25-30

At that season Jesus answered and said, I thank Thee, O Father, Lord of heaven and earth, that thou didst hide these things from the wise and understanding, and didst reveal them unto babes: yea, Father, for so it was well-pleasing in thy sight. All things have been delivered unto me of my Father: and no one knoweth the Son, save the Father; neither doth any know the Father, save the Son, and he to whomsoever the Son willeth to reveal him. Come unto me, all ye that labor and are heavy laden, and I will give you rest.Take my yoke upon you, and learn of me; for I am meek and lowly in heart: and ye shall find rest unto your souls. For my yoke is easy, and my burden is light.

426-427.

Interpretation

- Jesus thanked the Father that the wonderful laws of Mind and Spirit were not made plain to the intellectually wise, because they would use them to further their personal ambitions. We see this exemplified in the present widespread movement of mental healing. The law is being appropriated by such persons, and they are using it to perpetuate the old mortal ways in money-making, exalting the powers of personality, and the like. They will fall short. It is only those who are innocent and childlike, willing to give up all of self and selfish aims (babes) who will have the mastery revealed unto them. It is the obedient son only who has delivered unto him all the things of the Father.

• All those who labor to build up mortal limitations, and thereby become heavy laden, are invited to come unto the Christ and have surcease for their souls. All those who are striving to sustain the demand of mortality, according to the worldly standard, are bidden to come to this meek and lowly Christ within and find rest.

428-429.

Luke 7:36-50

And one of the Pharisees desired him that he would eat with him. And he entered into the Pharisee's house, and sat down to meat. And behold, a woman who was in the city, a sinner; and she knew that he was sitting at meat in the Pharisee's house, she brought an alabaster cruse of ointment, and standing behind at his feet, weeping, she began to wet his feet with her tears, and wiped them with the hair of her head, and kissed his feet, and anointed them with the ointment. Now when the Pharisee that had bidden him saw it, he spoke within himself, saying, This man, if he were a prophet, would have perceived who and what manner of woman this is that touched him, that she is a sinner.

430-431.

Luke 7:41-50

And Jesus answering said unto him, Simon, I have somewhat to say unto thee. And he saith, Teacher, say on. A certain leader had two debtors: the one owed five hundred shillings, and the other fifty. When they had not wherewith to pay, he forgave them both. Which of them therefore will love him most? Simon answered and said, He, I suppose, to whom he forgave the most. And he said unto him, Thou hast rightly judged. And turning to the woman, he said unto Simon, Seest thou this woman? I entered into thy house, thou gavest me no water for my feet: but she hath wetted my feet with her tears, and wiped them with her hair. Thou gavest me no kiss: but she, since the time I came in, hath not ceased to kiss my feet. My head with oil thou didst not anoint: but she hath anointed my feet with ointment. Wherefore I say unto thee, Her sins, which are many, are forgiven; for she loved much: but to whom little is forgiven, the same loveth little.

And he said unto her, Thy sins are forgiven. And they that sat at meat with him began to say within themselves Who is this that even forgiveth sins? And he said unto the woman, Thy faith hath saved thee; go in peace.

Interpretation

•   This is a lesson on spiritual judgment and divine forgiveness. Within the individual consciousness the woman symbolizes a feminine state of mind, evidently one that had been in darkness and was now coming into the light of Spirit. She also represents humility, service, and compassion, that are willing to lay her all at the feet of the Christ in serving Him.

•   The Pharisaical mind, here represented by Simon, represents an intellectual state of consciousness that holds to its old precepts and refuses to let in the thought that there is such a thing as the forgiving love of Jesus Christ. The Pharisee also represents one who does not realize that the spirit of loving service and humility of mind must be possessed before he can enter into the kingdom of the heavens.

•   Understanding alone is cold and indifferent. It must have the precious, fragrant ointment of love poured out upon it.

•   The lender forgave both the debtors. Under divine law the one who has forgiven the larger debt would naturally feel a greater love and tenderness toward the lender. The great lesson for the Pharisaical mind is to see through the eyes of God and behold the good and the beautiful and the pure everywhere and cease clamoring over the shortcomings of the natural man.

Luke 8:1-3

And it came to pass soon afterwards, that he went about through the cities and villages, preaching and bringing the good tidings, of the kingdom of God, and with him the twelve, and certain women who had been healed of evil spirits and infirmities: Mary that was called Magdalene, from whom seven demons had gone out, and Joanna the wife of Chuzas Herod's steward, and Susanna, and many others, who ministered unto them of their substance.

Interpretation

•   The I AM and the faculties, "the twelve," in ministering successfully to the various thought centers in the organism (cities and villages), need the sustaining assistance of the soul (the feminine, or love nature), which has first been lifted up from mortal expression to spiritual expression. This is represented by "certain women...who ministered unto them of their substance."

Mark 3:20-21

And the multitude came together again, so that they could not so much as eat bread. And when his friends heard it, they went out to lay hands on him: for they said, He is beside himself.

Mat. 12:22-23

Then was brought unto him one possessed with a demon, blind and dumb: and he healed him, insomuch that the dumb man spoke and saw. And all the multitudes were amazed, and said, Can this be the son of David?

Mark 3:22

And the scribes that came down from Jerusalem said, He hat Beelzebub, and, By the prince of the demons casteth he out the demons.

Mat. 12:25-32

And knowing their thoughts he said unto them, Every kingdom divided against itself is brought to desolation; and every city or house divided against itself shall not stand: and if Satan casteth out Satan, he is divided against himself; how then shall his kingdom stand? And if I by Beelzebub cast out demons, by whom do your sons cast them out? Therefore shall they be your judges. But if I by the Spirit of God cast out demons, then is the kingdom of God come upon you. Or how can one enter into the house of the strong man, and spoil his goods, expect he first bind the strong man? And then he will spoil his house. He that is not with me is against me, and he that gathereth not with me scattereth. Therefore I say unto you, Every sin and blasphemy shall be forgiven unto man; but the blasphemy against the Spirit shall not be forgiven. And whosoever shall speak a word against the Son of man, it shall be forgiven him; but whosoever shall speak against the Holy Spirit, it shall not be forgiven him neither in this world, nor in the that which is to come.

Interpretation

•   The word went around that Jesus cast out devils by the prince of devils, Beelzebub.

•   According to this narrative he went so far that even his friends thought he was beside himself, and they sought to restrain him.

•   When man frees himself from the trammels of sacerdotal imposition, the first impression is that he is crazy, or possessed of some evil tendency. It was universally taught that diseased people were under the spell of demons, or devils, sent upon them by the prince of devils, Beelzebub. Here they were charging that Jesus was casting these devils out and healing all manner of diseases by Beelzebub. Then it was He called their attention to their fanaticism blinding their common sense. For a few centuries our men of material science have taught that diseases were material in character and cause. They have built up a science with matter and material law as cause and cure. Men have accepted their conclusions and millions never doubt their accuracy. Yet all this science is an assumption and imposition upon men.

•	The whole science of material reasons for material diseases must go, because there never was a material disease, consequently there could never be a material remedy. All diseases are mental and the remedy must be of like character.

•	The fact is that we are fast getting back to the understanding of Jesus' time in this matter of the cause of disease. There are all shades and degrees of these demons, their name is "legion," but they all have their origin in wrong states of mind.

•	Often when the Christ heals an error state of consciousness the Pharisaical thoughts within us refuse to see the words of the Christ, and begin quibbling and grumbling. They give credence to the "evil spirits," over which Beelzebub is supposed to rule. The central idea in this scripture id the inconsistency and stubborn ignorance of attributing good acts to evil causes.

•	Jesus said that the charge that good was done by evil was blasphemy, and that it was the sin against the Holy Spirit, which could not be forgiven. It is a very serious matter to attribute good works to evil sources because it betrays a deplorable lack of understanding of Truth. We should recognize and acknowledge the good wherever it is manifest. If we see evil in good works it is proof that we have evil in our minds, and we cannot be wholly purified until we cast it out.

•	Our work today is to spiritualize the external religious thoughts within us until they, too, are imbued with the Spirit of the Lord and behold the good and beautiful everywhere.

446.

Mat. 12:33-37

Either make the tree good, and its fruit good; or make the tree corrupt: for the tree is known by its fruit. Ye offspring of vipers, how can ye, being evil, speak good things? For out of the abundance of the heart the mouth speaketh. The good man out of his good treasure bringeth forth good things: and the evil man out of his evil treasure bringeth forth things. And I say unto you, that every idle word that men shall speak, they shall give account thereof in the day of judgment. For by thy words thou shalt be justified, and by thy words thou shalt be condemned.

447-448.

Interpretation

•	Every word and every combination of words has back of it an idea, and the power of the word is primarily in that idea. There is an omnipresent invisible substance so very sensitive that whatever word is spoken makes its impress therein. Therefore, a negative or an evil word sent forth has its effect in the life of the one uttering that word. Oily, deceitful, seemingly constructive words uttered for a false purpose are doubly evil and the one sending them forth must pay the penalty.

•   Therefore, if man has unfolded an evil consciousness he must reap fruit of like character. But if only constructive up building words are registered in the consciousness, good fruit will be the result.

449-450.

Mat. 12:38-42

Then certain of the scribes and Pharisees answered him, saying, Teacher, we would see a sign from thee. But he answered and said unto them, An evil and adulterous generation seeketh after a sign; and there shall no sign be given to it but the sign of Jonah the prophet: for as Jonah was three days and three nights in the belly of the whale; so shall the Son of man be three days and three nights in the heart of the earth. The men of Nineveh shall stand up in the judgment with this generation, and shall condemn it: for they repented at the preaching of Jonah; and behold, a greater than Jonah is here. The queen of the south shall rise up in the judgment with this generation, and shall condemn it; for she came from the ends of the earth to hear the wisdom of Solomon; and behold, a greater than Solomon is here.

451-453.

Interpretation

•   The religious thoughts pertaining to the realm of form (Pharisees) do not know that Truth comes into expression in the consciousness through understanding; they seek a sign in the external realm. No sign of the presence of Christ can be given to such a consciousness, for the things of Spirit are spiritually discerned. Those who asked for a "sign" of the power of Truth were in a mixed or adulterated state of mind, and all the signs in the world would not have convinced them.

•   Jonah represents a state of consciousness that is spiritually quickened, but that does not have the power to put Spirit into action. One meaning of the name Nineveh is "exterior growth." Nineveh represents living in the exterior without the knowledge of God, which usually leads to confusion. The men of Nineveh represent potential thoughts of wisdom that have not as yet recognized that which is constructive from that which is not constructive.

•   The queen of the south represents the subconscious mind, which is awakened when the wisdom of Spirit begins its work in the consciousness. This awakening stirs up both the good and the evil thoughts in man and he must choose or judge them, not by intellectual wisdom (Solomon) but by that "greater than Solomon," the Son of God.

Mat. 12:43-45

But the unclean spirit, when he is gone out of the man, passeth through waterless places, seeking rest, and findeth it not. Then he saith, I will return into my house whence I came out; and when he is come, he findeth it empty, swept, and garnished, Then goeth he, and taketh with himself seven other spirits more evil than himself, and they enter in and dwell there: and the last state of that man becometh worse than the first. Even so shall it be also unto this evil generation.

Interpretation

•   Whenever we deny a negative condition, we set up a mental vacuum. If a positive force is not set into activity immediately, still greater negation is encountered. One negative, unclean thought returns with seven others and the condition is worse than at the beginning.

Luke 11:27-28

And it came to pass, as he said these things, a certain woman out of the multitude lifted up her voice, and said unto him, Blessed is the womb that bare thee, and the breasts which thou didst suck. But he said, Yea rather, blessed are they that hear the word of God, and keep it.

Interpretation

The woman here represents a thought still on the natural plane of consciousness, but with its face turned toward the light. She perceives that Jesus is indeed the inspired teacher of God and thus pronounces upon him the blessing stated in this Scripture. Jesus called her attention to principle, that God really blesses those who lay hold of His Word and apply it in all life's activities.

Mat. 12:46-50

While he was yet speaking to the multitude, behold, his mother and his brethren stood without, seeking to speak to him. And one said unto him, Behold, thy mother and thy brethren stand without, seeking to speak to thee. But he answered and said unto him that told him, Who is my mother? And who are my brethren? And he stretched forth his hand towards his disciples, and said, Behold, my mother and my brethren! For whosoever shall do the will of my Father who is in heaven, he is my brother, and sister, and mother.

Interpretation

• Jesus was revealing the fact that the spiritual is stronger than any human connection. Jesus was not disowning His mother and His brothers, but He was making it very clear to His followers that those who were living under the light of Spirit were doing the will of the Father, were his "brother, and sister, and mother."

460-462.

Mark 4:21-25

And he said unto them, Is the lamp brought to be put under the bushel, or under the bed, and not to be put on the stand? For there is nothing hid, save that it should be manifested; neither was anything made secret, but that it should come to light. If any man hath to hear, let him hear. And he said unto them, Take heed what ye hear: with what measure ye mete it shall be measured unto you; and more shall be given unto you. For he that hath, to him shall be given: and he that hath not, from him shall be taken away even that which he hath.

Interpretation

• Jesus spoke these words to His disciples. His disciples are the persons in every age who faithfully follow His teachings. They compose the True Christ Church, in its outer sense, no matter to which denomination of the Christian Church they belong. Even if their names are not found on any church book, they still belong to the church of Christ.
• No person who has come into a consciousness of His Sonship—the Christ within him as his life, wisdom, love, and overcoming power—can possibly hide his light. He will be serving mankind very efficiently in some way, and his service will bless and uplift others. Thus many such persons will surely be instruments through whom Christ will establish His kingdom here among men.

463-469.

Mat. 13:1-7

On that day went Jesus out of the house, and sat by the sea side. And there were gathered unto him great multitudes, so that he entered into a boat, and sat; and all the multitude stood on the beach. And he spoke to them many things in parables, saying, Behold, the sower went forth to sow; and as he sowed, some seeds fell by the way side, and the birds came and devoured them: and others fell upon the rocky places, where they had not much earth: and when the sun was risen, they were scorched; and because they had no root, they withered away. And others fell upon the thorns; and the thorns grew up and choked them: and others fell upon the good ground, and yielded fruit, some a hundredfold, some sixty, some thirty. He that hath ears, let him hear.

And the disciple came, and said unto him, Why speakest thou unto them in parables? And he answered and said unto them, Unto you it is given to know the mysteries of the kingdom of heaven, but to them it is not given. For who-so-ever hath, to him shall be given, and he shall have abundance, but whosoever hath not, from him shall be taken away even that which he hath. Therefore speak I to them in parables; because seeing they see not, and hearing they hear not, neither do they understand. And unto them the prophecy of Isaiah, which saith,

> By hearing ye shall hear, and shall in no wise understand;
> And seeing ye shall see, and shall in no wise perceive;
> For this people's heart is waxed gross,
> And their eyes are dull of hearing, And their eyes they have closed;
> Lest haply they should perceive with their eyes, And hear with their ears,
> And understand with their heart, And should turn again,
> And I should heal them.
> But blessed are your eyes, for they see; and your ears, for they hear. For verily say unto you, that may prophets and righteous men desired to see the things which ye see, and saw them not; and to hear the things which we hear, and heard them not.

Luke 8:11

Now the parable is this: The seed is the word of God.

Mat. 13:19-23

When any one heareth the word of the kingdom, and understandeth it not, then cometh the evil one, and snatcheth away that which hath been sown in his heart. This is he that was sown by the way side. And he that was sown upon the rocky places, this is he that heareth the word, and straightway with joy receiveth it; yet hath he not root in himself, but endureth for a while; and when tribulation or persecution ariseth because of the word straightway he stumbleth. And he that was sown among the thorns, this is he that heareth the word; and the care of the world, and the deceitfulness of riches, choke the word, and he becometh unfruitful. And he that was sown upon the good ground, this is he that heareth the word, and understandeth It; who verily beareth fruit, and bringeth forth, some a hundred fold, some sixty, some thirty.

Mark 4:26-29

And he said, So is the kingdom of God, as if a man should cast seed upon the earth; and should sleep and rise night and day, and the seed should spring up and grow, he knoweth not how. The earth beareth fruit of herself; first the blade, then the ear, then the full grain in the ear. But when the fruit is ripe, straightway he putteth forth the sickle, because the harvest is come.

Interpretation

•   Most people think that the Word referred to by Jesus is accomplished by preaching or talking with ecclesiastical authority. But Jesus says, "A sower went forth to sow." Nothing is said about this official capacity as a sower of good seed. Then whoever gives forth the true word is an authorized sower.

•   Whoever you are, if you are telling the Truth about God and His kingdom, you are His preacher, fully supplied with all the credentials of the highest dignitary in ecclesiastical orders.

•   "In the morning sow thy seed, and in the evening withhold not thy hand." Tell these glad tidings of the now here kingdom of Good. Although the words you send forth may not all find reception in the minds of those who listen, you are to speak just as if you expected them to. The farmer always plants with the expectation of getting crop, no matter how often he is disappointed. You may find that some of the Truth you have sown has fallen by the wayside, some on rocky ground, some among thorns, but a share has found a resting place in good ground and will surely bring an increase.

•   It is marvelous to realize the power of the word—yes, every word, but the Word of Truth above all. A renowned physical scientist said that the sensitive plate of nature is so delicate that even the passing shadow of a cloud is registered upon the earth, and its impress could be reproduced had we the proper appliances. Think of this and compared it with the mightiest engraver of life, the spoken word, and you can in a measure conceive how important is what you say.

•   The spoken word has a special field of action in the realm of forms. Thought moves on the next or inner plane, where the vibratory forces have not crystallized into visible things. The corporeal body of man, the earth, and all the shapes upon it are made up of aggregations of little spheres held in suspense by the action of the mind. These little spheres do not touch one another, but are in constant motion. They have no entity in themselves—they are the visible pictures of ideas held in mind. When mind thinks they respond on the plane of energy, being vitalized and devitalized according to the thought of strength or weakness held in mind.

•   When thought forms itself into words, its vibrations go forth into direct contact with these little spheres and they are broken up, whirled about, transformed, and re-formed with startling swiftness. If the Word is sent forth with intensity, and the conviction of Truth is held in mind, a force is exerted upon bodies far and near that is of tremendous import. When you speak words of Truth to a listening mind you are absolutely building into the brain new cells and tearing down old ones. Not only this, but the new cells are propagating centers of life and intelligence that will grow and increase to all eternity. Physical scientists tell us that from a single protoplasmic cell might be grown a whole universe of worlds. In similar manner the single idea of Truth which you implant in another mind may increase beyond all computation.

- Then let us remember always to sow good seed regardless of the field. "The seed is the word of God." The parables in which Jesus spoke were understood by the disciples; they were spiritually alive and ready to receive the great Truth which reveals how man's spiritual word brings forth the fruit with increase. But it is practically useless to try to spiritualize any state of consciousness before it is prepared to receive the quickening power of the Word. People functioning wholly on this plane of existence are blinded to spiritual things. "Seeing they see not, and hearing they hear not."

- In one functioning in a negative state of consciousness the soil of the mind is always shallow and unproductive or else rough and rocky, which makes his life tedious and hard.

- Jesus here reveals very clearly the results one may expect when he shuts himself away from the real understanding of Spirit. But he who sows the seed in good soil "Heareth the word and understandeth it" and results are satisfactory indeed.

- It is safe to say that all people who are at all illumined are glad to hear the Truth that they may profit thereby.

- In this Scripture Jesus gives His own metaphysical interpretation of the parable just preceeding. We are indeed blessed when we are established in a strong, positive, constructive state of consciousness and are rooted and grounded in the belief that Spirit is the one and only power in all the earth. When the Word is set into activity in such a consciousness it is bound to bring forth the fruit of the Spirit multiplied thirty, sixty, and a hundredfold.

478-479.

Mat. 13:24-30

Another parable set he before them, saying, The kingdom of heaven is likened unto a man that sowed good seed in his field: but while men slept, his enemy came and sowed tares among the wheat, and went away. But when the blade sprang up and brought forth fruit, then appeared the tares also. And the servants of the house-holder came and said unto him, Sir, didst thou not sow good seed in thy field? Whence then hath it tares? And he said unto them, An enemy hath done this. And the servants say unto him, Wilt thou then that we go and gather them up? But he saith, Nay; lest haply while ye gather up the tares, ye root up the wheat with them. Let both grow together until the harvest: and in the time of the harvest I will say to the reapers, Gather up first the tares, and bind them in bundles to burn them; but gather the wheat into my barn.

480-485.

Interpretation

- Metaphysical teachers find that their most difficult work is the persuading of students to recognize heaven as a condition of the mind. Jesus evidently experienced like difficulty in making himself understood, which accounts for the numerous parables and comparisons he gave of the kingdom of heaven. The comparisons He used were illustrative of some condition pertaining to the kingdom, and never did He give description of it as a place located in some distant heavenly realm.

• Yet in spite of these oft-repeated illustrations by Jesus, showing the kingdom of heaven to be a state of consciousness, the great mass of Christians today are teaching that it is a place, to which those people who accept Jesus as their savior go when they die. There is no authority in the Bible for such doctrine. If such a place existed, Jesus would certainly have described it plainly, instead of giving parable after parable and illustration after illustration, showing it to be a state of consciousness to be attained by man.

• If heaven is a place, Jesus, of all others, should have described it so that the millions whom He knew would hang upon His every word as truth, might have no doubt about it. But He knew the truth and gave the only description of heaven which men, immersed in the belief that forms are real, could understand—that is, by comparing it to the various conditions about them with which they were familiar.

• Heaven is described first, as a condition where there shall remain only the good. The evil is likened unto tares sown among wheat, which is allowed to grow with the good seed until the harvest, then destroyed, leaving the good only. Those who have lived in the delusion of time and place as real have assumed that this "harvest" was a great judgment day sometime in the future. But Jesus put a negative to this when He said, "The kingdom of God is within you." It must be that there is a state in the mind of humanity where this kingdom of goodness and harmony is supreme.

• This state is the "good seed" which is sown in the soil of mind, to be cultivated, increased and a harvest returned to the Giver. The "tares" are the failures, the shortcomings, which result through negligence on man's part. "While men slept" the enemy sowed the tares.

• It is in the mind that these states are active or inactive. This is the kingdom which man rules and through which he will bring forth heaven. Heaven is already there on one plane of mind, but it must be established on all planes. The so-called evil has place in certain stages of growth, or the Master would not have recommended that it be left alone. Yet man must know that the "harvest" is taking place every day, every hour, every moment, and that the good thoughts and the evil thoughts are constantly coming into a state where they are ripe for the harvest.

486.

Mat. 13:31-32

Another parable set he before them, saying, The kingdom of heaven is like unto a grain of mustard seed, which a man took, and sowed in his field: which indeed is less than all seeds; but when it is grown, it is greater than the herbs, and becometh a tree, so that the birds of the heaven come and lodge in the branches thereof.

Interpretation

• The mustard seed comparison is to show the capacity of the apparently small thought of Truth to develop in consciousness until it becomes the abiding place of a higher range of thoughts (birds of the air).

Mat. 13:33-35

Another parable spoke he unto them; The kingdom of heaven is like unto leaven, which a woman took, and hid in three measures of meal , till it was all leavened. All these things spoke Jesus in parables unto the multitudes; and without a parable spoke he nothing unto them: that it might be fulfilled which was spoken through the prophet, saying, I will open my mouth in parables; I will utter things hidden from the foundation of the world.

Interpretation

• The "leaven" is the Truth and the "woman" is the soul. When a word of Truth seems to be hidden by the inner mind, it is not idle, but is quietly spreading from point to point. This process continues until the whole consciousness is vitalized by Spirit. People who have for years had this hidden word of Truth at work in them are quick to respond to a larger exposition of the Divine Law, and we recognize that they are ripe for the truth. Those who can lay hold of these deep truths are awakened so they can see and hear spiritually as well as physically. Those who are not ready for the deep fundamental truths of Being take them literally instead of taking them symbolically. A prophet is one who reads out of the thoughts of the present mind and can determine in what these thoughts are bound to culminate. He is one who foretells that which is to come.

Mat. 13:36-43

Then he left the multitudes, and went into the house: and his disciples came unto him, saying, Explain unto us the parable of the tares of the field. And he answered and said, He that soweth the good seed is the Son of man; and the field is the world; and the tares are the sons of the evil one; and the enemy that sowed them is the devil: and the harvest is the end of the world; and the reapers are angels. As therefore the tares are gathered up and burned with fire; so shall it be in the end of the world. The Son of man shall send forth his angels, and they shall gather out of his kingdom all things that cause stumbling, and them that do iniquity, and shall cast them into the furnace of fire: there shall be the weeping and the gnashing of teeth. Then shall the righteous shine forth as the sun in the kingdom of their Father. He that hath ears, let him hear.

493-495.

Interpretation

• Jesus was the greatest metaphysician that ever lived and often gave His own spiritual interpretation. The reapers or the angels are our helpful, constructive thoughts that gather in the good, and our devils or enemies symbolize our rebellious, opposing thoughts—that gather in evil.

• It is this sifting process that finally establishes in the whole consciousness the good only, and man gets the joys of the kingdom of heaven as he goes along. If he is industrious in separating the "tares" from his good thoughts, he will bring that peace and harmony which is his in Spirit right out into visibility, and the kingdom of heaven will be established in his mind and body.

• When enough men have thus been faithful, the earth itself will take on this peace and harmony and all violence will cease. There will be no wars and no cyclones. The gentle rain of heaven will fall as a dew over all the face of the earth, and all the desert places will bring forth abundantly. Poverty and famine will vanish. Disease will be no more and death fall upon none. The bodies of men will not grow old, but increase in lightness and symmetry with every added spiritual thought until gravity no longer holds them to earth, and millions will build abodes in the air all about this beautiful planet. This is the kingdom of heaven to be established by man with this world as the center of operation.

496.

Mat. 13:44

The kingdom of heaven is like unto a treasure hidden in the field; which a man found, and hid; and in his joy he goeth and selleth all that he hath, and buyeth that field.

497-501.

Interpretation

• When the tremendous possibilities of the mind of the Spirit (God) are discerned by man, he often tries to turn it to pecuniary profit. This is painfully in evidence among New Thought people in this age. The treasure they know is hid in the field of mind, and, when they discover it, they sell all and buy that field. They turn all their forces of mind and body to the gaining of prosperity through the occult law. Some of them succeed amazingly—for a time, but there is a law of righteousness, mentioned by Jesus, which they sometimes forget. If acquisitiveness is large and spirituality small in a man, he is almost sure to try to use his new found domain for pecuniary profit in some way. The laws of the kingdom are so little understood by beginners that they at first make blunders that a fuller understanding adjusts.

• For example, a man of ordinary honesty took a course of New Thought lessons, in which he was taught that he could bring about any desired change in himself or his affairs by sending forth his silent thoughts. He had a house and lot which he had for some time been on the point of selling to a man who needed the home, but was timid in closing up the deal.

• The New Thought student decided that here was a fine opportunity to use his new science, so he began treating his customer to close up the purchase and pay over the money. The very night that he began treatments he dreamed that he went into a large room where many men were sitting at tables with various gambling devices, and he had a revolver in each hand. His house customer sat at a table near the door, and our New Thoughter pointed his pistols at his head and told him to hold up his hands; then he proceeded to rob him of his money. He then went from table to table, robbing each one of everything in sight. When he had completed the "hold-up" he backed out the door, and woke himself up running down the street.

• This dream was so clearly a warning from the Spirit of what his science treatments were, and what they would lead to, that he was very careful thereafter how he in any way used the law to take advantage of another man, or move any one to do anything for selfish ends.

• Yet riches and honor are promised to those who enter into the kingdom of God, and the fact that some men try to use the Divine Law of prosperity in worldly ways should not deter the sincere truth seeker from entering into possession of that which is rightfully his. We may blunder in our ignorant use of the Law, but honesty of purpose will draw to us the Spirit of Truth, "who will guide you into all Truth."

• The treasure hid in the field is the logical truth that all that is belongs to Being, and can be brought forth by one who gives up the without and looks within for the real value.

502.

Mat. 13:45-46

Again, the kingdom is like unto a man that is a merchant seeking goodly pearls: and having found one pearl of great price, he went and sold all that he had, and bought it.

503.

Interpretation

• The merchant is one who is seeking the jewel of the soul, or spiritual good, through exchange of thought, discussion, and argument. He also must give up all these so-called values for the pearl of great price.

Mat. 13:47-52

Again, the kingdom of heaven is like unto a net, that was cast into the sea, and gathered of every kind: which, when it was filled, they drew up on the beach; and they sat down, and gathered the good into vessels, but the bad they cast away. So shall it be in the end of the world: the angels shall come forth, and sever the wicked from among the righteous, and shall cast them into the furnace of fire: there shall be the weeping and the gnashing of teeth.

Have ye understood all these things? They say unto him, Yea. And he said unto them, Therefore every scribe who hath been made a disciple to the kingdom of heaven is like unto a man that is a householder, who bringeth forth out of his treasure things new and old.

506-507.

Interpretation

• The net cast into the sea represents that state of mind that seeks for Truth in many places and gets much that has to be thrown away.
• The end of the word represents the point in consciousness where the true thoughts are in the majority and the error thoughts have lost their power. This is the final consummation of the regenerative process and everything that has been stored up in consciousness is brought forth and becomes of visible, practical value to the man. This is represented by the "householder" who brings forth his "things new and old."

508-509.

Mark 6:1-6

And he went out from thence: and he cometh into his own country; and his disciples follow him. And when the Sabbath was come, he began to teach in the synagogue: and many hearing him were astonished, saying, Whence hath this man these things? And, What is the wisdom that is given unto this man, and what mean such mighty works brought by his hands? Is not this the carpenter, the son of Mary, the brother of James, and Joses, and Judas, and Simon? And are not his sisters here with us? And they were offended in him. And Jesus said unto them, A prophet is not without honor, save in his own country and among his own kin, and in his own house. And he could there do no mighty works, save that he laid his hands upon a few sick folks, and healed them. And he marveled because of their unbelief. And he went about the villages teaching.

Interpretation

Jesus Christ's own country was Nazareth, which symbolizes the inferior or un-enlightened mentality. When a thought-force goes out from this state of mind and rises into the realm of Spirit and takes on spiritual qualities and returns to its native surroundings to do its redemptive, uplifting work, that old error state of consciousness refuses it. ("Is not this the carpenter's son?") It is best to leave it alone until it feels the need.

Spirit cannot do its perfect work unless there is an earnest desire in that state of consciousness for redemption. One cannot force truth. The soul must unfold and come into the understanding of the law. Until that time arrives one cannot grasp an understanding of the spiritual law. To try to force this on another is casting pearls before swine.

Luke 8:22

Now it came to pass on one of these days that he entered into a boat, himself and his disciples, and he said unto them, Let us go over unto the other side of the lake: and they launched forth. And leaving the multitude, they take him with them, even as he was, in the boat. And other boats were with him. And there ariseth a great storm of wind, and the waves beat into the boat, insomuch that the boat was now filling. And he himself was in the stern, asleep on the cushion: and they awake him, and say unto him, Teacher, carest thou not that we perish? And he awoke, and rebuked the wind, and said unto the sea, Peace, be still. And the wind ceased, and there was a great calm. And he said unto them, Why are ye fearful? Have ye not yet faith? And they feared exceedingly, and said one to Another, Who then is this, that even the wind and the sea obey him?

Interpretation

• Jesus gained the power to quell the storm by first gaining perfect control over His own mind. Then as He continued to work in harmony with the law, even the winds and the waves obeyed Him. When the race as a whole unfolds this soul capacity, the very laws of nature will change. There will be no earthquakes or storms, but all races of people will dwell in peace and joy and contentment.

• In individual consciousness the storms, or disturbances in nature, first take place in the mind of man. Through the activity of his own thoughts he has the key to control his demonstrations. First he must gain dominion over all his thought-people. Then gradually he will gain the mastery over nature.

•   In this Scripture the sea represents the universal race thought. The boat represents the body of man. The disciples, those who have received spiritual quickening, are his faculties. Jesus Christ represents the I AM, the spiritual identity in man. When we go to sleep the I AM withdraws from the conscious mind. This is symbolized by Jesus' being asleep in the bow of the boat, or the spiritual man was not in action. The storm on the sea, where the waves rolled so high, symbolizes a brain storm in which some thought of violence has entered. If allowed to go on without control the waves will destroy the body temple. The power to produce peace and harmony is centered in the I AM, or in man's consciousness of mastery and dominion. It is brought into activity through declarations of Truth, and denials of all inharmonious conditions. When we quicken this power things begin to happen. By declaring the activity of the spiritual man, by praising God and giving thanks for the victory, the I AM is fully aroused and begins its perfect work. The law is, "In all thy ways acknowledge him, and he will direct thy paths."

518-522.

Mark 3:1-20

And they came to the other side of the sea, into the country of the Gerasenes. And when he was come out of the boat, straightway there met him out of the tombs a man with an unclean spirit, who had his dwelling in the tombs: and no man could any more bind him, no, not with a chain; because that he had been often bound with fetters and chains, and the chains had been rent asunder by him, and the fetters broken in pieces: and no man had strength to tame him. And always, night and day, in the tombs and in the mountains, he was crying out, and cutting himself with stones. And when he saw Jesus from afar, he ran and worshipped him; and crying out with a loud voice, he saith, What have I to do with thee, Jesus, thou Son of the Most High God? I adjure thee by God, torment me not. For he said unto him, Come forth, thou unclean spirit, out of the man.

And he asked him, what is thy name? and he saith unto him, My name is Legion; for we are many. And he besought him much that he would not send them away out of the country. Now there was there on the mountain side a great herd of swine feeding. And they besought him, saying, Send us into the swine, that we may enter into them. And he gave them leave.

And the unclean spirits came out, and entered into the swine: and the herd rushed down the steep into the sea, in number about two thousand; and they were drowned in the sea. And they that fed them fled, and told it in the city, and in the country. And they came to see what it was that had come to pass. And they come to Jesus, and behold him that was possessed with demons sitting, clothed and in his right mind, even him that had the legion; and they were afraid. And they saw it declared unto them how it befell him that was possessed with demons, and concerning the swine. And they began to beseech him to depart from their borders. And as he was entering into the boat, he that had been possessed with demons besought him that he might be with him. And he suffered him not, but saith unto him, Go to thy house unto thy friends, and tell them how great things the Lord hath done for thee, and how he had mercy on thee. And he went his way, and began to publish in Decapolis how great things Jesus had done for him: and all men marveled.

523.

Interpretation

• The name Gerasenes means "fortunate;" "organized;" "fortified;" and has the same interpretation as Gadarenes, (Mat. 8: 28). Gerasenes represent strongly organized thoughts of energy and power in the subconscious realm of mind in man. When freed from carnal desires and warring tendencies, these thoughts will work mightily for the good of the individual, but in their unredeemed or error-possessed state they are very violent and destructive. In this instance, evidently they were undisciplined and therefore are in an unbalanced state of consciousness.

• The swine represent greed. Sense consciousness would preserve them. When the indwelling Christ denies them, they pass down into the eliminative organs. "And he said unto (the evil spirits) Go. And they came out, and went into the swine; and behold, the whole herd rushed down the steep into the sea, and perished in the waters." However the selfish states of mind that are established in consciousness want to continue and cling to their old way of thinking. When, however, the spiritual vibrations come in and break up the old cohesions, some of them pass away.

524-528.

Mark 5:21-37

And when Jesus had crossed over again in the boat unto the other side, a great multitude was gathered unto him; and he was by the sea. And there cometh one of the rulers of the synagogue, Jairus by name; and seeing him, he falleth at his feet, and beseecheth him much, saying, My little daughter is at the point of death: I pray thee, that thou come and lay thy hands on her, that she may be made whole, and live. And he went with him; and a great multitude followed him, and they thronged him.

And a woman, who had an issue of blood twelve year, And had suffered many things of many physicians, and had spent all that she had, and was nothing bettered, but rather grew worse, having heard the things concerning Jesus, came in the crowd behind, and touched his garment. For she said, If I touch but his garments, I shall be made whole. And straightway the fountain of her blood was dried up; and she felt in her body that she was healed of her plague. And straightway, Jesus, perceiving in himself that the power proceeding from him had gone forth, turned him about in the crowd, and said,

Who touched my garments? And his disciples said unto him, Thou seest the multitude thronging thee, and sayest thou, Who touched me? And he looked about to see her that had done this thing. But the woman fearing and trembling, came and fell down before him, and told him all the truth. And he said unto her, Daughter, thy faith hath made thee whole; go in peace, and be whole of thy plague.

While he yet spoke, they come from the ruler of the synagogue's house, saying, Thy daughter is dead: why troublest thou the Teacher any further? But Jesus, not heeding the word spoken, saith unto the ruler of the synagogue, Fear not, only believe. And he suffered no man to follow with him, save Peter, and James, and John the brother of James.

Mat. 9:23

And when Jesus came into the ruler's house, and saw the flute-players, and the crowd making a tumult,

Mark 5:38c, 39b

and many weeping and wailing greatly, he saith unto them, Why make ye a tumult, and weep? The child is not dead, but sleepeth. And they laughed him to scorn. But he, having put them all forth, taketh the father of the child and her mother and them that were with him, and goeth in where the child was. And taking the child by the hand, he said unto her, Talitha cumi; which is, being interpreted, Damsel, I say unto thee, Arise. And straightway the damsel rose up, and walked; for she was twelve years old. And they were amazed straightway with a great amazement. And he charged them much that no man should know this: and he commanded that something should be given her to eat.

529-532.

Interpretation

•   Here we have an account of the healing power of faith. No one knows what faith is, neither does anyone know what electricity is. A certain unwavering attitude of the mind has been again and again observed to bring results, and it has been named faith. A wider knowledge of the character of the mind, and the substance forming power of thought, affords a degree of understanding about the mental constituency of faith. Confidence in a certain thing causes us to become attached to it, and this gradually builds a thought structure which works from its own center. This faith center is, according to Paul, "the substance of things hoped for."

•   Men have faith in very many things that are not worthy. The wise follow Jesus' injunction: "Fear not. Only believe." But faith is a thing of growth and those who have not planted it in their minds look to others for help.

•   The woman who had been ill so many years touched the hem of Jesus' garment and was healed. Her faith was in the personality—she wanted to touch the healer. The same attitude is found among a class who in this day want the healer to lay hands on them. A vitalizing virtue can be transferred from healer to patient, but it is not the highest form of healing and should be employed only in very rare cases. Jesus did no voluntarily use this method— the woman crept up behind Him and surreptitiously tapped the great aura of vitality that surrounded Him.

• The bringing to life of Jairus's daughter was in line with the methods used by modern healers. Jesus said, "the damsel is not dead but sleepeth." The crowd laughed Him to scorn. Then admitting to the room only Peter, James, John, and the parents of the child, He reaffirmed the truth that the little girl was not dead but asleep. Taking her by the hand Jesus commanded her to arise, and her spirit returned and she arose immediately.

533-534.

Mat. 9:27-34

And as Jesus passed by from thence, two blind men followed him, crying out, and saying, Have mercy on us, thou son of David. And when he was come into the house, the blind men came to him: and Jesus saith unto them, Believe ye that I am able to do this?

They said unto him, Yea, Lord. Then touched he their eyes, saying, According to your faith be it done unto you. And their eyes were opened. And Jesus strictly charged them saying, See that no man know it. But they went forth, and spread his fame in all that land.

And as they went forth, behold, there was brought to him a dumb man possessed with a demon. And when the demon was cast out, the dumb man spoke: and the multitudes marveled, saying, it was never so seen in Israel. But the Pharisees said, By the prince of the demons casteth he out demons.

535-536.

Interpretation

• Jesus laid great store by faith. When the two blind men asked him for healing, he said, "Believe he that I am able to do this?" Healers of every kind find that faith is necessary to success.

• The casting of the devil out of the dumb man was considered the greatest of marvelous works. The man was not only dumb but possessed with a devil also. Jesus recognized all false conditions in the body as primarily false states of mind. He commanded them to "come out," and they obeyed. This method is being applied in many ways by healers in this day, and those who scoffed and called these methods superstition are now accepting and using them because of their efficiency.

Mat. 9:35-38

And Jesus went about all the cities and the villages, teaching in their synagogues, and preaching the gospel of the kingdom, and healing all manner of disease and all manner of sickness. But when he saw the multitudes, he was moved with compassion for them, because they were distressed and scattered, as sheep not having a shepherd. Then saith he unto his disciples, The harvest indeed is plenteous, but the laborers are few. Pray ye therefore the Lord of the harvest, that he send forth laborers unto his harvest.

538-539.

Interpretation

• To know himself, man must open up the undiscovered country within himself. He must first appreciate the largeness of his God-given identity—the I AM. This step in spiritual evolution is represented by Jesus' going about through all the cities and villages, teaching, preaching, and healing. These movements of Jesus represent the I AM in its universal capacity as a teacher and harmonizer of its own mental and bodily conditions.

• But there is yet no organized harmony—the people (thoughts) "were scattered, as sheep not having a shepherd." The I AM must have agents to instruct the great throng of thoughts that surge about the consciousness—that is, the faculties of the mind must be spiritually disciplined and their right relations established, so that it will not be necessary for one's special attention to be directed toward faculties in order to have them function in spiritual ways. They must be educated, and then they will do the Master's will obediently, whether he is consciously present or not.

540-547.

Mat. 10:1, 5-42

And he called unto him his twelve disciples, and gave them authority over unclean spirits, to cast them out, and to heal all manner of disease and all manner of sickness.

These twelve Jesus sent forth, and charged them, saying, Go not into any way of the Gentiles, and enter not into any city of the Samaritans; but go rather to the lost sheep of the House of Israel. And as ye go, preach, saying, The kingdom of heaven is at hand. Heal the sick, raise the dead, cleanse the lepers, cast out demons: freely ye received, freely give.

Get you no gold, nor silver, nor brass in your purses; no wallet for your journey, neither two coats, nor shoes, nor staff: for the laborer is worthy of his food. And into whatsoever city or village ye shall enter, search out who in it is worthy; and there abide till ye go forth. And as ye enter into the house, salute it. And if the house is worthy, let your peace come into it: for if it be not worthy, let your peace return to you. And whosoever shall not receive you, nor hear your words, as ye go forth out of that house or that city, shake off the dust of your feet. Verily I say unto you, It shall be more tolerable for the land of Sodom and Gomorrah in the day of judgment, than for that city.

Behold I send you forth as sheep in the midst of wolves, be ye therefore wise as serpents and harmless as doves. But beware of men: for they will deliver you up to councils, and in their synagogues they will scourge you; yea and before governors and kings shall ye be brought for my sake, for a testimony to them and to the Gentiles. But when they deliver you up, be not anxious how or what ye shall speak: for it shall be given you in that hour what ye shall speak. For it is not ye that speak, but the Spirit of your Father that speaketh in you. And brother shall deliver up brother to death, and the father his child: and children shall rise against parents, and cause them to be put to death. And ye shall be hated of all men for my name's sake: but he that endureth to the end, the same shall be saved. But when they persecute you in this city, flee into the next: for verily I say unto you, Ye shall not have gone through the cities of Israel, till the Son of man become.

A disciple is not above his teacher, nor a servant above his lord. It is enough for the disciple that he be as his teacher, and the servant as his lord.

If they have called the master of the house Beelzebub, how much more them of his household!

Fear them not therefore: for there is nothing covered, that shall not be revealed; and hid, that shall not be known. What I tell you in the darkness, speak ye in the light; and What ye hear in the ear, proclaim upon the house-tops.

Be not afraid of them that kill the body, but are not able to kill the soul: but rather fear him who is able to destroy both soul and body in hell.

Are not two sparrows sold for a penny? And not one of them shall fall on the ground without your Father: but the very hairs of your head are all numbered. Fear not, therefore: ye are of more value than many sparrows.

Everyone therefore who shall confess me before men, him will I confess also before my Father who is in heaven. Think not that I came to send peace of the earth: I came not to send peace, but a sword. For I came to set a man at variance against his father, and the daughter against her mother, and the daughter in law against her mother in law; and a man's foes shall be they of his own household. He that loveth father or mother more than me is not worthy of me; and he that loveth son or daughter more than me is not worthy of me. And he that doth not take his cross and follow after me is not worthy of me.

He that findeth his life shall lose it; and he that loseth his life for my sake shall find it.

He that receiveth you receiveth me, and he that receiveth me receiveth him that sent me. He that receiveth a prophet in the name of a prophet shall receive a prophet's reward: and he that receiveth a righteous man in the name of a righteous man shall receive a righteous man's reward. And whosoever shall give to drink unto one of these little ones a cup of cold water only, in the name of a disciple, verily I say unto you he shall in no wise lose his reward.

548-559.

Interpretation

• The specific work of the faculties is in consciousness. The I AM roams the universe through and can teach and heal wherever it wishes, but the disciples, or faculties, are not expected to act outside of the individual consciousness.

• "Go not into the way of the Gentiles and enter not into any city of Samaritans." If in healing another you lose vitality you are letting your strength (Andrew) go "into the way of the Gentiles." This is magnetic healing, which is forbidden by the Christ.

• You are authorized to speak the word of strength to that faculty in another, because it is a true statement, and the law will be fulfilled in divine order.

• "Get you no gold, nor silver, nor brass in your purses, no wallet for your journey, neither two coats, nor shoes, nor staff, for the laborer is worthy of his food."

• This scripture metaphysically interpreted means that we must place our entire faith in Spirit. We are not to depend upon materiality in any of its forms but know and realize that the living Word within us can and does demonstrate our every need both physically and spiritually.

• The I AM, in what might be termed missionary trips, represents the Word of Truth going into various parts of the consciousness, proclaiming the doctrine of the Christ. In some of these states of consciousness there is both good and error stored away. When the I AM enters these various states of consciousness its work is to search out that which is worthy and establish spiritual supremacy therein. But if error is discovered, which refuses to see the light, it should be left to its own destruction. "Verily I say unto you, It shall be more tolerable for the land of Sodom and Gomorrah in the day of judgment, than for that city."

• To go forth as sheep symbolizes going forth in the consciousness of purity, innocence, guilelessness, and divine obedience. This state of consciousness can penetrate into the consciousness of devouring, selfish, hungering, opposing thoughts and yet not be affected by them.

• "For it is not ye that speak, but the Spirit of your Father that speaketh in you." In prayer we take with us a Word of Truth, go into the silence, and contact God-Mind, then realize that Word of Truth until God-Mind satisfies the logic of our soul. This realization has the power itself to speak forth the Word of God.

• When Jesus spoke of the relationship of the disciple and teacher, and the servant and his lord, He was referring to the specific law He had in mind when He said, "I and my Father are one." The teacher here referred to is of course the spiritual teacher, the Spirit of God, which is always greater than the disciple; in like manner, the Lord is always greater than the servant.

• We must establish ourselves in the Christ principle and let the Christ reveal one step at a time in order to go forward.

• Beelzebub is the negative ego in man's consciousness, the man of flesh. Another name for this mortal ego in man is "Satan," which is to be watched as he is destructive and does not live on the spiritual plane at all.

• God Mind is everywhere present and God Mind is divine intelligence. Therefore, "there is nothing covered, that shall not be revealed." It is impossible to conceal anything from Spirit. Spirit sees everything and knows everything, is the source of all activity. It is possible for us to go into the silence and realize divine intelligence until the very spirit of light permeates our whole being and we know whatever we desire to know.

• Jesus said to fear him who is able to destroy both soul and body rather than those who can kill the body only. It is possible for the soul to get so material, to become so wrapped up in worldly affairs, that it entirely crowds out the spiritual. Such a soul might disintegrate. However, it would require millions of years of adverse thought to accomplish such a condition.

• In using the sparrows for an illustration, Jesus is calling attention to how very little and cheap the sparrow is, and yet the Father takes notice of every one of them. Man being the head of all activity of the earth is the most important creation. Therefore man should esteem himself as God's masterpiece. The importance of man is revealed in Jesus' words, "The very hairs of your head are all numbered."

• Jesus then spoke of confessing Him before the Father. To confess is to acknowledge. When we acknowledge our spiritual nature before men we open the way for that nature to receive in larger measure from the Father—man's spiritual source. To grow spiritually we must keep up the contact with the fountainhead, God the Father. Herein Jesus stated a law of spiritual unfoldment that would transform the institutions of learning the world over. Children should be taught that they come forth from Spirit, exist in spiritual life, and can express more and more of that life as they think about its presence in the body and in everything they do. This instruction about omnipresent life as a principle, which man incorporates into his body by thought and recognition, would be followed by the acknowledgment of divine mind always present as the source and inspiration of man's intelligence.

• All is Spirit. The "I" referred to in Verses 34 to 38 is the superman, or spiritual man, or the Christ man. The Spiritual man is not subject to the discord of human.

560-563.

Luke 9:7-9

Now Herod the tetrarch heard of all that was done: and he was much perplexed, because that it was said by some, that John was risen from the dead; and by some, that Elijah had appeared; and by others, that one of the old prophets was risen again. And Herod said, John I beheaded: but who is this, about whom I hear such things? And he sought to see him.

Mark 6:17-29

For Herod himself had sent forth and laid hold upon John, and bound him in prison for the sake of Herodias, his brother Philip's wife; for he had married her. For John said unto Herod, It is not lawful for thee to have thy brother's wife. And Herodias set herself against him, and desired to kill him; and she could not; for Herod feared John, knowing that he was a righteous and holy man, and kept him safe. And when he heard him, he was much perplexed; and he heard him gladly. And when a convenient day was come that Herod on his birthday made a supper to his lords, and the high captains, and the chief men of Galilee; and when the daughter of Herodias herself came in and danced, she pleased Herod and them that sat at meat with him; and the king said unto the damsel, Ask of me whatsoever thou wilt, and I will give it thee. And he sware unto her, Whatsoever thou shalt ask of me, I will , unto the half of my kingdom. And said unto her mother, What shall I ask? The head of John the Baptizer. And she came straightway with haste unto the king, and asked, saying, I will that thou forthwith give me on a platter the head of John the Baptist. And the king was exceeding sorry; but for the sake of his oaths, and of them that sat at meat, he would not reject her. And straightway the king sent forth a soldier of his guard, and commanded to bring his head: and he went and beheaded him in the prison, and brought his head on a platter, and gave it to the damsel; and the damsel gave it to her mother. And when his disciples heard thereof, they came and took up his corpse, and laid it in a tomb."

564-572.

Interpretation

• When we first come into a realization of our needs spiritually, and decide to reform, there is a great sifting of thought and act. We see many things distorted, and often allow our sins to assume large proportions under the searchlight of the Spirit. This zeal to reform and change our mode of thought in a most radical way is John the Baptist. It condemns error in most unmeasured terms, and grows indignant over the immoral practices of the people. Just here we have to be careful. Whatever you condemn you must meet and fight in some form. A challenge means a duel, unless there is apology or explanation or cowardice. This holds good in every mental challenge we make.

• When we denounce the sins of the people, those sinful thoughts rise up and give us battle. It does not make any difference how flagrant the sin, nor how just the demonstration, the opposition comes just the same. It is a question of your strength and ability to meet the error in the spirit in which you have denounced it. In God there is no "righteous indignation." God does not deal with sin by getting angry and excited over it, and the wise man learns that he must deal with all things as God would. God's arms are always open—the vilest sinner may return.

- A certain little woman of the writer's acquaintance has a habit of indulging in this "righteous indignation" over certain forms of error, sometimes in herself and sometimes in others, which is invariably followed by a pain in the back of her head, and a nervous spell as a consequence. Thus her good intention, John, is beheaded because she does not use judgment in her reforms. If you have a pain in the back of your head and nervous headaches, you may find the cause in denunciation of evil, either in yourself or others.

- The law does not allow us to kill off the error state of consciousness as a whole. Every part of man has its place in the economy of Being. Sensation is a legitimate part of physical consciousness and has a ruling identity, represented by Herod. This is that temporal ruler in consciousness called personality. It is not wholly evil as some teach, but has fallen into certain selfish habits of thought. What is needed is purification based upon understanding; and not denunciation and punishment. Although Herod is a libertine, and guilty of the grossest sins against morality, John is not justified in his wholesale denouncement. Hence, when we denounce and rant against sin, the law does not protect us. It is found that those who go out to fight the sins of the world are usually overcome. "Resist not evil," said Jesus. The only successful reform is that based upon education and love.

- The personality is involved with many planes of consciousness, and in this allegory of Herod and his liaisons is brought out some of the phases of sense lust. Sensation is necessary, but it should be curbed and ruled instead of allowed to have its own sweet way. Its way seems sweet, but ends in bitterness if we give up wholly to the enjoyment of the sweetness without meditation or thought about its character and relation to the whole man. Lust is the excess of pleasure. But that same pleasure indulged in with moderation and an understanding mind becomes lasting joy. The only source of understanding is God, so we find that we must dedicate every pleasure of soul or body to God, and do all in His name.

- When one gives up to sense delight in many forms of outward pleasure, the mind almost unconsciously becomes bound to these forms of enjoyment. These are the oaths of Herod that have gone forth from his mind, and which he has to make good wherever he has expressed them. The Hindu mystics claim that this world is an illusion in a sort of dancing light called the astral light, in which the senses whirl in confusion. This is symbolized in this scripture by the daughter of Herodias, the dancing girl, whose gyrations intoxicated Herod until he was willing to give her half his kingdom. But this siren of the sense world does not choose material possessions; she seeks to wean man wholly from the reform elements in his consciousness, and plunges him into greater depths of sensuality by bringing about an entire severance of the head, or the understanding of spiritual things, from the body.

Mark 6:30-44

And the apostles gather themselves together unto Jesus; and they told him all things, whatsoever they had done, and whatsoever they had taught. And he saith unto them, Come ye yourselves apart into a desert place, and rest a while. For there were many coming and going, and they had no leisure so much as to eat. And they went away in the boat to a desert place apart. And the people saw them going, and many knew them, and they ran together there on foot from all the cities, and outwent them. And he came forth and saw a great multitude, and he had compassion on them, because they were as sheep not having a shepherd: and he began to teach them many things. And when the day was now far spent, his disciples came unto him, and said, The place is desert and the day is now far spent; send them away, that they may go into the country and villages round about, and buy themselves somewhat to eat. But he answered and said unto them, Give ye them to eat. And they say unto him, shall we go and buy two hundred shillings worth of bread, and give them to eat? And he said unto them, How many loaves have ye? go and see.

And when they knew they say, Five, and two fishes. And he commanded them that all should sit down by companies upon the green grass. And they sat down in ranks, by hundreds, and by fifties. And He took the five loaves and the two fishes, and looking up to heaven, he blessed, and brake the loaves; and he gave to the disciples to set before them; and the two fishes divided he among them all. And they all ate, and were filled, And they took up broken pieces, twelve basketfuls, and also of the fishes. And they that ate the loaves were five thousand men."

Interpretation

• The multitude of thoughts (the people) have to be fed by the increasing spiritual word. The faculties (disciples) functioning through the intellect do not see how so many mouths can be fed in an apparently desert place. If one listens to the intellect at this stage in development, there will be neglect of duty and a shirking of exercise of power by I AM. The faculties or disciples of the mind function through fixed centers in consciousness, and they are not at this period in full realization of the power and capacity of the I AM. Yet it is though these faculties that the I AM reaches the outlying fields of thought, or "people." Giving thanks increases thought substance with mighty swiftness.

• The five loaves represent the senses that have taken form or become substance in consciousness, as feeling, tasting, smelling, hearing, seeing; and the fishes are ideas not yet in manifestation. In Scripture symbology fish always represent ideas not yet brought into visibility.

• By declaring our senses to be spiritual, and speaking to every one of them the increasing word, we multiply their capacity and give through their increase a sustaining vigor and vitality to the whole organism. This is done through the simple word of the I AM, backed by realization of its spiritual capacity. We cannot in our own power perform this miraculous increase, but when we look up to heaven and bless and break, and give to our disciples, all our thoughts are fed by this divine manna, and there is an abundance left over.

580-582.

Mat. 14:22-33

And straightway he constrained the disciples to enter into the boat, and to go before him unto the other side, till he should send the multitudes away. And after he had sent the multitudes away, he went up into the mountain apart to pray: and when even was come, he was thee alone. But the boat was now in the midst of the sea, distressed by the waves; for the wind was contrary. And in the forth watch of the night he came unto them, walking upon the sea. And when the disciples saw him walking on the sea, they were troubled, saying, It is a ghost; and they cried out for fear. But straightway Jesus spoke unto them saying, Be of good cheer; it is I; be not afraid. And Peter answered him and said, Lord, if it be thou, bid me come unto thee upon the waters. And he said, Come. And Peter went down from the boat, and walked upon the waters to come to Jesus. But when he saw the wind, he was afraid; and beginning to sink, he cried out, saying, Lord save me. And immediately Jesus stretched forth his hand, and took hold of him, and saith unto him, O thou of little faith, wherefore didst thou doubt? And when they were gone up into the boat, the wind ceased. And they that were in the boat worshipped him, saying, Of a truth thou art the Son of God."

583-590.

Interpretation

•   Water represents mental potentiality. The race thoughts have formed a sea of thought, and to walk over it safely requires that one have a faith in himself. Faith is necessary to accomplish so great a work comes from understanding—understanding of God and man, and the Law of Mastery given to man.

•   God is substance; sub, under; stare, to stand. He is the underlying principle of the universe, upholding all things by the Word of His power, by the Omnipresent energy that permeates all creation. Such an understanding of God establishes the mind firmly in faith and the feet walk surely over the sea of mind.

•   Doubt of the omnipotence of Spirit is the real root of both mental and physical weakness. Faith in one's self is a power-builder, but where this faith links itself with the Mighty One of the universe, and feels His sustaining presence, all adverse conditions are overcome. To walk the waves of troubled thought without sinking down into them requires the established faith of Jesus in the power of Spirit. Peter represents faith in its various stages of development. When our faith in the power of Spirit to sustain us under all conditions is but partially developed, we are apt to sink into the thought waves about us when they become boisterous.

• The world is full of ambitious people, people who seem to have success before them. They start out bravely, but are swept under by elements weak as water. Could these people but know they mighty power right at hand, and when they begin to sink, cry out with faith as Peter did "Lord, save me," they would be raised up above adverse conditions about them.

• The great majority try to walk the waves of life in their own personal strength, but they go down in a troubled sea in the end. Ability with them is not of the unlimited Christ character, but a mere mortal standard.

• The difference between the successful men and women of the world and the failures is not one of brain structure, nor mental ability, nor physical strength, but always confidence in the true self. Even those who have been taught of the Master are still filled with doubts and fears when storms arise, and instead of a reality, He seems an apparition. But the Master Christ Mind is not an apparition, but a mighty power, and when we have faith in it, all the discordant elements of our lives are quieted, and we reduce to harmony and wholeness everything our peace-giving thoughts touch.

• It is not necessary that we walk on material water to follow Jesus. These are lessons in spiritual overcoming. When we have found the Spirit of the law the material expression adjusts itself. We live constantly in a sea of thought that is moved upon by every impulse of the mind. There are greater storms on land than on sea, and they are far more destructive because of the many minds reached by the psychic waves. An everyday the saving grace, "Be of good cheer: it is I; be not afraid."

• Jesus the Master was Lord of heaven and earth. His faith and understanding gave him the mastery over all the elements and over every form of mortal thought. When union is made between the Master Mind and the mind of man, consciousness realizes its true Self and the dominion which was man's from the beginning is restored to him. He is no longer weak and negative, subject to conditions and circumstances, but is powerful and masterful, and walks triumphantly over all the waters of ignorance and error.

• If you link your fortune with Christ, you cannot fail, you cannot be defeated. It does not make any difference how great the disaster which may seem to have befallen you, if you join hands with the living Christ within and about you in the realms invisible, and invoke his almighty succor, you will make your seeming defeat a stepping-stone to higher things.

591-592.

Mark 6:53-56

And when they had crossed over, they came to the land unto Gennesaret, and moored to the shore. And when they were come out of the boat, straightway the people knew him, and ran round about that whole region, and began to carry about on their beds those that were sick, where they heard he was. And wheresoever he entered, into villages, or into cities, or into the country, they laid the sick in the marketplaces, and besought him that they might touch if it were but the border of his garment: and as many as touched him were made whole."

593-594.

Interpretation

•   In individual consciousness Jesus and His disciples represent the indwelling Christ with its twelve spiritual faculties. Genessaret means the way of divine life. We are related both within the consciousness and without to all creation through the universal life principle. In this state of consciousness there are those thoughts that have allowed the life radiation to die out. However, when the Christ penetrates into this region the highest thought forces there in command call together all the weak, wavering ones and they are instantly healed by the Christ touch. When we recognize our unity with the one life, and with all life, we are on the way to true exaltation and rulership and abundant substance.

595-599.

Mark 7:1-23

And there are gathered together unto him the Pharisees, and certain of the scribes, who had come from Jerusalem and had seen that some of his disciples ate their bread with defiled, that is, unwashen, hands. (For the Pharisees, and all the Jews, except they wash their hands diligently eat not, holding the tradition of the elders; and when they come from the marketplace except they bathe themselves, they eat not; and many other things there are, which they have received to hold washings of cups, and pots, and brasen vessels). And the Pharisees and the scribes ask him, Why walk not thy disciples according to the tradition of the elders, but eat their bread with defiled hands? And he said unto them, Well did Isaiah prophesy of your hypocrites, as it is written, This people honoreth me with their lips, But their heart is far from me. But in vain do they worship me, Teaching as their doctrines the precepts of men. Ye leave the commandment of God, and hold fast the tradition of men. And he said unto them, Full well do ye reject the commandment of God, that said, Honor thy father and thy mother; and, he that speaketh evil of father, or mother, let him die the death: but ye say, if a man shall say to his father or his mother, That wherewith thou mightest have been profited by me is Corfan that is to say, Given to God; ye no longer suffer him to do aught for his father or his mother; making void the word of God by your tradition, which ye have delivered: and many such things ye do. And he called to him the multitude again, and said unto them, Hear me all of you, and understand: there is nothing from without the man, that going into him can defile him; but the things which proceed out of the man are those that defile the man. And when he was entered into the house from the multitude, his disciples asked of him the parable. And he sayith unto them, Are ye .so without understanding also? Perceive ye not, that Whatsoever from without goeth into the man, it cannot defile him; because it goeth not into his heart, but into his belly, and goeth out into the draught? This he said making all meats clean. And he said, That which proceedeth out of the man, that defileth the man. For from within, out of the heart of men, evil thoughts proceed, fornication, thefts, murders, adulteries, covetings, wickedness, deceit, lasciviousness, an evil eye, railing, pride, foolishness: all these evil things proceed from within, and defile the man.

600-603.

Interpretation

•   The Pharisees represent thoughts that arise out of the subsciousness [subconscious – Ed.], binding man to external forms of religion without giving him understanding of their real meaning.

•   Religionists who have become unbalanced through giving undue attention to the forms of religious rites, lose sight of the principle back of the symbols. Standards of life and action for Christian people have gone through many transformations, but the crystallizations in the realm of forms are found on every side.

•   One of the Pharisaical forms was not to eat with unwashen hands. Jesus came teaching and demonstrating a far different doctrine. It is really the innermost thoughts of man's consciousness that build or defile. Spiritual man is a man that lives, moves, and has his being on the invisible plane of existence. If you look at things, persons, etc. you are not looking at the source. Good or evil is conceived in man and not outside of man. Only that which is based on principle can stand. Jesus' teachings were founded on principle. He expressed them in sound words. Constructive thinking and constructive living are the only powers that lead to Truth's house where the adversary cannot make his appearance.

•   Man functions on two planes, the formless and the formed. When he keeps the balance between these, all goes well. The equilibrium is disturbed by too much attention to the one or the other. An excess of attention to the formless brings about diffusion and incoherency, while much thought about the realm of forms leads to narrowness and constrictions in a multitude of ways.

•   The intellectual man is always looking for difference whereby he can prove his superiority. The spiritual man looks back of mere forms, and seeks to harmonize and balance and establish the consciousness of satisfaction and peace. The true; metaphysician sees the good in all people and recognizes that only that which comes from the heart is truly worthwhile. He sees the realities of Truth.

604-606.

Mark 7:24-26

And from thence he arose, and went into the borders of Tyre and Sidon. And he entered into a house, and would have no man know it; and he could not be hid. But straightway a woman, whose little daughter had an unclean spirit, having heard of him, came and fell down at his feet. Now the woman was a Greek, a Syropheonician by race. And she besought him that he would cast forth the demon out of her daughter.

Mat. 15:23-25

He answered her not a word. And his disciples came and besought him, saying, Send her away; for she crieth after us. But he answered and said, I was not sent but unto the lost sheep of the house of Israel. But she came and worshipped him, saying, Lord, help me.

Mark 7:27-30

And he said unto her, Let the children first be filled: for it is not meet to take the children's bread and cast it to the dogs. But she answered and saith unto him, Yea, Lord; even the dogs under the table eat of the children's crumbs. And he said unto her, For this saying go thy way; the demon is gone out of thy daughter. And she went unto her house, and found the child laid upon the bed, and the demon gone out.

607-612.

Interpretation

• The name Tyre means strength, and the name Sidon means beast of prey. Tyre and Sidon represent the region of man which may be termed body sensation. This realm in its intellectual aspect is designated in Scripture as Greek. It has not been illumined by Spirit, and is considered too material to be worthy of spiritualization. This is the way nearly all people look upon the body and its sensations. As shown in this Scripture they go into it consciously; "He entered into a house, and would have no man know it;" but we can't get away from our thoughts, "He could not be hid."
• The Greek woman represents the unspiritualized love, natural to body. Its daughter is physical sensation, which has been sensualized by impure thoughts.
• At a certain stage in spiritual unfoldment one may decide that a high spiritual thought force is too holy to operate in the lower forms of sense consciousness in order to redeem it. The disciples besought Jesus to send the woman away and thus refuse to heal the daughter. Jesus' reply "I was not sent but unto the lost sheep of the house of Israel," reveals that the whole man must be redeemed and that the "holier than thou" idea is no part of true Christianity.
• Whenever the illuminated I AM centers its attention anywhere in the body there is at once a quickening of intelligence and a reaching out for higher things by consciousness functioning there. Every part of the organism is under the control of a set of thoughts that direct and care for that particular function. The nerves are under the control of an ego that thinks about nerves; the muscles, bones, blood, in fact every department of the man, each has its distinct thought center. So we are made up of many men and women, because

both the masculine and feminine qualities are equally distributed, and they all work together in harmony when divine order is established.

• We really use all those different parts of our being, but not understandingly. In our ignorance we dissipate the natural purity and strength of these obedient people who form our soul and body. But when we become illuminated by the Spirit a reform sets in, and they then all reflect the new light that has come to us, especially so when we concentrate our minds upon the centers, or "enter into a house."

• Yet there lingers in the mind that old idea, borrowed from the limited vision of the Jew, that the Spirit does not include the body in its redemptive process. But the body cries out for cleansing and purification. "Even the dogs under the table eat of the children's crumbs." Good common sense should teach us that life is continuous throughout nature, a stream proceeding from the highest to the lowest.

• This understanding of the unity and purity of the one life brings healing to the demonized sense consciousness. "She found the child laid upon the bed, and the demon gone out."

613-614.

Mark 7:31-37

And again he went out from the borders of Tyre, and came through Sidon unto the sea of Galilee, through the midst of the borders of Decapolis. And they bring unto him one that was deaf, and had an impediment in his speech; and they beseech him to lay his hands upon him. And he took him aside from the multitude privately, and put his fingers into his ears and he spat, and touched his tongue; and looking up to heaven, he sighed and saith unto him, Ephphatha, that is Be opened. And his ears were opened, and the bond of his tongue was loosed, and he spake plain. And he charged them that they should tell no man: but the more he charged them, so much the more a great deal they published it. And they were beyond measure astonished, saying, He hath done all things well; he maketh even the deaf to hear, and the dumb to speak.

615-623.

Interpretation

• All physical acts are first performed in the mind. The once strongest man in the world, Sandow, said in an interview: "It is in the mind -- all a matter of mind. The muscles really have a secondary place. A man with strong concentration of mind will develop quicker in the quality of his muscles than will he who cannot concentrate his mind upon the matter. The whole secret of my system lie in concentration of mind." This testimony from a man who was a muscular giant is important because of the emphasis he put upon the mind as the source of power.

- But the mind does not necessarily have to confine its working power to fleshly muscles. A magnet the size of a man's arm will lift as much scrap iron as twenty men, when it is charged with electricity.
- Metaphysicians find that there is an energy even finer than electricity through which the mind acts -- they call it Spirit. When the mind concentrates upon Spirit there is an inflow of this finer force, and the whole man, Spirit, soul, body, is charged like a magnet.
- The name Decapolis means "ten cities." In symbology a center represents a group of thoughts, or a thought center in consciousness. Metaphysically interpreted this journey of Jesus means that the I AM (Jesus) withdrew its attention from the outer centers (borders of Tyre) and concentrated upon the inner centers (the "midst of the borders of Decapolis"). These ten thought centers are of the soul, and when lined up by a developed mind exert great power.
- Deafness is usually caused by inability of nerves in carrying sound waves. Back of this is the mind that prevents the natural inflow and outflow of universal life. Continuous thought about self and selfish interests throws the life force to the nerve centers and they become clogged. The blood and serums are congested in the mucous linings, and medical men classify the various conditions that arise as disease. The remedy for such is a quickening of the life flow in the body, and opening of the mind to Truth.
- Jesus may have treated the deaf and dumb man just as described in the scripture. He had purified and raised to a high rate of vibration all the elements of his organism. He was like a highly electrified magnet, which could impart its power to other magnets in a state of partial inertia. Energy flow from his finger tips and his saliva was a quickening, purifying serum. When he had set going the physical machinery of hearing and speech, his next and most important move was to impart the consciousness of Spirit, which He did. "He looked up to heaven," he sighed and saith, "Eph-pha-tha, that is, Be opened."
- Galilee means a "circle." In the realm of the unlimited, the circle becomes a sphere, which is the emblem of infinity. Jesus' entrance into Galilee may be said to represent the increased activity of Truth coming down into the subconscious realm and bringing about the realization of Christhood. The vast region of the subconscious may well be compared with the sea of Galilee. Again and again, after a period of mighty works, Jesus withdrew into Galilee. So does the spiritual I AM withdraw into Galilee (consciousness of endless activity), in order to came into closer contact with God, the source or all energy.
- The great multitudes that followed Jesus are the legions of thoughts that swarm the mind, seeking harmony. These thoughts are harmonized and unified by contact with the high spiritual consciousness of the I AM; and while no single one of these various thought entities can grasp or comprehend the healing and uplifting work of the I AM, all recognize its origin in Spirit. Man knows that his good comes from his clinging fast to his highest concept of what is true and noble; that "true worth is in being, not seeming."

• Jesus is still with us, doing His mighty works. "Lo, I am with you always." We must have faith in the spiritual power of our minds, then the way is opened for the healing of our deafness and dumbness. We should all be hearing the voice of the Spirit and speaking the words of Truth. We need this treatment daily until our minds and ears are opened. Enter into the "midst" of your consciousness and quicken the power dormant there. Then throw it out to ears and tongues, saying as you do so, "In the name of Jesus Christ, Be opened."

624-625.

Mark 8:1-9

In those days, when there was again a great multitude, and they had nothing to eat, he called unto him his disciples, and saith unto them, I have compassion on the multitudes because they continuo with me now three days, and have nothing to eat: and if I send them away fasting to their homes, they will faint on the way; and some of them are come from far. And his disciples answered him, Whence shall one be able to fill these men with bread here in a desert place? And he asked them, How many loaves have ye? And they said, seven. And he commanded the multitude to sit down on the ground: and he took the seven loaves, and having given thanks, he brake, and gave to his disciples, to set before them; and they set them before the multitude. And they had a few small fishes: and having blessed them, he commanded to set these also before them. And they ate, and were filled: and they took up, of broken pieces that remained over, seven baskets. And they were about four thousand: and he sent them away.

626-627.

Interpretation

• The loaves symbolize universal substance, and fishes represent ideas of increase. We follow Jesus in this demonstration of the law whenever we enter into the realization of substance, know our oneness with it and use our power to bring it into manifestation. The practical application of this truth is made, first in our own consciousness when we make union with substance, and, through our twelve spiritual faculties, pass it out to all of the cells of the body. In this way the body is fed and nourished with the living Word, the bread from heaven.

• From the universal substance, through man's power to realize-and use it, every need is supplied. Faith makes the substance tangible, and through the power of thought, we form the substance into whatever we may need.

628-629.

Mark 8:10-12

And straightway he entered into the boat with his disciples, and came into the part of Dalmanutha. And the Pharisees came forth, and began to question with him, seeking of him a sign from heaven, trying him. And he sighed deeply in his spirit, and said, Why doth this generation seek a sign?

Mat. 16:2b-4

When it is evening, ye say, It will be fair weather; for the heaven is red. And in the morning, It will be foul weather today; for the heaven is red and lowering. Ye know how to discern the face of the heaven; but ye cannot discern the signs of the times. An evil and adulterous generation seeketh after a sign; and there shall no sign be given unto it; but the sign of Jonah. And he left them, and departed.

630-632.

Interpretation

• The name Dalmanutha means "overhanging branch;" "bucket." Dalmanutha represents a faculty in consciousness that has only a limited understanding of, and capacity to contain the waters of life (bucket).

• Pharisees and Sadducees symbolize narrowness, self-righteousness, hardness of heart, argumentativeness, crystallization in old religious rites and ceremonies. It is this state of consciousness that opposes and tries to tear down the constructive work of Spirit. It is able to discern the letter of the law, but not the spirit; the signs of the times in the outer but not in the inner. The spiritual sign is always given, but can only be discerned by the spiritually quickened soul.

• Jesus did not stay long in Dalmanutha, because the Pharisees met Him at once and began to question Him and ask for a sign. (And He left them, and departed.) This means that the I AM cannot remain in such limited, doubting condition of mind, but departs quickly.

• There are Pharisees at every turn, tempting believers to do some great thing, like the healing instantly of some well known case in their community, to the end that everybody may believe. Such people are usually sincere in their claim that some such marvelous work will prove a sign to the unbelieving of the power of the Spirit. But every experienced healer knows the futility of such methods to convince people of Truth. Truth has entrance to the mind through the understanding.

633-634.

Mark 8:14-21

And they forgot to take bread; and they had not in the boat with them more than one loaf. And he charged them, saying, Take heed, beware of the leaven of the Pharisees and the leaven of Herod. And they reasoned one with another, saying, We have no bread. And Jesus perceiving it saith unto them, Why reason ye, because ye have no bread? do ye not yet perceive, neither understand? have ye your heart hardened? Having eyes, see ye not? and having ears, hear ye not? and do ye not remember? When I brake the five loaves among the five thousand, how many baskets full of broken pieces took ye up? They say unto him, Twelve. And when the seven among the four thousand, how many basketfuls of broken pieces took ye, up? And they say unto him, Seven. And he said unto them, Do ye not yet understand?

Matt. 16:12

Then understood they that he bade them not beware of the leaven of bread, but of the teaching of the Pharisees and Saducees.

635-637.

Interpretation

• "The disciples came to the other side and they forgot to take bread." At this point the I AM withdrew and departed to another side of consciousness.

• Leaven always means expansion. Whatever line of thought is received into consciousness goes on working until it is rooted out by another line of thinking or until it changes one's whole consciousness and manifests fully in the outer life.

• Like all genuine teachers of Truth, Jesus tried to get the attention of his people away from material things, in order that they might realize the spiritual. He refused to display his power like a necromancer, or juggler. He was a teacher of the science of mind, which He could demonstrate at the opportune moment. When they way (say – Ed.), "We have no bread," He told them to beware of the limited thoughts (leaven of the Pharisees and Herod). When we confined the Divine Law to the customary avenues of expression, and scoff at anything beyond, we are letting the leaven of Herod work to our undoing. When the mind is raised up through affirmations of God omnipresent substance and life, we are not only fed, but there is a surplus. This is the teaching of Jesus, and it has always been exemplified by His faithful followers. It is not the outward demonstration that counts, but the increase of substance in mind and body that always follows the faithful application of the law.

638.

Mark 8:22-26

And they come unto Bethsaida. And they bring to him blind man, and beseech him to touch him. And he took hold of the blind man by the hand, and brought him out of the village; and when he had spit on his eyes, and laid his hands upon him, he asks him, Seeth thou aught? And he looked up, and said, I see men: for I behold them as trees walking. Then again he laid his hands upon his eyes; and he looked steadfastly, and was restored and saw all things clearly. And he sent him away to his home, saying, Do not even enter into the village.

Interpretation

• Blind eyes represent blind understanding, and the treatment spiritually interpreted will quicken darkened minds. "He took the blind man by the hand and brought him out of the village." Segregate your thoughts from everyday associations. To the evil minded the act of spitting upon another is an expression of contempt, but to the spiritually minded it is the very reverse. The saliva of a Christ-man can be transmuted into a free energy that will melt away the scum called cataract. Repeated treatments are often necessary because of the density of the thought of darkness and inability to understand.

• The Christ Mind, or superconsciousness, exists in all people; the difference between a Christ-man and a natural man is in development. It is really an easy matter to realize this higher principle if one gives it the proper attention. There must be a daily withdrawal from the common trend of thought. The mind must be lifted up by use of spiritual thoughts and words. The time thus spent will bring great returns, so great that all comparisons are odious.

Mat 16:13-20

Now when Jesus came into the parts of Caesarea Philippi, he asked his disciples, saying, Who do men say that the Son of man is? And they said, Some say John the Baptist; some, Elijah: and others, Jeremiah, or one of the prophets. He said unto them, But who say ye that I am? And Simon Peter answered and said, Thou art the Christ, the Son of the living God. And Jesus answered and said unto him, Blessed art thou, Simon Barjonah; for flesh and blood hath not revealed it unto thee, but my Father who is in heaven.

But I also say unto thee, thou art Peter, and upon this rock I will build my church; and the gates of Hades shall not prevail against it. I will give thee the keys of the kingdom of heaven: and whatsoever thou shalt bind on earth shall be bound in heaven; and whatsoever thou shalt loose on earth shall be loosed in heaven. Then charged he the disciples that they should tell no man that he was the Christ.

Interpretation

• Prayer is a collecting of the faculties and a focusing of the thought on a higher plane of mind activity than that on which one ordinarily dwells. Complete concentration of the mind in prayer is best gained in the solitude of one's own thought and in silence, apart from all outer distractions. Under conditions such as these, clear thinking is possible, and the universal storehouse of ideas opens its treasure to one.

Mat. 16:21-23

From that time began Jesus to show unto his disciples that he must go unto Jerusalem, and suffer many things of the elders and chief scribes, and be killed, and the third day be raised up. And Peter took him, and began to rebuke him, saying, Be it far from thee, Lord: this shall never be unto thee. But he turned, and said unto Peter, Get thee behind me, Satan: thou art a Stumbling block unto me: for thou mindest not the things of God, but the things of men.

646-649.

Interpretation

•   This mighty revelation that man is in fact the very Son of the living God is too stupendous for even the illuminated one to comprehend and retain at once. Before this truth can become a constant factor in mind it suffers many things at the hands of the "elders" and "chief priests" and "scribes" which represent the traditional beliefs and ruling religious ideas dominant in the mind. Many of these beliefs have been fixed in mind from childhood, and do not yield at once to the spiritual idea. Instead they assert their power to extinguish spiritual understanding for a season. It is "killed" but shall after the third day be raised up."

•   The spiritual idea contains the germ of living Truth, and the earnest desire for Truth sets the latent forces of the subconsciousness *(subconscious – Ed.)* to work, and the result is an awakening of the conscious mind to a clearer understanding of spiritual reality.

•   These three-days represent three movements of mind, which may be designated "perception," "realization," "manifestation." The realizing degree has its part in the subjective consciousness and is accompanied with more or less darkness. The clear light of first perception is obscured, yet we know that changes are going on in consciousness, and if we are wise, we will accompany the Christ down into the tomb of matter within us and assist in every way in overcoming the hereditary sins of the flesh. Truth rises again to the conscious mind and establishes itself.

•   The disciples, or faculties of the mind, have been built up largely on the outer plane of consciousness, and they do not understand the necessity of the crucifixion of personality. Peter, especially, rebukes such a proposition, but the Supreme One recognizes this thought as a stumbling-block to that final giving up that precedes the transfiguration. Thus faith in the perpetuity of mortality is a stumbling-block to spiritual development.

650-651.

Mat. 16:24-27a

Then said Jesus unto his disciples, If any man would come after me, let him deny himself, and take up his cross, and follow me. For whosoever would save his life shall lose it: and whosoever shall lose his life for my sake shall find it. For what shall a man be profited, if he shall gain the whole world, and forfeit his life? or what shall a man give in exchange for his life? For the Son of man shall come in the glory of His Father with his angels;

Mark 6:38

For whosoever shall be ashamed of me and my words in this adulterous and sinful generation, the Son of man also shall be ashamed of him, when he cometh in the glory of his Father with the holy angels.

Mat. 16:27b-28

...then shall he render unto every man according to his deeds, Verily I say unto you, There are some of them that stand here, who shall in no wise taste of death, till they see the Son of man coming in his kingdom.

652-654.

Interpretation

• In order that spiritual man may be supreme in consciousness, mortal man must be crucified. We must give up devotion to the personal life if we want the spiritual life. The two are incompatible and cannot both survive. This becomes clearer to the inner consciousness as the universal character of the Christ man is revealed, hence the teaching of the necessity of a crucifixion of the man that appears to sense consciousness to have existence independent of God.

• Mortality and mortal ideas fall far short of Spirit, and they must all be surrendered before we can enter into eternal life. The old version says it is the soul that is lost but the new gives it as life. It is not a question of preparing the soul for heaven after death, but a demonstration of life right here and now.

• To gain spiritual life and spiritual consciousness we must concentrate our energies and our desires on winning through to the spiritual realm and makin ourselves at home there. This means denying ourselves all indulgence in less interests and activities and recognizing only the claims of the higher. "If any man would come after me, let him deny himself, and take up his cross, and follow me." Daily. The personal self sets up counter currents which put life at cross-purposes with spiritual development. Steady, daily denial of the claims of the personal self constitutes our "cross." The loss of personal life is the only way to find eternal life. The acceptance of this might truth takes away the consciousness of death, and reveals the Son of God coming into his kingdom here and now.

655-658.

Mat. 17:1-2

And after six days Jesus taketh with him Peter, and James, and John his brother, and bringeth them up into a high mountain apart: and he was transfigured before them; and his face did shine as the sun, and his garments became white as the light.

Luke 9:30-33

And behold, there talked with him two men, who were Moses and Elijah; who appeared in glory, and spake of his decease which he was about to accomplish at Jerusalem. Now Peter and they that were with him were heavy with sleep; but when they were fully awake, they saw his glory, and the two men that stood with him. And it came to pass, as they were parting with him, Peter said unto Jesus, Master, it is good for us to be here: and let us make three tabernacles; one for thee, and one for Moses, and one for Elijah: not knowing what he said.

Mat. 17:5-8

While he was yet speaking, behold, a bright cloud overshadowed them: and behold, a voice out of the cloud, saying, This is my beloved Son, in whom I am well pleased; hear ye him. And when the disciples heard it, they fell on their face, and were sore afraid. And Jesus came and touched them and said, Arise, and be not afraid. And lifting up their eyes, they saw no one, save Jesus only.

Mark 9:9-13

And as they were coming down from the mountain he charged them that they should tell no man what things they had seen, save when the Son of man should have risen again from the dead. And they kept the saying, questioning among themselves what the rising again from the dead should mean. And they asked him, saying, How is it that the scribes say that Elijah must first come? And he said unto them, Elijah indeed cometh first, and restoreth all things: and how it is written of the Son of man, that he should suffer many things and be set at naught? But I say unto you, that Elijah is come, and they have also done unto him whatsoever they would, even as it is written of him.

Mat. 17:13

Then understood the disciples that he spake unto them of John the Baptist.

659-671

Interpretation

• Going up into the mountain to pray means an elevation of thought and aspiration from the mortal to the spiritual viewpoint. When the mind is exalted in prayer the rapid radiation of mental energy causes a dazzling light radiation from all parts of the body, and especially the head.

• To pray effectively one must have faith (Peter), love (John), and judgment (James). These accompanying the I AM (Jesus) in prayer, reveal the law of denial (Moses) and affirmation (Elijah), which eventually does away with the personality, and brings forth the Christ.

• Even our so-called physical bodies reveal a radiant body, (which Jesus referred to as sitting on the throne of His glory), which interlaces the trillions of cells of the organism and burns as brightly as the electric light. Jesus gave His disciples a glimpse of His radiant body when He was transformed before them.

• "His face did shine as the sun, and his garments became white as the light."

• Jesus was a very advanced soul and His radiant body was developed in a larger degree than any one in our race evolution, but we all have that body and its development is in proportion to our spiritual culture. In Jesus His body of light glowed while He was praying. Jesus did not go down to corruption but He, by the intensity of His spiritual devotions, transformed every cell into its innate atomic light and power. When John was in the Spirit of devotion Jesus appeared to him and "his eyes were as a flame of fire; and his feet like burnished brass." Jesus lives today in that body of glorified electricity in a kingdom that interpenetrates the earth and its environment. He called it the kingdom of the heavens.

• We do not have to look to the many experiences of the spiritually illumined recorded in the Bible to prove the existence of this super substance. People everywhere are discovering it, as they always have in every age and clime. Men will continue to pray, and prayer releases the innate glory of the soul, so we must be taught how to establish our identity in the Christ and through it gain the mastery of the stored up riches of the man invisible.

• The metaphysical literature of our day is very rich with experiences of those who have found through various channels the existence of the radiant body. The latest is Angelo Morgan's book "Behold The Angel!" This book is a radical departure from Miss Morgan's well-known poetical vein. She is specific and to the point in announcing her revelations. She says in the preface:

• "This is a book about the radiant body, the living Self of every human being; the immortal structure which is the real self even now in this moment of time."

• "The author through intense conviction and the validity of recent experience, writes in concrete terms of what to her is as real as flesh, bone, blood, and muscles. There is behind this veil of flesh an actual flame-like structure invisible to our everyday limited perception. When I say it is radiant, I mean it literally. It is vividly alive, glorious as the sunrise."

• She tells of numerous instances in which she saw hands and feet and other parts of her body lighted or really transformed by the flame invisible.

• This convincing confession of Miss Morgan prompts me to tell of my development of the radiant body, during half a century's experience. It began when I was mentally affirming statements of truth. Just between my eyes, just above, I felt a "thrill" that lasted a few moments, then passed away. I found I could repeat this experience with affirmations. As time went on I could set up this "thrill" at other points in my body and finally it became a continuous current throughout my nervous system. I called it the Spirit, and found that it was connected with a universal life force whose tributary source was Jesus Christ. As taught in the Bible we have through wrong ways of thinking and living lost contact with the Parent Life. Jesus Christ, a transcendent soul, incarnated in the flesh and thereby introduced us by His Word into the original Father life. He said, "If ye abide in me and my words abide in you, you shall never see death."

• I have believed that and affirmed His words until they have become organized in my body and I absolutely feel that I shall never pass out of this organism. Sometimes when I make this claim of eternal life in the body I am asked if I expect to live always in this flesh. My answer is that I realize that the flesh is in broken down every day and its cells transformed into energy and life, and a new body is being formed of a very superior quality. That new body in Christ will be my future habitation. I shall not fly away to some heaven in the skies but help to make heaven here.

• I have found that the kingdom of God is within men and that we are wasting our time, and defeating the work of the Spirit, if we look for it anywhere else. The appearance of Moses and Elijah may also be said to represent the two processes through which the picture of the purified man is to be objectified or demonstrated in real life. The first is the Mosaic or evolutionary process of nature, through which there is a steady upward trend of all things. The other is the ability of the spiritual discerner of Truth (the prophet Elijah) to make conditions rapidly change on the mental plane, to be in due season worked out in substance. Thus we are told in the Scriptures that Elijah must first come and restore all things. The mind must first be set right through spiritual understanding, after which comes the demonstration.

• Faith, love, judgment are "heavy with sleep," when we begin our devotions. Then they become awakened through the exalted exercise of thought, and take on a degree of spirituality, but they do not fully understand the law of Divine unity which exists in the higher spiritual realm. Faith would erect three tabernacles, or temporary thought bodies, not yet realizing the body of Christ, which is a unit: hence the accompanying voice out of the cloud, "This is my beloved Son, in whom I am well pleased; hear ye him."

• Telling no man of any of the things which they had seen, represents the inability of the mind to express the revelations of the spiritual. There are no occult secrets to those who are spiritually quickened. Yet no language can explain that which occurs on a plane of consciousness in which the conditions and relations are far different from the material. The limited mind cannot grasp the powers of the unlimited. For example, it sounds like a fairytale to say that in a certain exalted state of prayer and affirmation we can treat every receptive person in a moment of time and bring greater results than through repeated denials and affirmations on the lower planes of consciousness. Yet this is absolutely true and is but an expression of the radiant comprehension and power of the Superconsciousness, or Mind of the Spirit.

• Many also refer to this Scripture as proof of reincarnation. John the Baptist was Elijah come again.

Mark 9:14-27

And when they came to the disciples, they saw a great multitude about them, and scribes questioning with them. And straightway all the multitude, when they saw him, were greatly amazed, and running to him saluted him, And he asked them, What question ye with them? And one of the multitude answered him, Teacher, I brought unto thee my son, Who hath a dumb spirit; and wheresoever it taketh him, it dasheth him down: and he foamoth, and grindeth his teeth, and pineth away: and I spake to thy disciples that they should cast it out; and they were not able. And he answereth them and saith, O faithless generation, how long shall I be with you? how long shall I bear with you? bring him unto me. And they brought him unto him: and when he saw him, straightway the spirit tare him grievously; and he fell to the ground, and wallowed foaming. And he asked his father, how long time is it since this hath come unto him? And he said, From a child. And oft-times it hath cast him both into the fire and into the waters, to destroy him: but if thou canst do anything, have compassion on us, and help us. And Jesus said unto him, If thou canst! All things are possible to him that believeth. Straightway the father of the child cried out, and said, I believe; help thou mine unbelief. And when Jesus saw that a multitude came running together, he rebuked the unclean spirit, and saying unto him, Thou dumb and deaf spirit, I command thee, come out of him, and enter no more into him. And having cried out, and tore him much, be came out: and the body became as one dead: insomuch that the more part said, He is dead. But Jesus took him by the hand, and raised him up; and he arose.

Luke 9:43a

And they were all astonished at the majesty of God.

Mat. 17:19-21

Then came the disciples to Jesus apart, and said, Why could not we cast it out? And he saith unto them, Because of your little faith: for verily I say unto you, If ye have faith as a grain of mustard Seed, ye shall say unto this mountain, Remove him to yonder place; and it shall remove; and nothing shall be impossible unto you. But this kind goeth not out save by prayer and fasting.

Interpretation

• Epilepsy is caused by contention of sense over spiritual supremacy. "The flesh lusteth against the Spirit, and the Spirit against the flesh; for these are contrary the one to the other; that ye may not do the things that ye would."
• The epileptic boy represents one in which the fleshly ego or the lusts of the sense mind have assumed such proportions in the personality that is has lost even its physical poise and for the time being is a maniac. Jesus, representing the supreme spiritual entity, has power to restore the poise and

equilibrium of the mind under divine law and this accomplishes the so-called miracle of healing. God created man and gave him balanced faculties and the ability to unfold and establish himself as a sane harmonious perfect expression of the divine idea. Jesus attained this perfection and through it gained authority and power sufficient to help others to the same place in consciousness. We all have this capacity and express its power to the extent of our spiritual unfoldment.

• Man in his natural capacity, no matter how highly developed may be, cannot control the contention of sense over Spirit. The Christ awakens the powers of the spiritual man however, and the combination breaks down resistance, and the soul becomes open and receptive to the higher laws. Harmony is restored.

• What man has to do is to realize his ability to awaken his spiritual identity which is the image and likeness of God. He must awaken his power to declare his Christhood, and redeem every opposing force. In this way the error manifestation is changed into harmonious life activity. Jesus' disciples could not cast out the demons of personality. He told them that it could only be accomplished through fasting and prayer. The inference is that they must raise their spiritual power through denying their negative thoughts and affirming the positive.

678.

Mat. 17:22-23

And while they abode in Galilee, Jesus said unto them, The Son of man shall be delivered up into the hands of men; and they shall kill him, and the third day he shall be raised up. And they were exceeding sorry.

679-680.

Interpretation

• In this Scripture Jesus was referring to the experience one passes through going from the natural to the spiritual consciousness.

• The name Galilee means "energy of life;" "power;" "force;" "soul energy." Galilee represents life activity.

• Jesus' abiding in Galilee symbolizes a continual expression of the activity of Truth, which always brings about a realization of Christhood, after personality has been denied and the praise of God has been set up. In this transformation the natural man is killed and lies in the grave three days, at the end of which time he is resurrected on the spiritual plane.

681.

Mat. 17:24-27

And when they were came to Capernaum, they that received the half-shekel came to Peter, and said, Doth not your teacher pay the half-shekel? He saith, Yea. And when he came into the house, Jesus spake first to him, saying,

What thinkest thou, Simon? the kings of the earth, from whom do they receive toll or tribute? from their sons or from strangers? And when he said, From strangers, Jesus said unto him, Therefore the sons are free. But, lest we cause them to stumble, go thou to the sea, and cast a hook, and take up the fish that first cometh up; and when thou hast opened his mouth, thou shalt find a shekel: that take, and give unto them for me and thee.

683-684.

Interpretation

•   In individual consciousness Capernaum represents the coming into an understanding of the comforting power of Spirit.

•   The fish is the most fecund of all the products of nature and represents the idea of accumulation, of increasing, multiplying power. We often use the fish to represent the increasing capacity or the production of the earth. Jesus used the fish to exemplify the fecundity of spiritual ideas. The mouth has to do with the expression of the word. The piece of gold in the fish's mouth represents the power of the true word to increase the fecundity of nature. The king of the earth here corresponds to God, The sons are Sons of God. The Sons of God are free from taxation. But though we are exempt we have power to supply the tax. This means that Jesus, although He is the Son of God, and those who understand the divine law, are free from earth's bondage, yet may conform to it in certain states of unfoldment. By this same law we can use our spiritual ability to bring prosperity and success into our affairs.

685-688.

Mark 9:35b-36

And when he was In the house he asked them, What were ye reasoning on the way. But they held their peace: for they had disputed one with another on the way, who was the greatest. And he sat down, and called the twelve; and he saith unto then, If any man would be first, he shall be last of all, and servant of all. And he took a little child, and set him in the midst of them: and taking him in his arms, he said unto them,

Mat. 18:3b-7

Verily I say unto you, Except ye turn, and become as little children, ye shall in no wise enter into the kingdom of heaven. Whosoever therefore shall humble himself as this little child, the same is the greatest in the kingdom of heaven. And whoso shall receive one such little child in my name receiveth me: but whoso shall cause one these little ones that believe on me to stumble, it is profitable for him that a millstone should be hanged about his neck, and that he should be sunk in the depths of the sea.

Woe unto the world because of occasions of stumbling! for it must needs be that the occasions come; but woe to that man through whom the occasion cometh!

Mark 9:43-50

And if thy hand cause thee to stumble, cut it off: it is good for thee to enter into life maimed, rather than having thy two hands to go into hell, into the unquenchable fire. where their worm dieth not, and the fire is not quenched. And if thy foot cause thee to stumble, cut it off: it is good for thee to enter into life halt, rather than having thy two feet to be cast into hell, where their worm dieth not, and the fire is not quenched. And if thine eye cause thee to stumble, cast it out: it is good for thee to enter into the kingdom of God with one eye, rather than having two eyes to be cast into hell; where their worm dieth not, and the fire is not quenched. For every one shall be salted with fire. Salt is good: but if the salt have lost its saltiness, wherewith will ye season it? Have salt in yourselves, and be at peace one with another.

689-693

Interpretation

• In the spiritually quickened soul, through the activity of God Mind, the personal ego is also quickened and comes forth to assert its greatness. In our sane moments we realize that none is great save God and that he who would be great must be servant of all. The little child symbolizes a meek and lowly attitude of mind that is receptive and obedient to spiritual law, and to perfect faith. The soul must possess these qualities in order that God Mind may find full, free, and unhampered expression through it.

• Mortal man's idea of the kingdom of heaven is a government where the officers and rulers are patterned after the kingdoms of earth. But the kingdom of God is of a very different character. It is a condition in which Divine Mind supplies ideals for all the thoughts of man's mind. The greatest in this kingdom is he who is most humble and receptive to the divine ideals. Christ is the servant of humanity. He humbled himself and became the least among men that He might save them from the works of their ignorance. Whoever turns from the pride and arrogance of mortality and accepts the Christlike spirit is receiving Christ. This is the teaching of Jesus. The humble Christlike spirit is necessary to those who desire to enter the presence of Divine Mind.

• It is a dangerous thing to kill our innocent, childlike thoughts. It is better to be very negative; better to go to the very depths of the sea of mortality than to cause a single spiritual thought of childlike receptivity to be obstructed in consciousness.

• It is the will of Divine Mind that all that makes up human consciousness shall be raised to the heavenly degree -- that not even one of these little ones should perish.

• In this Scripture Jesus was also making very clear the significance of the "single eye." He was revealing the great importance of letting Spirit come first under all circumstances. Physical handicaps are nothing in comparison with spiritual shortcomings. Eliminate external impediments to spiritual progress – cut them out and enter into spirituality at any cost. Some people are very eager to know all about the higher law -- they study occultism, spiritualism, and mesmerism, for the purpose of gaining power, and for the satisfying of a certain human curiosity. This is the "eye" that should be plucked out. This lust for knowledge and power blunts the sweet innocence of the little child within, and often leads to sins that have to be atoned for in the purifying fires of the soul.

694.

Mark 9:38-41

John said unto him, Teacher, we saw one casting out demons in thy name; and we forbade him, because he followed not us. But Jesus said, Forbid him not: for there is no man who shall do a mighty work in my name, and be able quickly to speak evil of me. 40 For he that is not against us is for us. For whosoever shall give you a cup of water to drink, because ye are Christ's, verily I say unto you, he shall in no wise lose his reward.

695.

Interpretation

•   Here again Jesus the Master was teaching the universality of the law. There is one grand principle of life, and regardless of creed or sect whoever applies the principle gets results.

696-697.

Mat. 18:15-20

And if thy brother sin against thee, go, show him his fault between thee and him alone: if he hear thee, thou hast gained thy brother. But if he hear thee not, take with thee one or two more, that at the mouth of two witnesses or three every word may be established. And if he refuse to hear them, tell it unto the church: and if he refuse to hear the church also, let him be unto thee as the Gentile and the publican. Verily I say unto you, what things soever ye shall bind on earth shall be bound in heaven; and what things so ever ye shall loose on earth shall be loosed in heaven. Again I say unto you, that if two of you shall agree on earth as touching anything that they shall ask, it shall be done for them of my Father who is in heaven. For where two or three are gathered together in my name, there am I in the midst of them.

698.

Interpretation

•   Our spiritual unfoldment determines our relationship with our fellowmen. When we have loosed ourselves from a limitation in the invisible, the law is that we are also freed in the world of manifestation. When two or three are truly gathered together in the name of Jesus Christ they inadvertently dwell in the realm of Absolute Principle where Jesus Christ dwelt, thus harmonizing their ideas with His understanding of Divine Mind.

699-701.

Mat. 18:21-35

Then came Peter and said to him, Lord, how oft shall my brother sin against me, and I forgive him? until seven times? Jesus saith unto him, I say not unto thee, Until seven times; but, Until seventy times seven. Therefore is the kingdom of heaven likened unto a certain king, who would make a reckoning with his servants. And when he had begun to reckon, one was brought unto him, that owed him ten thousand talents. But forasmuch as he had not wherewith to pay, his lord commanded him to be sold, and his wife, and children, and all that he had, and payment to be made. The servant therefore fell down and worshipped him, saying, Lord, have patience with me, and I will pay thee all. And the lord of that servant, being moved with compassion, released him, and forgave him the debt. But that servant went out, and found one of his fellow-servants, who owed him a hundred shillings: and he laid hold on him, and took him by the throat, saying, Pay what thou owest. So his fellow-servant fell down and besought him, saying, Have patience with me, and I will pay thee. And he would not: but went and cast him into prison, till he should pay that which was due. So when his fellow-servants saw what was done, they were exceeding sorry, and came and told unto their lord all that was done. Then his lord called him unto him, and saith to him, Thou wicked servant, I forgave thee all that debt, because thou besoughtest me: shouldest not thou also have had mercy on thy fellow-servant, even as I had mercy on thee? And his lord was wroth, and delivered him to the tormentors, till he should pay all that was due. So shall also my heavenly Father do unto you, if ye forgive not everyone his brother from your hearts.

702-704.

Interpretation

•   Forgiving offences to the uttermost is necessary in order that you may be God-like and bring down this kingdom of the heavens unto the earth. The measure of the wrong or injury done you by another should not be taken into consideration. The Jews thought it was God-like to forgive seven times, but Jesus said, "seventy times seven," which implies unlimited forgiveness. Thus is shown the relation of man to his fellowmen and the Principle of Being. We live in and think through a universal ether that is more sensitive to our thought vibrations than the most finely-keyed musical instrument to the vibrations of sound. This is the translucent substance of the "kingdom of the heavens," and it records every emotion, every thought, every word sent out by us. A feeling of thought or anger, or revenge, or injury of any kind toward another, sets awhirl with violent discord this mother substance, this white Shekinah, and the beautiful forms which it is constantly pushing out from the center of being are broken and distorted. It is here that man incurs the great debt to Mother Nature of "ten thousand talents," and which hecan never pay through his own effort; yet the wisdom and love attributes of being may be called into expression by man, and through their soothing and harmonizing power all this turmoil may be reduced to order. Thus the great debt which man owes is paid by God.

705-707.

Mat. 19:1-12

And it came to pass when Jesus had finished these words, he departed from Galilee, and came into the borders of Judaea beyond the Jordan; and great multitudes followed him; and he healed them there.   And there came unto him Pharisees, trying him, and saying, Is it lawful for a man to put away his wife for every cause?   And he answered and said, Have ye not read, that he who made them from the beginning made them male and female,   and said, For this cause shall a man leave his father and mother, and shall cleave to his wife; and the two shall become one flesh?   So that they are no more two, but one flesh. What therefore God hath joined together, let not man put asunder. They say unto him, Why then did Moses command to give a bill of divorcement, and to put her away?   He saith unto them, Moses for your hardness of heart suffered you to put away your wives: but from the beginning it hath not been so.   And I say unto you, Whosoever shall put away his wife, except for fornication, and shall marry another, committeth adultery: and he that marrieth her when she is put away committeth adultery.   The disciples say unto him, If the case of the man is so with his wife, it is not expedient to marry.   But he said unto them, Not all men can receive this saying, but they to whom it is given.   For there are eunuchs, that were so born from their mother's womb: and there are eunuchs, that were made eunuchs by men: and there are eunuchs, that made themselves eunuchs for the kingdom of heaven's sake. He that is able to receive it, let him receive it.

708-710.

Interpretation

•   For the sake of spiritual discipline men and women take control of human desire for sexual expression and use it as a lever to raise the whole consciousness into the kingdom of the heavens or into pure spiritual consciousness. Jesus said, "He that is able to receive it, let him receive it." Thus we perceive that Jesus plainly taught that there is a divine marriage which has received the sanction of God from the very beginning; also that there is a divine asceticism which is recognized by Divine Mind and is one of the avenues through which the soul can be raised to pure spiritual consciousness in advance of race evolution.

•   A true marriage under spiritual law brings about perfect unity in mind and body, while human relationships are of little or no value. Spiritually interpreted, man symbolizes wisdom and woman symbolizes love. Under the divine law of evolution these twain are united and in order to fulfill the law must work together.

•   It has been universally observed that men and women who are harmoniously united grow to resemble each other. This unity is based upon understanding and love which manifest through every avenue, even to the flesh. "The two shall become one flesh."

•   Moses represents the intellectual phase of the law. The hardness of their hearts represents a lack of love. Divine marriage is the union of harmonious souls. Whenever two divinely married persons separate and seek other alliances, they break the divine law. An alliance between persons who are not divinely united is adultery, and leads to corruption of spiritual life.

711.

Mark 10:13-16

And they were bringing unto him little children, that he should touch them: and the disciples rebuked them. But when Jesus saw it, he was moved with indignation, and said unto them, Suffer the little children to come unto me; forbid them not: for to such belongeth the kingdom of God. Verily I say unto you, Whosoever shall not receive the kingdom of God as a little child, he shall in no wise enter therein. And he took them in his arms, and blessed them, laying his hands upon them.

712-713.

Interpretation

•   Jesus was continually talking about the kingdom of heaven or "heavens," as it is written in the original. The disciples in material consciousness looked upon this kingdom as a new government which Jesus was to establish in Judaea. This is typical of the illuminated intellect. Many perceive the truth but do not enter into tangible consciousness of its presence, because they do not make a place in their minds for the new and higher ideas.

•   This realm of the heavens lies all about us and within us. Its matrix lies all about us. Within mind are all the ideas that make for harmony in existence. This realm of the heavens may be projected into existence in just one way and that is through the mind of man by letting it enter into him. To do this the mind must become receptive. It must take that attitude which will let the divine ideas flow in.

714-716.

Mark 10:17-27

And as he was going forth into the way, there ran one to him, and kneeled to him, and asked him, Good Teacher, what shall I do that I may inherit eternal life? And Jesus said unto him, Why callest thou me good? none is good save one, even God. Thou knowest the commandments, Do not kill, Do not commit adultery, Do not steal, Do not bear false witness, Do not defraud, Honor thy father and mother. And he said unto him, Teacher, all these things have I observed from my youth. And Jesus looking upon him loved him, and said unto him, One thing thou lackest: go, sell whatsoever thou hast, and give to the poor, and thou shalt have treasure in heaven: and come, follow me. But his countenance fell at the saying, and he went away sorrowful: for he was one that had great possessions. And Jesus looked round about, and saith unto his disciples, How hardly shall they that have riches enter into the kingdom of God! And the disciples were amazed at his words. But Jesus answereth again, and saith unto them, Children, how hard is it for them that trust in riches to enter into the kingdom of God! It is easier for a camel to go through a needle's eye, than for a rich man to enter into the kingdom of God. And they were astonished exceedingly, saying unto him, Then who can be saved? Jesus looking upon them saith, With men it is impossible, but not with God: for all things are possible with God.

717-720.

Interpretation

•   Jesus considered spiritual understanding and the power which accompanies it of more importance than great riches, piety, and careful observance of the moral law. The rich young man who had, in addition to his riches, been a strict observer of the law as laid down by Moses, was told to sell what he had, to give to the poor, and to come and follow Jesus.

•   The rich young man may be likened to personality. It is that in us which lays store by the things of form and shape. Personality is ambitious for eternal life and strives to attain it without sacrificing the selfish attachment to things of sense, while unselfishness liberates it. Personality does not know the real good. It follows the letter of the commandments, and in this is commended; but there is one lack -- it must give up its belief in the all-importance of earthly possessions.

•   When personality attaches itself to material riches, it really believes in a power other than God. It trusts the resources of the visible rather than those of the invisible, and thus weakens its spiritual faculties. All the powers of the mind must be developed spiritward before man can rise to the higher consciousness called heaven. If we trust in riches, trust in God is weakened.

•   It is possible, but rare, for one to have large possessions and yet be able to enter into the consciousness of eternal life. The necessary condition is a contact between man and his Creator as to the disposition of his riches. If a man would covenant with God to give all his possession to the furtherance of the good, dedicating everything to that end and making himself a steward of the Father, he might enter into the kingdom.

721.

Mat. 19: 27-30

Then answered Peter and said unto him, Lo, we have left all, and followed thee; what then shall we have? And Jesus said unto them, Verily I say unto you, that ye who have followed me, in the regeneration when the Son of man shall sit on the throne of his glory, ye also shall sit upon twelve thrones, judging the twelve tribes of Israel. And every one that hath left houses, or brethren, or sisters, or father, or mother, or children, or lands, for my name's sake, shall receive a hundredfold, and shall inherit eternal life. But many shall be last that are first; and first that are last.

722-723

Interpretation

•   Giving up all trust in the help of relations and earthly possessions and following the guidance of the higher self bring as a final reward a consciousness of the real, upon which these outer conditions rest. According to Rotherham's translation, the last clause of verse 29 of this chapter reads, "manifold shall receive, and life age-abiding shall inherit."
•   Those who seem to have first place from the worldly standpoint shall be last in the final test, and those who seem least shall be given first place. On every hand we see quiet spiritual workers who are laying up in the heavens of the mind a store of true thoughts that must eventually precipitate into visibility and make them spiritual lights.

724-726

Mat. 20:1-16

For the kingdom of heaven is like unto a man that was a householder, who went out early in the morning to hire laborers into his vineyard. And when he had agreed with the laborers for a shilling a day, he sent them into his vineyard. And he went out about the third hour, and saw others standing in the marketplace idle; and to them he said, Go ye also into the vineyard, and whatsoever is right I will give you. And they went their way. Again he went out about the sixth and the ninth hour, and did likewise. And about the eleventh hour he went out, and found others standing; and he saith unto them, Why stand ye here all the day idle? They say unto him, Because no man hath hired us. He saith unto them, Go ye also into the vineyard. And when even was come, the lord of the vineyard saith unto his steward, Call the laborers, and pay them their hire, beginning from the last unto the first. And when they came that were hired about the eleventh hour, they received every man a shilling. And when the first came, they supposed that they would receive more; and they likewise received every man a shilling. And when they received it, they murmured against the householder,   saying, These last have spent but one hour, and thou hast made them equal unto us, who have borne the burden of the day and the scorching heat. But he answered and said to one of them, Friend, I do thee no wrong: didst not thou agree with me for a shilling? Take up that which is thine, and go thy way; it is my will to give unto this last, even as unto thee. Is it not lawful for me to do what I will with mine own? or is thine eye evil, because I am good? So the last shall be first, and the first last.

Interpretation

• Here Jesus illustrates the law-making power of man in the kingdom of mind.

• The householder, or landlord, represents man, and the vineyard represents the body. The "kingdom of heaven" includes both mind and body and Jesus illustrates in many parables how a cultivation and adjustment of both are necessary in order that the law may be fulfilled.

• Physiologists have discovered that the body is a perfect beehive of little workers, and they express astonishment at the intelligence displayed by cells and corpuscles in their labors. All that goes on in the organism is directed by man consciously or unconsciously and his every thought sets up action in the cells and they do what he wills.

• A thought oft repeated settles back into the subconsciousness (subconscious – Ed.) and a function is established that builds up a definite tissue. Desire is a phase of will, and when the mind of man, or animal, or even the plant, desires to attain a certain end the necessary machinery of mind and body are set into action to bring it about.

• When man learns that he has power to make harmony or "heaven," in his "vineyard," or body, he is energetic, he is out "early in the morning."

• In the kingdom of mind time cuts no figure. The compensation is the same whether it be the third or the eleventh hour when the thought was put to work. The more one uses thoughts along the right lines the more expert he becomes. This being true it is plain that the last thought shall be first and the first last, because the last has the larger capacity.

Mark 10: 32-34

And they were on the way, going up to Jerusalem; and Jesus was going before them: and they were amazed; and they that followed were afraid. And he took again the twelve, and began to tell them the things that were to happen unto him,   saying, Behold, we go up to Jerusalem; and the Son of man shall be delivered unto the chief priests and the scribes; and they shall condemn him to death, and shall deliver him unto the Gentiles: and they shall mock him, and shall spit upon him, and shall scourge him, and shall kill him; and after three days he shall rise again.

Interpretation

• Jesus going up to Jerusalem represents man in the regeneration reaching a place in his development where the old states of mind must be wholly erased and in its stead a new and higher man established.

- Before the new house (body) is built the old must be demolished. A new set of ideas builds a new body and it replaces the old body of weakness, disease and death. When this takes place there is great commotion in mind—the religious thoughts are full of condemnation and the secular thoughts would crush out entirely the claimant of life beyond their ken. In destroying the life in the physical body they destroy their only avenue of expression. Thus error in its ignorance destroys itself.

733.

Luke 9:51-56

And it came to pass, when the days were well-nigh come that he should be received up, he steadfastly set his face to go to Jerusalem, and sent messengers before his face: and they went, and entered into a village of the Samaritans, to make ready for him. And they did not receive him, because his face was as though he were going to Jerusalem. And when his disciples James and John saw this, they said, Lord, wilt thou that we bid fire to come down from heaven, and consume them? But he turned, and rebuked them. And they went to another village.

734.

Interpretation

- When the spiritual I AM, here represented by Jesus is approaching its great demonstration, and has the assurance that every preparation is completed, it steadfastly presses on, and refuses to deviate from its course. If error is discovered and refuses to see the light, it is not the work of man to call down judgment upon such conditions, but he should leave it to its own destruction.

735-736.

Luke 9:57-62

And as they went on the way, a certain man said unto him, I will follow thee whithersoever thou goest. And Jesus said unto him, The foxes have holes, and the birds of the heaven have nests; but the Son of man hath not where to lay his head. And he said unto another, Follow me. But he said, Lord, suffer me first to go and bury my father. But he said unto him, Leave the dead to bury their own dead; but go thou and publish abroad the kingdom of God. And another also said, I will follow thee, Lord; but first suffer me to bid farewell to them that are at my house. But Jesus said unto him, No man, having put his hand to the plow, and looking back, is fit for the kingdom of God.

Interpretation

•   Jesus went to the other side of consciousness or withdrew from the push and pull of the outer world and rested in the peace of Spirit. The scribe who said, "I will follow thee wither-so-ever thou goest" represents the memory of what took place.

•   The son of man is Spirit lifted up in the Christ, and when he realizes who he is, he does not have to depend upon materiality as the foxes and the birds.

•   In Spirit, there is no thought of dying, or bidding farewell, or burial, or looking back. We rest in Omnipresence where all is life and joy.

Mat. 20:20-21

Then came to him the mother of the sons of Zebedee with her sons, worshipping him, and asking a certain thing of him. And he said unto her, What wouldest thou? She saith unto him, Command that these my two sons may sit, one on thy right hand, and one on thy left hand, in thy kingdom

Mark 10:38-45

But Jesus said unto them, Ye know not what ye ask. Are ye able to drink the cup that I drink? or to be baptized with the baptism that I am baptized with? And they said unto him, We are able. And Jesus said unto them, The cup that I drink ye shall drink; and with the baptism that I am baptized withal shall ye be baptized: but to sit on my right hand or on my left hand is not mine to give; but it is for them for whom it hath been prepared. And when the ten heard it, they began to be moved with indignation concerning James and John. And Jesus called them to him, and saith unto them, Ye know that they who are accounted to rule over the Gentiles lord it over them; and their great ones exercise authority over them. But it is not so among you: but whosoever would become great among you, shall be your minister; and whosoever would be first among you, shall be servant of all. For the Son of man also came not to be ministered unto, but to minister, and to give his life a ransom for many.

Interpretation

•   The workers in the vineyard of Jesus Christ think that their intellectual attainments fit them for any place in the spiritual kingdom, when they lack that first and most important evidence of complete dedication—the abnegation of self and a readiness to do whatever the Spirit bids.

•   Many states of mind have to be dealt with by one who arouses all the power in the conscious and subconscious realms. The soul, represented the mother of Zebedee's children, wants her offspring to have first place in the new kingdom. This ambition of the soul is evident when we think our abilities should be given due recognition in the spiritual kingdom, without considering their experience or training -- under spiritual law. When asked if they were able to drink the cup of the spiritually minded, and be baptized with his baptism, they lightly answer, "We are able."

• But are they ready to give up pride, ambition for place or preferment, and become like common servants in the house? Workers in the vineyard of Jesus Christ find few who are willing to serve as He served.

• To drink of the cup means to take in faith, believing, before one can fully understand. Only those who are prepared in the principle can understand the law of principle. The working out of the law places each where he belongs.

• Every priest in the Catholic church must pass through the serving state before he can enter a higher; so the neophyte in the secret religions of the Orient must serve in the most menial duties before he is considered a safe custodian of the higher forces of the soul and mind.

745-746.

Mark 10:46-52

And they come to Jericho: and as he went out from Jericho, with his disciples and a great multitude, the son of Timaeus, Bartimaeus, a blind beggar, was sitting by the way side. And when he heard that it was Jesus the Nazarene, he began to cry out, and say, Jesus, thou son of David, have mercy on me. And many rebuked him, that he should hold his peace: but he cried out the more a great deal, Thou son of David, have mercy on me. And Jesus stood still, and said, Call ye him. And they call the blind man, saying unto him, Be of good cheer: rise, he calleth thee. And he, casting away his garment, sprang up, and came to Jesus. And Jesus answered him, and said, What wilt thou that I should do unto thee? And the blind man said unto him, Rabboni, that I may receive my sight. And Jesus said unto him, Go thy way; thy faith hath made thee whole. And straightway he received his sight, and followed him in the way.

747-749.

Interpretation

• Bartimaeus represents a phase of the darkened mentality in man. This blinded, polluted, and poverty-stricken state of mind is the outcome of the race habit of attributing honor and precedence to old established beliefs and customs (Bartimaeus was a Jew) to the exclusion of present spiritual inspiration. But this ignorant phase of the mentality is groping for light, which is realized through Jesus Christ, the Word of God expressed.

• As we proceed in our spiritual development we find certain laws at work in mind and body. When we perceive a truth, and obediently place ourselves in all ways necessary to the bringing forth of it, we observe an increase in power. Instead of being one of a multitude, we become leader, and the multitude follows, eager to be instructed and helped out of their darkness.

• There are many blind men in our minds but we do not know it until we become meek enough to receive Divine Wisdom. Then only can we clear up the ignorance and lack of perception within our own souls. To touch the eyes of one's own ignorance and darkness one must get the attention of the blind by mentally asking, "What will ye that I should do unto you?" they will nearly always answer, "Lord, that I may receive my sight." That is, the soul is always calling for more light, more understanding. Then "tough" the all-potential mind within you with your word of Truth that the Spirit gives to every man -- innate spiritual understanding. "Ask and ye shall receive." "I am the light of the world; ye are the light of the world."

750.

Luke 10:1

Now after these things the Lord appointed seventy others, and sent them two and two before his face into every city and place, whither he himself was about to come.

751-752.

Interpretation

• This Scripture teaches the coming of the I AM thought into the outer, or body consciousness, to establish truth there. The seventy represent the five senses, seeing, hearing, tasting, smelling, feeling, with two additional ones, thinking and intuitive perception. The brain is the thinking organ and the solar plexus is the perceiving organ. "Two by two" refers to the dual action of each of these senses. All the sense have to be trained in spiritual ways, and their efficiency must be multiplied. They must be freed from mortal limitation, that they may do their share in conveying the saving truth to the very cells of the body.

753-754.

Luke 10:2-9

And he said unto them, The harvest indeed is plenteous, but the laborers are few: pray ye therefore the Lord of the harvest, that he send forth laborers into his harvest. Go your ways; behold, I send you forth as lambs in the midst of wolves. Carry no purse, no wallet, no shoes; and salute no man on the way. And into whatsoever house ye shall enter, first say, Peace be to this house. And if a son of peace be there, your peace shall rest upon him: but if not, it shall turn to you again. And in that same house remain, eating and drinking such things as they give: for the laborer is worthy of his hire. Go not from house to house. And into whatsoever city ye enter, and they receive you, eat such things as are set before you: and heal the sick that are therein, and say unto them, The kingdom of God is come nigh unto you.

Interpretation

• "Carry no purse, no wallet, no shoes." The seventy are untried spiritual thoughts. While we keep our vision spiritual, our thoughts are radiant and unencumbered. We have no earthly attachments. We have no occasion for worry about how we are to be provided for. How grievously the world needs peace is evidenced by the recent war — the greatest war of history. Had the people of the world heard this command of Jesus and set forth daily the word, "Peace be to this house," the war would not have occurred. This is not mere assumption but can be demonstrated. The spirit of peace will become so manifest that man will find it almost impossible to realize that discord ever had a place in his mind or in the world about him. Peace is native to man, and the peaceful spirit springs up within him in the work of peace because the son of peace is there. That special line from the Scripture, "Salute no man on the way" really means not to stop and gossip but to use the mind only in constructive ways.

Luke 10:10-24

But into whatsoever city ye shall enter, and they receive you not, go out into the streets thereof and say, Even the dust from your city, that cleaveth to our feet, we wipe off against you: nevertheless know this, that the kingdom of God is come nigh. I say unto you, it shall be more tolerable in that day for Sodom, than for that city. Woe unto thee, Chorazin! woe unto thee, Bethsaida! for if the mighty works had been done in Tyre and Sidon, which were done in you, they would have repented long ago, sitting in sackcloth and ashes. But it shall be more tolerable for Tyre and Sidon in the judgment, than for you. And thou, Capernaum, shalt thou be exalted unto heaven? thou shalt be brought down unto Hades. He that heareth you heareth me; and he that rejecteth you rejecteth me; and he that rejecteth me rejecteth him that sent me. And the seventy returned with joy, saying, Lord, even the demons are subject unto us in thy name. And he said unto them, I beheld Satan fallen as lightning from heaven. Behold, I have given you authority to tread upon serpents and scorpions, and over all the power of the enemy: and nothing shall in any wise hurt you. Nevertheless in this rejoice not, that the spirits are subject unto you; but rejoice that your names are written in heaven. In that same hour he rejoiced in the Holy Spirit, and said, I thank thee, O Father, Lord of heaven and earth, that thou didst hide these things from the wise and understanding, and didst reveal them unto babes: yea, Father; for so it was well-pleasing in thy sight. All things have been delivered unto me of my Father: and no one knoweth who the Son is, save the Father; and who the Father is, save the Son, and he to whomsoever the Son willeth to reveal him. And turning to the disciples, he said privately, Blessed are the eyes which see the things that ye see: for I say unto you, that many prophets and kings desired to see the things which ye see, and saw them not; and to hear the things which ye hear, and heard them not.

761-764.

Interpretation

• Chorazin and Bethsaida represent types of mind that are not moved to repent and accept the Truth, whereas the admittedly undisciplined states of consciousness, represented by Tyre and Sidon, will confess and repent.

• Capernaum represents sympathy — the sympathy that shares the feeling of the sick and grieving, and accepts final the verdict of the human senses.

• Lightning represents spiritual quickening.

• In individual consciousness Spirit works from within (East) to the without (West).

• Also spiritual quickening comes with a universal baptism of the Holy Spirit. Many receive light from one great outpouring.

• This reveals that the Christ is not to come again as a person, but comes as a spiritual awakening. This truth is in direct opposition to the "second coming" of Jesus.

• Today there are those in every walk of life who are receiving spiritual quickening; a flash of intelligence (lightning) awakens the sleeping consciousness and new understanding results.

765-767.

Luke 10:25-37

And behold, a certain lawyer stood up and made trial of him, saying, Teacher, what shall I do to inherit eternal life? And he said unto him, What is written in the law? how readest thou? And he answering said, Thou shalt love the Lord thy God with all thy heart, and with all thy soul, and with all thy strength, and with all thy mind; and thy neighbor as thyself. And he said unto him, Thou hast answered right: this do, and thou shalt live. But he, desiring to justify himself, said unto Jesus, And who is my neighbor? Jesus made answer and said, A certain man was going down from Jerusalem to Jericho; and he fell among robbers, who both stripped him and beat him, and departed, leaving him half dead. And by chance a certain priest was going down that way: and when he saw him, he passed by on the other side. And in like manner a Levite also, when he came to the place, and saw him, passed by on the other side. But a certain Samaritan, as he journeyed, came where he was: and when he saw him, he was moved with compassion, and came to him, and bound up his wounds, pouring on them oil and wine; and he set him on his own beast, and brought him to an inn, and took care of him. And on the morrow he took out two shillings, and gave them to the host, and said, Take care of him; and whatsoever thou spendest more, I, when I come back again, will repay thee. Which of these three, thinkest thou, proved neighbor unto him that fell among the robbers?   And he said, He that showed mercy on him. And Jesus said unto him, Go, and do thou likewise.

768-772.

Interpretation

•   The central idea of this Scripture is "And who is my neighbor?" and Jesus illustrates it by the story of the waylaid traveler and the good Samaritan. Our neighbor is here shown to be farther removed than the one who lives next door, or those in whom we are personally interested.

•   The result of love to God and to our neighbor is the attainment of eternal life, according to this teaching of the Jewish scripture, and sanctioned by Jesus. The metaphysical interpretation is that we may get very close to God in spirit, but we must see the life of God manifest in externals also, before we shall compass the fullness of Being, and come into its completeness in consciousness. Religion easily falls into forms and thus loses it vitality – its life-giving quality. The early Christians had all the powers of the Spirit, and they performed miracles. But rites and ceremonies came with organizations and church building, and spiritual power gradually waned. This is the history of every religious organization. The founder is inspired and fires his disciples for a time. Then comes a period of temporal prosperity – and spiritual decadence.

•   The formalist overlooks the essence of things—he lacks compassion or love. When life lies bleeding, the priest and Levite pass by on the other side, but the quick sympathy of the unconventional is aroused and he does the right thing from inner impulse.

•   To lay hold of eternal life we must bind up its wounds wherever we find them, and we will find them wherever life flows, whether in man or beast.

•   God is life, and wherever the pulse of life beats there God is. Man cannot give nor take life, but so long as he thinks he can slay the living, and proceeds to do so in the man and beast, he will be at enmity with life. Those who would lay hold on "eternal life" must seek in every way to preserve the forms in which it manifests. The wounds of life are thus bound up.

•   We all have life, and it is God's eternal life, but it does not become ours in reality until we consciously realize it. The one who enters into eternal life, as did Jesus, must lay hold on that life omnipresent and make it one with his body. This is the secret of inheriting eternal life.

•   Have compassion upon the life in the body of every living creature, and especially in your own body. Declare life perpetually abiding in the organism. Bind up some of the wounds through which you are dissipating the life of your organism. Robbers are at work upon your body every day. They are the lusts of passion and appetite. Drive them off and bind up the wounds. Put the body in the "inn" of your pure thought and pay the price through overcoming.

Luke 10:38-42

Now as they went on their way, he entered into a certain village: and a certain woman named Martha received him into her house. And she had a sister called Mary, who also sat at the Lord's feet, and heard his word. But Martha was cumbered about much serving; and she came up to him, and said, Lord, dost thou not care that my sister did leave me to serve alone? bid her therefore that she help me. But the Lord answered and said unto her, Martha, Martha, thou art anxious and troubled about many things: but one thing is needful: for Mary hath chosen the good part, which shall not be taken away from her.

Interpretation

• Martha and Mary represent the outer and the inner phases of the soul's activity in welcoming the spiritual teacher, Christ. The soul, established in love, is always quick to discern the presence of true thoughts, and it welcomes the spiritual teacher. The feminine side of the soul is most receptive to spiritual wisdom.

• Martha represents the outer activity of the soul in receiving the higher self; Mary, the inner receptivity. Martha desires to show her love by service; Mary by learning at Jesus' feet.

• Both these activities are necessary, but we must take heed lest in our desire to serve we forget our times of communion with our indwelling Lord. We must not set greater value upon active service than upon quiet, loving receptivity to the Spirit of Truth within.

• The feet represent that part of the understanding which connects us with earthly conditions. Mary, sitting at Jesus' feet, represents the soul learning the lessons of life from the higher self. When the learning of life is first place in consciousness, the service that follows becomes simple and easy. But when Martha, the activity of service, is given precedence, anxiety and irritation result, because there is a seeming separation from the source of love and life, and a lack is sensed in consciousness. Truly, "to obey is better than sacrifice." An understanding of Truth must precede all real and effective service.

Luke 19:11-27

And as they heard these things, he added and spake a parable, because he was nigh to Jerusalem, and because they supposed that the kingdom of God was immediately to appear. He said therefore, A certain nobleman went into a far country, to receive for himself a kingdom, and to return. And he called ten servants of his, and gave them ten pounds, and said unto them, Trade ye herewith till I come. But his citizens hated him, and sent an ambassage after him, saying, We will not that this man reign over us. And it came to pass, when he was come back again, having received the kingdom, that he commanded these servants, unto whom he had given the money, to be called to him, that he might know what they had gained by trading. And the first came before him, saying, Lord, thy pound hath made ten pounds more. And he said unto him, Well done, thou good servant: because thou wast found faithful in a very little, have thou authority over ten cities. And the second came, saying, Thy pound, Lord, hath made five pounds. And he said unto him also, Be thou also over five cities. And another came, saying, Lord, behold, here is thy pound, which I kept laid up in a napkin: for I feared thee, because thou art an austere man: thou takest up that which thou layedst not down, and reapest that which thou didst not sow. He saith unto him, Out of thine own mouth will I judge thee, thou wicked servant. Thou knewest that I am an austere man, taking up that which I laid not down, and reaping that which I did not sow;   then wherefore gavest thou not my money into the bank, and I at my coming should have required it with interest? And he said unto them that stood by, Take away from him the pound, and give it unto him that hath the ten pounds. And they said unto him, Lord, he hath ten pounds. I say unto you, that unto every one that hath shall be given; but from him that hath not, even that which he hath shall be taken away from him. But these mine enemies, that would not that I should reign over them, bring hither, and slay them before me.

782-791.

Interpretation

•   Jesus had taught that the kingdom of God would not come in a form whereby it could be observed externally; that men should not look here or there in the outer for it, because it is within. But the old established religious thoughts that belong solely to the intellectual consciousness, the Pharisees, cannot comprehend the inner overcoming and that establishing of the Truth in consciousness which cause one to become aware of the kingdom.

•   As soon as one attains a certain degree of intellectual understanding of Truth, he becomes self-righteous, Pharisaical; he is inclined to think that he has all the Truth and should demonstrate at once the fullness of the kingdom in his outer life. But he must learn to use aright the beginning of Truth that has been revealed to him, that he may become worthy of a place in the kingdom. And so we have the parable given in this lesson.

•   The parable is very similar to the parable of the talents, given in Matthew 25:14-30. Divine Mind is portrayed as a nobleman who gave ten pounds to his ten servants, and "went into a far country, to receive for himself a kingdom, and to return." In reality Divine Mind always has been the one ruler of the universe and man, but man in mortal consciousness has not known this. Therefore, the sovereignty of the Great King must be established; the consciousness of man must learn to respond wholly to the will of God.

•   This scripture shows how the soul increases its capacity to know Divine Mind. We are the offspring of Divine Mind, and we must come into conscious oneness with it. Involved in us is the capacity to evolve, or to bring form divinity.

• The number ten refers to the expression of the senses in man. There are five senses; each sense has two avenues of expression. The pounds symbolize capacities, which we can increase.

• In regeneration Truth is made clear to the individual, and he learns the law of mind increase. He learns that all of his avenues of expression and all of his capacity are fundamentally spiritual. The "increase" comes through the realization of spiritual capacity and reality of the causes. The development of perception, comprehension, discrimination, judgment, and intuition, or soul-consciousness, is the multiplication of the senses (pounds) which was commended by the Lord. As the capacities of mind are increased, dominion is gained over more and more of the aggregation of thoughts (cities) within.

• Those who do not understand how to increase their mental capacities through right thought become timid and cautious.

• Millions have been cowards and incompetents by fear of making blunders. It is better to make mistakes than to remain inactive. The world is full of people who carefully put their talents in a napkin and have kept it out of sight. They are more or less bitter because others have succeeded while they have failed. To them, the Lord is hard and sever (severe – Ed.); they even think him unjust.

• The cause of failure is not incapacity, but refusal to use the talents which are inherent. Potential capacity is really all that man possesses. Man's work is to develop in character those potentialities. The increase that comes when the inner forces are set to work pleases the Lord and brings the servant into dominion.

• The citizens who hate the righteous king (Divine Mind), and who will not have him rule over them, are the carnal thoughts in the individual that are "not subject to the law of God." They oppose the rulership of the spiritual I AM (the Divine Will), and are destroyed, denied out of the consciousness of the one who comes into his Christ dominion.

• "To him that hath shall be given, and from him that hath not shall be taken away, even that which he hath."

• This text refers to two states of consciousness in man. "Him that hath" is one who has entered into the realization of spiritual substance. Through the Divine Law, all things are added unto him. "Him that hath not" is one who has no understanding of spiritual realities, but thinks that material possessions are real, and worth his time and effort to gain. All that he gains is in the external. It is transitory because it does not have back of it the enduring, abiding, eternal substance. He therefore loses all that he has apparently accumulated.

• It appears to be a hard law that would take away from a man that which he seems to have, simply because he fails to increase it. But such must be the judgment executed upon the slothful servant. If the potential capacities (pounds) are not righteously used by the individual, they are lost to consciousness, and their substance is absorbed by the servants (senses) who make selfish use of what has been given them.

792-793

Luke 19:28

And when he had thus spoken, he went on before, going up to Jerusalem.

Luke 19:41-44

And when he drew nigh, he saw the city and wept over it, saying, If thou hadst known in this day, even thou, the things which belong unto peace! but now they are hid from thine eyes. For the days shall come upon thee, when thine enemies shall cast up a bank about thee, and compass thee round, and keep thee in on every side, and shall dash thee to the ground, and thy children within thee; and they shall not leave in thee one stone upon another; because thou knewest not the time of thy visitation.

794

Interpretation

• 	When the intellect refuses to accept the Christ, spiritual man is killed out and must suffer the consequences.

795-796

Luke 20:1-8

And it came to pass, on one of the days, as he was teaching the people in the temple, and preaching the gospel, there came upon him the chief priests and the scribes with the elders; and they spake, saying unto him, Tell us: By what authority doest thou these things? or who is he that gave thee this authority? And he answered and said unto them, I also will ask you a question; and tell me: The baptism of John, was it from heaven, or from men? And they reasoned with themselves, saying, If we shall say, From heaven; he will say, Why did ye not believe him? But if we shall say, From men; all the people will stone us: for they are persuaded that John was a prophet. And they answered, that they knew not whence it was. And Jesus said unto them, Neither tell I you by what authority I do these things.

797-798

Interpretation

• 	Jesus was trying to teach the chief priests and elders to do something for themselves. He told them He could not explain in definite language what to do from the plane of the natural man, symbolized by John the Baptist, but that they must use their inspiration. They had the same source of inspiration that

He contacted – God. They should know for themselves that all authority is from God. On one occasion Jesus said, "It is not I, but the Father within me, he doeth the works."

• Metaphysically interpreted, the indwelling Christ, symbolized by Jesus is endeavoring to teach the highest religious thoughts in authority – the chief priests and the elders – how to go to the one invisible source and find out for themselves that all authority is from God.

799-800.

Mat. 21:28-32

But what think ye? A man had two sons; and he came to the first, and said, Son, go work today in the Vineyard. And he answered and said, I will not; but afterward he repented himself, and went. And he came to the second, and said, like wise. And he answered and said, I go, sir; and went not. Which of the two did the will of his father? They say, the first. Jesus saith unto them, Verily I say unto you, that the publicans and the harlots go into the kingdom of God before you. For John came until you in the way of righteousness, and ye believed him not; but the publicans and the harlots believed him: and ye, when ye saw it, did not even repent yourselves afterward, that ye might believe him.

801-803.

Interpretation

• The thoughts in the mind of each of us are attracted to a common center which is called

• I AM. The various classifications of thought segregate themselves according to their likes and dislikes, dominated, of course by the central I AM.

• I AM is the Son of God, and can do the will of God without interference from any outside source if it elects to do that will. In its ignorance it may become a sinner before it has claimed Divine Wisdom. Mind is the Vineyard of Being and all states of consciousness must be brought to fruitage by the Son or all-potential thought of God, in its free individuality. Wisdom and obedience are to be brought forth and when the Son is sincere and does the best he knows, he is on safer ground than one who has allowed his thoughts to crystallize around certain set forms of righteousness. These Pharisaical thoughts observe the letter and lose sight of the Spirit, but are so sure of their truth that they are immovable and do not obey the Divine command, "Go forward."

• Man's understanding of Truth is progressive, and Divine Mind is constantly setting before us higher and better standards of infinite compassion and forgiveness. Those who are truly repentant and strive obediently to do the will of God are fully forgiven regardless of the magnitude of their sins, and they thus get into the kingdom before the self-righteous.

Mat. 21:33-42

Hear another parable: There was a man that was a householder, who planted a vineyard, and set a hedge about it, and dug a winepress in it, and built a tower, and let it out to husbandmen, and went into another country. And when the season of the fruits drew near, he sent his servants to the husbandman, to receive his fruits. And the husbandmen took his servants, and beat one, and killed another, and stoned another. Again, he sent other servants more than the first: and they did unto them in like manner. But afterward he sent unto them his son, saying, They will reverence my son. But the husbandmen, when they saw the son, said among themselves, This is the heir; come, let us kill him, and take his inheritance. And they took him, and cast him forth out of the vineyard, and killed him. When therefore the lord of the vineyard shall come, what will he do unto those husbandmen? They say unto him, He will miserably destroy those miserable men, and will let out the vineyard unto other husbandmen, who shall render him the fruits in their seasons. Jesus saith unto them, Did ye never read in the scriptures, The stone which the builders rejected, The same was made the head of the corners; This was from the Lord, And it is marvelous in our eyes?"

807-808

Interpretation

• In this parable the householder represents the ruling identity in consciousness. The wine press symbolizes the divine source of life; the hedge stands for divine protection; the tower pertains to the divine perception of Truth. The husbandmen represent the faculties implanted by Divine Mind and the fruits of the vineyard denote the bringing forth of the various powers of consciousness.

• When the thoughts of the Spirit come to the faculties (Husbandmen) and claim recognition of the One Mind, they are killed out of consciousness. The sending of the son represents the descent into consciousness of the Christ Spirit. This is the heir, the Divine I AM, which the Pharisaical attitude refuses to receive in its full power and dominion, and to such a consciousness Christ is dead, and there is no prospect of that re-generation of the body which is brought about only through mental, spiritual, and even physical receptivity to a higher quickening life-energy.

809.

Mat. 21:43-44

Therefore I say unto you, The Kingdom of God shall be taken away from you, and shall be given to a nation bringing forth the fruits thereof. And he that falleth on this stone shall be broken to pieces: but on whomsoever it shall fall, it will scatter him as dust.

Interpretation

•   Here Jesus was referring to the real kingdom, which is the understanding of the power of the Spirit. The realm of causation is spiritual, which is in reality the kingdom of the heavens. The Pharisees, the intellectual man, claim to know and understand. They say it is a place in the heavens. To the metaphysician it is dynamic force, which cannot be expressed in terms of externality. It works at the very center of things. Those who interpret the kingdom of the heavens as form and shape lose it; it has no existence for them.

•   A new concept must be formed as to the nature of the kingdom of the heavens. To those who realize it as a spiritual force, of course the external sky heaven is broken to pieces.

•   When they try to realize it as omnipresent light and energy all their old standards are pulverized into powder. This is the stone that is cut out of the mountain of reality, or omnipresent energizing substance, referred to in 11 Daniel, 35th chapter. "And the stone that smote the image became a great mountain and filled the whole earth."

Mat. 22:1-14

And Jesus answered and spoke again in parables unto them, saying, The kingdom of heaven is likened unto a certain king, who made a marriage feast for his son, and sent forth his servants to call them that were bidden to the marriage feast; and they would not come. Again he sent forth other servants, saying Tell them that are bidden, Behold, I have made ready my dinner; my oxen and my fatlings are killed, and all things are ready: come to the marriage feast. But they made light of it, and went their ways, one to his own farm, another to his merchandise; and the rest laid hold on his servants, and treated them shamefully, and killed them. But the king was wroth; and he sent his armies, and destroyed those murderers, and burned their city. Then saith he to his servants, The wedding is ready, but they that were bidden are not worthy. Go ye therefore unto the partings of the highways, and as many as ye shall find, bid to the marriage feast. And those servants went out into the highways, and gathered together all as many as they found, both bad and good: and the wedding was filled with guests. But when the king came in to behold the guests, he saw there a man who had not on a wedding garment. And he saith unto him, Friend, How camest thou hither not having a wedding garment? And he was speechless. Then the king said to his servants, Bind him hand and foot, and cast him out into the outer darkness; there shall be the weeping and the gnashing of teeth. For many are called but few are chosen."

Interpretation

•   All students of Scriptures and especially of the New Testament, should be thoroughly informed of the laws of mind. If he does not know that all things come from thoughts, he will be constantly materializing the "heavens," and misunderstanding the teaching of Jesus. The Jews had not acquired this understanding and Jesus was compelled to compare the higher mental realms to material conditions and customs, in parables and allegories.

•   In our day we are finding inner powers of earth, water, and air that the ancient people knew not of, and through the use of these finer forces, the material world is being transformed. But still deeper than the inner powers of earth, air and water are mental and spiritual forces, which men can put into expression, and bring about more wonderful transformations that they have yet imagined.

•   If it were true Jesus could easily have said, "heaven is located on a certain star a billion miles away; it has golden streets and those who confess me will go there after they die and play harps throughout eternity." Or, he could have described the Spirit-world—a place where men go and progress on and on after they die, and death is the open door to this so-called higher life. But He knew that these were all figments of the imagination of people who were ignorant of the real relations existing between the inner and the outer of the One Omnipresent God Mind, and he again and again illustrated by familiar comparisons, with things of their daily life what the true heaven was and how very close the Father is to His offspring.

•   The very large number of people who have made the union with Spirit are the first invited guests to the feast of the king. Strange, but true, these are most often the ones who are so taken up with exercising their superior abilities in material ways that they ignore the call of the Spirit.

•   Nearly all the world's brilliant people have somewhere, at some time in the many lives they have lived, been quickened of the Spirit through some religious experience and a certain union made with God. These are the many who are called, but few of them choose to come.

•   Great religious reforms and revivals originate among the common people. The rich, the cultured and the worldly wise are slow to accept spiritual truths. They have acquired spiritual power and turned it into material avenues. But the "feast" the transcendently good things of the Spirit, are pressing upon men and when those who are best fitted to utilize them turn away, the Lord bestows them upon those from the "highways," 'both bad and good."

•   The guest without the "wedding garment," is one who is attempting to take advantage of the wedding feast without conforming to the requirements. In oriental countries every wedding guest is expected to wear a wedding garment, so in this wedding feast of the Lords, every guest should see to it that his is clothed in his right mind—a right understanding of the divine Principle and a careful conformity to it in thought and word. This will clothe a man with "robes of righteousness," which is the true "wedding-garment."

823.

Luke 11:1-4

And it came to pass, as he was praying in a certain place, that when he ceased, one of his disciples said unto him, Lord, teach us to pray, even as John also taught his disciples. And he said unto them, When ye pray, say Father, Hallowed be thy name, Thy kingdom come. Give us day by day our daily bread. And forgive us our sins; for we ourselves also forgive every one that is indebted to us. And bring us not into temptation."

824-825.

Interpretation

• The starting point in every prayer is the understanding of God's locality and character. The usual prayer is addressed to a great man away off in an indefinite place called heaven. This is not according to the instruction of Jesus. "The kingdom of God is within you," and also He said that the Father dwelt in Him, and spoke the words through him.
• This Spirit dwells in the spiritual realms all around, within and without us. "In him we live, and move, and have our being." The name, or character, of this omnipresent Spirit is wholeness or perfection. In every prayer this should be recognized by the praying mind.

826.

Luke 11:50b

And he said unto them, Which of you shall have a friend, and shall go unto him at midnight, and say to him, Friend, lend me three loaves: for a friend of mine is come to me from a journey, and I have nothing to set before him; and he from within shall say, Trouble me not: the door is now shut, and my children are with me in bed; I cannot rise and give thee? I say unto you, Though he will not rise and give him because he is his friend, yet because of his importunity he will arise and give him as many as he needeth.

827.

Interpretation

• This is a lesson in persistency. Prayer does not affect God, but prayer broadens and deepens the soul consciousness so that God Mind can express through it to a greater degree. Thus we grow by persistently asking and realizing.

Luke 11:9-13

And I say unto you, Ask, and it shall be given you; seek, and ye shall find; knock and it shall be opened unto you. For every one that asketh receiveth; and he that seeketh findeth; and to him that knocketh it shall be opened. And of which of you that is a father shall his son ask a loaf, and he give him a stone? Or a fish, and he for a fish give him a serpent? Or if he shall ask an egg, will he give him a scorpion? If ye then, being evil, know how to give good gifts unto your children, how much more shall your heavenly Father give the Holy Spirit to them that ask him? One is your Father, even he who is in heaven. If ye then...know how to give good gifts unto your children, how much more shall your Father who is in heaven give good things to them that ask him?"

Interpretation

• Jesus' teaching concerning God was that God is wise, kind, loving, ever-present, guiding, protecting, providing Father, and we must learn really to know Him as such.

Luke 11:33-36

No man, when he hath lighted a lamp, putteth it in a cellar, neither under the bushel, but on the stand, that they which enter in may see the light. The lamp of thy body is thine eye: when thine eye is single, thy whole body also is full of light; but when it is evil, thy body also is full of darkness. Look therefore whether the light that is in thee be not darkness. If therefore thy whole body be full of light, having no part dark, it shall be full of light, as when the lamp with its bright shining doth give thee light."

Luke 11:37-39

Now as he spoke, a Pharisee asketh him to dine with him: and he went in, and sat down to meat. And when the Pharisee saw it, he marveled that he had not first bathed himself before dinner. And the Lord said unto him, Know ye the Pharisees cleanse the outside of the cup and of the platter; but your inward part is full of extortion and wickedness. Ye foolish ones, did not he that made the outside make the inside also? But give for alms those things which are within; and behold, all things are clean unto you."

Interpretation

• The spiritually minded man has more than he can do to keep up soul unfoldment and many times does not give so much attention to outer forms and ceremonies or even to his surroundings. He knows as he unfolds from principle within that the outer things will take care of themselves.
• The Pharisaical man who is largely on the intellectual plane oftentimes is filled with thoughts of "extortion and wickedness" but keeps up a wonderful outward appearance.
• Jesus was calling attention to these two different phases of unfoldment. "Ye foolish ones, did not he that made the outside make the inside also."

Luke 12:1-9

In the meantime, when the many thousands of the multitude were gathered together, insomuch that they trod one upon another, he began to say unto his disciples first of all, Beware ye of the leaven of the Pharisees, which is hypocrisy. But there is nothing covered up, that shall not be revealed; and hid, that shall not be known. Wherefore whatsoever ye have said in the darkness shall be heard in the light; and what ye have spoken in the ear in the inner chambers shall be proclaimed upon the housetops.

And I say unto you my friends, Be not afraid of them that kill the body, and after that have no more that they can do. But I will warn you whom ye shall fear: Fear him, who after he hath killed hath power to cast into hell; yea, I say unto you, Fear him. Are not five sparrows sold for two pence? And one of them is forgotten in the sight of God. But the very hairs of your head are all numbered, Fear not: ye are of more value than many sparrows. And I say unto you, before men him shall the Son of man also confess before the angels of God: but he that denieth me in the presence of men shall be denied in the presence of the angels of God.

Interpretation

• Jesus said to fear him who is able to destroy both soul and body rather than those who can kill the body only. It is possible for the soul to get so material, to become so wrapped up in worldly affairs, that it entirely crowds out the spiritual. Such a soul might disintegrate. However, it would require millions of years of adverse thought to accomplish such a condition.
• Jesus pointed out that if God took care of the sparrows, representing something unimportant, that He surely would take care of His masterpiece of creation—man.

Luke 12:10

And everyone who shall speak a word against the Son of man, it shall be forgiven him: but unto him that blasphemeth against the Holy Spirit it shall not be forgiven.

Interpretation

• Jesus said that ascribing good works to evil sources (the demons) was the unforgivable sin.

Luke 12:11-12

And when they bring you before the synagogues, and the rulers, and the authorities, be not anxious how or what ye shall answer, or what ye shall say: for the Holy Spirit shall teach you in that very hour what ye ought to say.

Interpretation

• In prayer we take with us a Word of Truth, go into the silence, and contact God Mind, then realize that Word of Truth until God Mind satisfies the logic of our soul. This realization has the power in itself to speak forth the Word of God.

Luke 12:13-15

And one out of the multitude said unto him, Teacher, bid my brother divide the inheritance with me. But he said unto him, Man, who made me a judge or a divider over you? And he said unto them, Take heed, and keep yourselves from all covetousness: for a man's life consisteth not in the abundance of the things which he possesseth.

Interpretation

• This Scripture explains itself. Jesus was simply setting forth the Truth that God is our supply and support, and that we should not covet what another has called forth from the universal storehouse, but manifest our own needs.

Luke 12:16-34

And he spoke a parable unto them, saying, The ground of a certain rich man brought forth plentifully: and he reasoned within himself, saying, What shall I do, because I have not where to bestow my fruits? And he said, This will I do; I will pull down my barns, and build greater; and there will I bestow all my grain and my goods. And I will say to my soul, Soul, thou hast much goods laid up for many years; take thine ease, eat, drink, be merry. But God said unto him, Thou foolish one, this night is thy soul required of thee; and the things which thou hast prepared, whose shall they be? So is he that layeth up treasure for himself and is not rich toward God. And he said unto his disciples, Therefore I say unto you, Be not anxious for your life, what ye shall eat; nor yet for your body, what ye shall put on. For the life is more than the food, and the body than the raiment. Consider the ravens, that they sow not, neither reap; which have no store-chamber nor barn; and God feedeth them: of how much more value are ye than the birds!

And which of you by being anxious can add a cubit unto the measure of his life? If then ye are not able to do even that which is least, why are ye anxious concerning the rest? Consider the lilies, how they grow: they toil not, neither do they spin; yet I say unto you, Even Solomon in all his glory was not arrayed like one of these. But if God doth so clothe the grass in the field, which today is, and tomorrow is cast into the oven; how much more shall he clothe you, O ye of little faith? And seek not ye what ye shall eat, and what ye shall drink, neither be ye of doubtful mind. For all these things do the nations of the world seek after: but you Father knoweth that ye have need of these things. Yet seek ye his kingdom, and those things shall be added unto you. Fear not, little flock; for it is your Father's good pleasure to give you the kingdom. Sell that which ye have, and give alms; make for yourselves purses which wax not old, a treasure in the heavens that faileth not, where no thief draweth near, neither moth destroyeth. For where your treasure is, there will your heart be also.

852.

Interpretation

• There is a spiritual law against hoarding. Also there is an omnipresent law through which we may demonstrate abundance. By laying up for the future we are delaying the day of our real spiritual salvation. Thus in this parable of the rich fool Jesus is making it very clear that the man who pulls down his barns to build greater ones in order to store away his earthly good is really unfolding a selfish state of mind that will shortly cost him dearly.

Luke 12:35-41

Let your loins be girded about, and your lamps burning; and be ye yourselves like unto men looking for their lord, when he shall return from the marriage feast; that, when he cometh and knocketh, they may straightway open unto him. Blessed are those servants, whom the lord when he cometh shall find watching: verily I say unto you, that he shall gird himself, and make them sit down to meat, and shall come and serve them. And if he shall come in the second watch, and if in the third, and find them so, blessed are those servants. But know this, that if the master of the house had know what hour the thief was coming, he would have watched, and not have left his house to be broken through. Be ye also ready: for in an hour that ye think not the Son of man cometh. And Peter said, Lord, speakest thou this parable unto us, or even unto all?

Interpretation

•   This scripture exemplifies the steps man takes in scientific silence. A word of Truth, concentrated upon, penetrates into spiritual consciousness, and we realize that we are more firmly established in our consciousness with our Source. With the lamp of faith burning, we wait expectantly for the realization that we are definitely unified with the perfect mind of God.

•   In this state of consciousness when the Lord knocks, the door is opened instantly, and we realize that union where the blessings of Spirit are poured out upon us. Blessed indeed is the man if at the second watch and the third watch is still found waiting.

•   Those who are watching for Christ and are led by the Spirit of Truth feel and know that He is present and is within them. They are already tasting and seeing the glories of His kingdom. It is being set up within them and they are becoming established in its peace, joy, and wholeness, daily realizing more and more of His spiritual substance.

Luke 12:42-48

And the Lord said, Who then is the faithful and wise steward, who his lord shall set over his household, to give them their portion of food in due season? Blessed is that servant, whom his lord when he cometh shall find so doing. Of a truth I say unto you, that he will set him over all that he hath. But if that servant shall say in his heart, My lord delayeth his coming; and shall begin to beat the menservants and the maidservants, and to eat and drink, and to be drunken; the lord of that servant shall come in a day when he expecteth not, and in a hour he knoweth not, and shall cut him asunder, and appoint his portion with the unfaithful. And that servant, who knew his lord's will, and made not ready, nor did according to his will, shall be beaten with many stripes; but he that knew not, and did things worthy of stripes, shall be beaten with few stripes. And to whomsoever much is given, of him shall much be required: and to whom they commit much, of him will they ask the more.

859-860.

Interpretation

• The servants of the Lord are the elemental forces of Being, ever at hand to carry out His demands. The servant of the Lord is the faithful and wise steward who is always awake to the movements of Spirit, ready and willing to do its bidding.

• Every phase of the earth is the expression of God, and full redemption cannot take place until man and the whole earth are as perfect as the ideas in Divine Mind that are back of them. In other words, God must be as perfect in expression, in the outer as He is in what is commonly known as the invisible realm.

• It was necessary for Jesus to depart from the sight of the outer or sense man and go into the inner realm, thus opening the way for man to enter into this same Christ consciousness, to commune with the Father, and to be preserved, spirit, soul, and body, as Jesus Christ was. Our whole man must be redeemed and spiritualized just as Jesus Christ was if we are to be where He is.

861-863.

Luke 12:49-59

I came to cast fire upon the earth; and what do I desire, if it is already kindled? But I have a baptism to be baptized with; and how am I straitened till it be accomplished! Think ye that I have come to give peace in the earth? I tell you, Nay; but rather division: for there shall be from henceforth five in one house divided, three against two, and two against three. They shall be divided, father against son, and son against father; mother against daughter, and daughter against her mother; mother in law against her daughter in law, and daughter in law against her mother in law. And he said to the multitudes also, When ye see a cloud rising in the west, straightway ye say, There cometh a shower; and so it cometh to pass. And when ye see a south wind blowing, ye say, There will be a scorching heat; and it cometh to pass. Ye hypocrites, ye know how to interpret the face of the earth and the heaven; but how is it that ye know not how to interpret this time? And why even of yourselves judge ye not what is right? For as thou art going with thine adversary before the magistrate, on the way give diligence to be quit of him; lest haply he drag thee unto the judge, and the judge shall deliver thee to the officer, and the officer shall cast thee into prison. I say unto thee, Thou shalt by no means come out thence, till thou have paid the very last mite.

Interpretation

• In order to interpret these words of Jesus we must assume that all is spiritual. The "I" refers to the Christ, the spiritual man. We know that the Christ does not enter into the human relationships. The Oriental uses strong language. We today find this unnecessary and we do not deny human relationships. The more we unfold the Christ nature, the closer we are to all people everywhere.

• When Jesus referred to Himself as a Divider of men, He meant that father shall be against son, mother against daughter, mother-in-law against daughter-in-law unless they are related spiritually. There is only one enduring relationship, and that is among those who are related spiritually. This grand truth breaks up the limited idea of human relationships. The human sense of life is the stepping-stone to the spiritual, but when man becomes quickened he enters a new consciousness governed by spiritual law.

Luke 13:1-9

Now there were some present at that very season who told him of the Galilaeans, whose blood Pilate had mingled with their sacrifices. And he answered and said unto them, Think ye that these Galilaeans were sinners above all the Galilaeans, because they have suffered these things? I tell you, Nay: but, except ye repent ye shall all in like manner perish. Or those eighteen, upon whom the tower of Siloam fell, and killed them, think ye that they were offenders above all the men that dwelt in Jerusalem? I tell you, Nay: but, except ye repent, ye shall all likewise perish. And he spoke this parable; A certain man had a fig tree planted in his vineyard; and he came seeking fruit thereon, and found none. And he said unto the vinedresser, Behold, these three years I come seeking fruit on this fig tree, and find none; cut it down; why doth it also cumber the ground? And he answering saith unto him, Lord, let it alone this year also, till I shall dig about it, and dung it: and if it bear fruit thence forth, well; but it not, thou shalt cut it down.

Interpretation

• This Scripture is very mystical and yet very simple. Jesus teaches that there is no discrimination between the different degrees of sin. If we are a sinner in one degree, we are a sinner in all.

• Paul explains that sin came into the world through one man and that one man can save us from all sin. We are saved through the Lord Jesus Christ. As taught in the parable of the fig tree, since it bore no fruit, the owner was minded to cut it down. But the vinedresser had a new inspiration. He said, "Let's cultivate it. Let's fertilize it. Let's see if we cannot grow something on this little tree that it may bring forth fruit." By the same law we have a way out through the cultivation of higher states of consciousness.

• Man fulfills the law of all good by believing in truth, honesty, justice, purity, loveliness, and knowing that these qualities are dominant in the minds of all people everywhere. In this way we demonstrate over all negations that come into our lives and into the lives of those we love and those with whom we associate.

871-872.

Luke 13:10-17

And he was teaching in one of the synagogues on the Sabbath day. And behold, a woman that had a spirit of infirmity eighteen years; and she was bowed together, and could in no wise lift herself up. And when Jesus saw her, he called her, and said to her, Woman, thou art loosed from thine infirmity. And he laid hands upon her: and immediately she was made straight, and glorified God. And the ruler of the synagogue, being moved with indignation because Jesus had healed on the Sabbath, answered and said to the multitude, There are six days in which men ought to work, in them therefore come and be healed, and not on the day of the Sabbath. But the Lord answered him, and said, Ye hypocrites, doth not each one of you on the Sabbath loose his ox or his ass from the stall, and lead him away to watering? And ought not this woman, being a daughter of Abraham, who Satan had bound, lo, these eighteen years, to have been loosed from this bond on the day of the Sabbath? And as he said these things, all his adversaries were put to shame: and all the multitude rejoiced for all the glorious things that were done by him.

873-875.

Interpretation

• The woman with the infirmity represents an attitude of mind in which the feminine qualities predominate, and thus has taken on too much humility and gradually lost the positive, masterful I AM power and dominion. Often man bows to outer authority because he does not possess knowledge along a certain line, because he is ignorant in a certain way. Every soul must do its own thinking. Every soul must assert its God-given authority and declare in the name of Jesus Christ that it is divinely balanced and poised. Every soul should realize that the one great source of wisdom is ever open to all alike and the ability is forthcoming to determine its affairs accurately and with power.

• Woman is sometimes burdened with grief until she is bowed to the earth. In this case Jesus, representing the indwelling Christ, by His strong words of authority (laying His hands upon her) lifted the burden and the soul was free.

• The ruler of the synagogue represents a higher intellectual thought, following the letter of the law, instead of being ruled by the Spirit. Jesus taught on all occasions that the Sabbath was made for man, and that it was perfectly legitimate for healing to take place on that day.

Luke 13:22-30

And he went on his way through cities and villages, teaching, and journeying on unto Jerusalem. And one said unto him, Lord, are they few that are saved? And he said unto them, Strive to enter in by the narrow door: for many, I say unto you, shall seek to enter in, and shall not be able. When once the master of the house is risen upon, and hath shut to the door, and ye being to stand without, and to knock at the door saying, Lord, open to us; and he shall answer and say to you, I know you not whence ye are; then shall ye begin to say: We did eat and drink in thy presence, and thou didst teach in our streets; and he shall say, I tell you, I know not whence ye are; depart from me, all ye workers of iniquity. There shall be weeping and gnashing of teeth, when ye shall see Abraham, and Isaac, and Jacob, and all the prophets, in the kingdom of God, and yourselves cast forth without. And they shall come from the east and west, and from the north and south, and shall sit down in the kingdom of God. And behold, there are last who shall be first, and there are first who shall be last.

Interpretation

•   Jesus was on His way to Jerusalem, traveling through cities and villages teaching Truth.
•   He represents the spiritual I AM with its face turned toward infinite peace (Jerusalem), spreading the gospel on its way.
•   The narrow door represents the I AM which functions through the mentality. The individuals who hold steadily to the I AM power and dominion—that narrow door through which spirituality enters—can teach all their thought people to come to that same standard. Then they are established in this kingdom that knows the Christ, but if they do not gain this mastery, there is weeping and gnashing of teeth.

Luke 13:31-33

In that very hour there came certain Pharisees, saying to him, Get thee out, and go hence: for Herod would fain kill thee. And he said unto them, Go and say to that fox, Behold, I cast out demons and perform cures to-day and to-morrow, and the third day I am perfected. Nevertheless I must go on my way to-day and to-morrow and the day following: for it cannot be that a prophet perish out of Jerusalem.

Interpretation

• At this time Jerusalem was the spiritual and cultural center of the world. However, it was infested with aliens. It was under the Roman yoke (domination of the greedy and warring man), and crime was rampant.

• Spiritually interpreted, the Pharisees represent our intellectual thoughts, which are warring with the indwelling Christ, symbolized by Jesus. These intellectual thoughts are trying to gain the power to dominate Jerusalem, the central station of peace within the soul. Herod, representing the ruling ego in sense consciousness, would kill out the Christ. However the indwelling Christ neither slumbers nor sleeps and knows all things; and since it always works from principle it knows what is best to be done.

• Jesus said, "Go and say to that fox, Behold I cast out demons and perform cures to-day and to-morrow, and the third day, I am perfected." Spiritually interpreted, this means that the first day we get a strong realization of Truth, the next day we make that realization a very part of the soul, the third day we come into the realization that we are established firmly in the consciousness that it is a part of our very life.

884.

Luke 14:1-6

And it came to pass, when he went into the house of one of the rulers of the Pharisees on a Sabbath to eat bread, that they were watching him. And behold, there was before him a certain man that had the dropsy. And Jesus answering spoke unto the lawyers and Pharisees, saying, Is it lawful to heal on the Sabbath, or not? But they held their peace. And he took him, and healed him, and let him go. And he said unto them, Which of you shall have an ass or an ox fallen into a well, and will not straightway draw him up on a Sabbath day? And they could not answer again unto these things.

885.

Interpretation

• Man does not exercise his dominion for various reasons, one of which is his tendency to reverence and observe the letter of the law instead of the spirit.

886-889.

Luke 14:7-24

And he spoke a parable unto those that were bidden, when he marked how they chose out of the chief seats; saying unto them, When thou art bidden of any man to a marriage feast, sit not down in the chief seat; lest haply a more honorable man than thou be bidden of him, and he that bade thee and him shall come and say to thee, Give this man place and then thou shalt begin with shame to take the lowest place. But when thou art bidden, go and sit down in the lowest place; that when he that hath bidden thee cometh, he may say to thee, Friend, go up higher: then shalt thou have glory in the presence of all that sit at meat with thee. For every one that exalteth himself shall be humbled; and he that humbled himself shall be exalted. And he said to him also that had bidden him, When thou makest a dinner or a supper, call not thy friends, nor thy brethren, nor thy kinsman, nor rich neighbors; lest haply they also bid thee again, and a recompense be made thee. But when thou makest a feast, bid the poor, the maimed, the lame, the blind: and thou shalt be blessed; because they have not wherewith to recompense thee: for thou shalt be recompensed in the resurrection of the just. And when one of them that sat at meat with him heard these things, he said unto them, Blessed is he that shall eat bread in the kingdom of God. But he said unto him, A certain man made a great supper; and he bade many: and he sent forth his servant at supper time to say to them that were bidden, Come; for all things are now ready. And they all with one consent began to make excuse. The first said unto him, I have bought a field, and I must needs go out and see it; I pray thee have me excused. And another said, I have bought five yoke of oxen, and I go to prove them; I pray thee have me excused. And another said, I have married a wife, and therefore I cannot come. And the servant came, and told his lord these things. Then the master of the house being angry said to his servant, Go out quickly into the streets and lanes of the city, and bring in thither the poor and maimed and blind and lame. And the servant said, Lord, what thou didst command is done, and yet there is room. And the lord said unto the servant, Go out into the highways and hedges, and constrain them to come in, that my house may be filled. For I say unto you, that none of those men that were bidden shall taste of my supper.

890-891

Interpretation

•   Jesus was trying to call their attention to the higher powers of Spirit. The main purpose of His coming to earth was to reveal to man that all power lay within him, and to show him how to attain and control the "kingdom of the heavens."

•   The feast at a wedding follows the ceremony and is dependent upon it. No wedding, no feast. In like manner, the feast of the heavenly things prepared by the Father is dependent upon the wedding or union of man with Spirit. This union must be made before man can partake of the heavenly feast.

892-893

Luke 14:25-30

Now there went with him great multitudes: and he turned, and said unto them, If any man cometh unto me, and hateth not his own father, and mother, and wife, and children, and brethren, and sisters, yea, and his own life also, he cannot be my disciple. Whosoever doth not bear his own cross, and come after me, cannot be my disciple. For which of you, desiring to build a tower, doth not first sit down and count the cost, whether he have wherewith to complete it? Lest haply, when he hath laid a foundation, and is not able to finish, all that behold begin to mock him, saying, This man began to build, and was not able to finish.

894.

Interpretation

•   The true meaning of this Scripture is that God must come first and we must be willing to put the Christ idea of love into every situation in our lives. It does not mean that we are not to honor and love father, mother, wife, children, sister, and brother; but it means that under all circumstances we should honor and love and adore the great source from which we came.

895.

Luke 14:31-35

Or what king, as he goeth to encounter another king in war, will not sit down first and take counsel whether he is able with ten thousand to meet him that cometh against him with twenty thousand? Or else, while the other is yet a great way off, he sendeth an ambassador, and asketh conditions of peace. So therefore whosoever he be of you that renounceth not all that he hath, he cannot be my disciple.

896.

Interpretation

•   The foregoing parables about the king who counts his soldiers before he goes to battle and the man who counts his money before he builds a house illustrate the fact that if any man comes after Christ, he must consider the cost of following him. If he is not willing to pay that price, he cannot be His disciple.

897-898.

Luke 15:1-10

Now all the publicans and sinners were drawing near unto him to hear. And both the Pharisees and scribes murmured, saying, This man receiveth sinners, and eateth with them.

And he spoke unto them this parable, saying, What man of you, having a hundred sheep, and having lost one of them, doth not leave the ninety and nine in the wilderness, and go after that which is lost, until he find it? And when he hath found it, he layeth it on his shoulders, rejoicing. And when he cometh home, he calleth together his friends and his neighbors, saying unto them, Rejoice with me, for I have found my sheep which was lost.

I say unto, that even so there shall be joy in heaven so we find that the shortest way is to go after these sinners and bring them to repentance.

Or what woman having ten pieces of silver if she lose one piece, doth not light a lamp, and sweep the house, and seek diligently until she find it? And when she hath found it, she calleth together her friends and neighbors, saying, Rejoice with me, for I have found the piece which I had lost. Even so, say unto you, there is joy in the presence of the angels of God over one sinner that repenteth.

899-905

Interpretation

• Some metaphysicians hold that error thoughts will perish of their own accord if we ignore them entirely and keep our attention fixed on the good only. This is undoubtedly a correct position, assuming that the error thoughts will not insist upon bobbing up now and then. But the experience of most people is that these sinner thoughts have a way of making themselves especially prominent after the Truth has come into consciousness, as in this Scripture. We are told, "Now all the publicans and sinners were drawing near unto him." So we find that the shortest way is to go after these sinners and bring them to repentance. This is called "demonstrating over error," or according to Jesus, "overcoming."

• This is called "demonstrating over error," or according to Jesus, "overcoming."

• Jesus lays unusual stress upon the necessity of "overcoming" in order to get into the kingdom of heaven; many times the expression is used in the Scripture, especially in Revelation. We are to be vigilant in correcting these thoughts that fall short of the divine ideal—the perfect man.

• But "the Pharisees and the scribes murmured, saying, this man receiveth sinners, and eateth with them. So today those who are in only the intellectual perception of Truth argue that when we search our faults and deny and affirm for them, that we are making too much of them, and that they will become prominent in consequence.

• However a deeper understanding of the law of thought shows us that every manifestation of the thinker partakes of his characteristics. Therefore every so-called evil, or sinner thought, has a certain quality of good in it; it has life and intelligence—it is a thinking entity itself, and must be dealt with just as you would deal with one of your children. So it is unwise to ignore these children of the mind, or give them a mental opiate, consoling ourselves that they are dead when they are in reality out in the wilderness of mortal realm— "lost sinners."

• The Truth is not afraid of being contaminated through association with sinners. Jesus did not associate with publicans to become one of them, but to raise them up. He did not compromise with wrong in any persons or class—He did not seek to gain favor with the publicans by avoiding the

Pharisees. Both classes were sinners, and He had an object in associating freely with them.

• The Pharisaical state of consciousness draws aside from sin, and through its assumption of righteousness, fails to detect some glaring error in its own thought. Search yourself, and see if you are short any sheep. It is a very pure character that is ninety-nine percent good, and most of us would be content to rest with that high standard, but Jesus says, "go after that one which is lost and find it."

• "There shall be joy in heaven over one sinner that repenteth, more than over ninety and nine righteous persons who need no repentence." Heaven is peace, and love, and justice, and goodness—it is the real of God and man. But if there is a part of the consciousness which has been outside of this heavenly condition, and we succeed in bringing it in, how we rejoice over the demonstration! Then we say to our friends and neighbors, "Rejoice with me, for I have found my sheep which was lost."

• We might compare the hundredth sheep to that part of consciousness which has been outside the kingdom of heaven. The will of the Father is for redemption of the entire consciousness.

906-910.

Luke 15:11-32

And he said, A certain man had two sons: and the younger of them said to his father, Father, give me the portion of thy substance that falleth to me. And he divided unto them his living. And not many days after, the younger son gathered all together and took his journey into a far country; and there he wasted his substance with riotous living. And when he had spent all, there arose a mighty famine in that country; and he began to be in want. And he went and joined himself to one of the citizens of that country; and he sent him into his fields to feed swine.

And he would fain have filled his belly with the husks that the swine did eat: and no man gave unto him. But when he came to himself he said, How many hired servants of my father's have bread enough and to spare, and I perish here with hunger! I will arise and go to my father, and say unto him, Father, I have sinned against heaven, and in thy sight: I am no more worthy to be called thy son: make me as one of thy hired servants. And he arose, and came to his father. But while he was yet afar off, his father saw him, and was moved with compassion, and ran, and fell on his neck, and kissed him. And the son said unto him, Father, I have sinned against heaven, and in thy sight: I am no more worthy to be called thy son. But the father said to his servants, Bring forth quickly the best robe, and put it on him; and put a ring on his hand, and shoes on his feet: and bring the fatted calf, and kill it, and let us eat, and make merry: for this my son was dead, and is alive again; he was lost, and is found. And they began to be merry. Now his elder son was in the field: and as he came and drew nigh to the house, he heard music and dancing. And he called to him one of the servants, and inquired what these things might be. And he said unto him, Thy brother is come; and thy father hath killed the fatted calf, because he hath received him safe and sound. But he was angry, and would not go in: and his father came out, and entreated him. But he answered and said to his father, Lo, these many years do I serve thee, and I never transgressed a commandment of thine; and yet thou never gavest me a kid, that I might make merry with my friends: but when this thy son came, who hath devoured thy living with harlots, thou killedest for him the fatted calf. And he said unto him Son, thou art ever with me, and all that is mine is thine. But it was meet to make merry and be glad: for this thy brother was dead, and is alive again; and was lost, and is found.

911-918.

Interpretation

The two sons represent soul consciousness and sense consciousness. Through the soul we are related to the Spirit, and through the sense to the flesh. These are mental states or thought aggregations. All the thoughts of a spiritual character gravitate together and form a state of consciousness that is pervaded by Spirit, and perpetually sustained by the Divine Mind. This is a spiritual soul, to whom the Father said, "Son, all that is mind is thine." The human soul is the "younger son." This thought aggregation finds its first pleasure in sense avenues. It is the exuberance of youth when every human sense is flooded with life. It draws freely from the one Source, the Father Mind, life, love, substance, power, and intelligence. These are the riches of God which are divided between the states of mind. These two souls, or states of thought, are referred to by Paul as the Spirit and the flesh at enmity, one warring against the other. It is not strictly correct to say that this higher plane of thought is the Spirit, but rather that it is the spiritual consciousness. The Spirit does not war against anybody or anything.

The mind that revels in pleasure of sense, gradually finds itself centering about the things about which it thinks so much. This is the law of thought action. What you think a great deal about, and like to do, you gradually become attached to, and in due course the attachment becomes so strong that you separate yourself from everything else. The constant thought of man about sense objects and sense pleasures gradually sunders him from the spiritual, and builds up a separate state of existence. This is the journey into the "far country." But being detached in consciousness from the real Source of existence, the sense consciousness gradually uses up its resources, in the lusts of the flesh, and not knowing how to go within and draw from the original fount, there is a "mighty famine in that country, and he began to be in want."

Then there is still further descent into sense conditions. The sense soul attaches itself to the realm of flesh, and tries to get sustenance out of it. The original text here indicates that he literally glued himself to the selfish personality of the flesh consciousness. He fed the swinish nature with the husks of life, and got no soul satisfaction. When we get down into the animal, and try to feed our souls with its mere outer covering of truth (husks) we starve. The human is eliminated until there is no man in it—"and no man gave unto him."

The coming to himself of the human soul is the awakening of understanding. Why should the body grow old and lose its life, "perish with hunger," when in the Father's house the hired servants have substance enough?

"I will arise and go to my Father." The mind that has been groveling in sense must rise to a higher range of thought and go, or continually send its thought, in spiritual ways. This journey back to Spirit is not completed in a day, but is a gradual step by step traveling, sometimes over rough roads.

"He arose and came to his father." The moment the thought rises to the contemplation of Spirit, there is a union with the Divine Mind—his father "fell on his neck and kissed him." Confession of sin is good for the self-centered man. It opens the door to higher things, and mellows the soul. An Eastern proverb is, "who draws near to me (God) an inch, I will draw near him an ell, and who walks to meet me, I will leap to meet him."

When we make the unity between the outer sense and the inner Spirit there is great rejoicing. The outer is flooded with vitality (the best robe), unending life (a ring on his hand), and understanding (shoes on his feet). The fatted calf represents the richness of strength always awaiting the needy soul. When all these relations have been established between the within and the without there is rejoicing. The dead man of sense is made alive in the consciousness of Spirit—the lost is found. "And they began to make merry."

(919-922) (Luke 16:1-13)

Note to Mr. Fillmore and Cora [from Unity Editorial/Publishing]: This interpretation seems inadequate. (Only 4 lines of interpretation for 3 pages of Scripture.)

919-922.

Luke 16:1-13

And he said unto the disciples, There was a certain rich man, who had a steward; and the same was accused unto him that he was wasting his goods. And he called him, and said unto him, What is this that I hear of thee? render the account of thy stewardship; for thou canst be no longer steward. And the steward said within himself, What shall I do, seeing that my lord taketh away the stewardship from me? I have not strength to dig: to beg I am ashamed. I am resolved what to do, that, when I am put out of the stewardship, they may receive me into their houses. And calling to him each of his lord's debtors, he said to the first, How much owest thou unto my lord? And he said, A hundred measures of oil. And he said unto him, Take thy bond, and sit down quickly and write fifty. Then said he to another, and how much owest thou? And he said, A hundred measures of wheat.

He said unto him, Take thy bond and write fourscore. And his lord commended the unrighteous steward because he had done wisely: for the sons of this world are for their own generation wiser than the sons of light. And I say unto you, make to yourselves friends by means of the mammon of unrighteousness; that, when it shall fail, they may receive you into the eternal tabernacles. He that is faithful in a very little is faithful also in much: and he that is unrighteous in a very little is unrighteous also in much.

If therefore ye have not been faithful in the unrighteous mammon, who will commit to your trust the true riches? And if ye have not been faithful in that which is another's, who will give you that which is your own? No servant can serve two masters: for either he will hate the one, and love the other: or else he will hold to one and despise the other. Ye cannot serve God and mammon.

922

Interpretation

• The rich man commended the dishonest steward because of his ability to think things through. When you begin thinking things through, you find that there is a principle back of all things and to bring good results you must work from principle.

923

Luke 16:14-17

And the Pharisees, who were lovers of money, heard all these things; and they scoffed at him. And he said unto them, Ye are they that justify yourselves in the sight of men; but God knoweth your hearts: for that which is exalted among men is an abomination in the sight of God. The law and the prophets were until John: from that time the gospel of the kingdom of God is preached, and every man entereth violently into it. But it is easier for heaven and earth to pass away, than for one tittle of the law to fall.

924

Interpretation

• The Pharisees symbolize the critical, intellectual phase of mind that always scoffs when any doctrine is presented that fails to exalt the letter of the law. There is a mighty truth revealed through the forgiving love of Jesus Christ, which the Pharisaical mind cannot accept.

925-927

Luke 16:19-31

Now there was certain rich man, and he was clothed in purple and fine linen, faring sumptuously every day: and a certain beggar named Lazarus was laid at his gate, full of sores, and desiring to be fed with the crumbs that fell from the rich man's table; yea, even the dogs came and licked his sores. And it came to pass, that the beggar died, and he was carried away by the angels into Abraham's bosom: and the rich man also died, and was buried. And in Hades he lifted up his eyes, being in torments, and seeth Abraham afar off, and Lazarus in his bosom. And he cried and said, Father Abraham, have mercy on me, and send Lazarus, that he may dip the tip of his finger in water, and cool my tongue; for I am in anguish in this flame.

But Abraham said, Son, remember that thou in thy lifetime receivedst thy good things, and Lazarus in like manner evil things: but now here he is comforted, and thou art in anguish. And besides all this, between us and you there is a great gulf fixed, that they that would pass from thence to you may not be able, and that none may cross over from thence to us. And he said, I pray thee therefore, father, that thou wouldst send him to my father's house; for I have five brethren; that he may testify unto them, lest they also come into this place of torment.

But Abraham saith, They have Moses and the prophets; let them hear them. And he said, Nay, father Abraham: but if one go to them from the dead, they will repent. And he said unto them, If they hear not Moses and the prophets, neither will they be persuaded, if one rise from the dead.

928-934.

Interpretation

•   In this parable Jesus describes the states of consciousness of one who passes through the change called death. The rich man and Lazarus represent the outer and the inner consciousness of the average worldly-minded person. The outer consciousness appropriates the attributes of soul and body and expresses them through sense avenues. "He was clothed in purple and fine linen, faring sumptuously every day." This condition typifies carnal riches.
•   Material selfishness starves the inner man and devitalizes the true or spiritual phase of the soul and body, which is described in the sentence, "A certain beggar named Lazarus was laid at his gate, full of sores, and desiring to be fed with the crumbs that fell from the rich man's table. The higher soul life is put out of the consciousness and fed with the dogs.
•   When death overtakes such a one, both the inner and the outer change environment. The material avenues are lost to the outer, and the carnal phase of the soul finds itself in a hell of animal desires without the flesh through which to express. "And in Hades he lifted up his eyes, being in torments."
•   Lazarus, the beggar, was "carried away by the angels into Abraham's bosom." The inner spiritual ego, drawn by its innate spiritual ideas, finds a haven or rest in the bosom of the Father, represented by Abraham.
•   (According to the best Bible authorities, "Abraham's bosom" represents a state of felicity, or celestial happiness. A good Bible translator also says that "Hades" means "The invisible land, the realm of the dead, including both Elysium and paradise for the good, and Tartarus, Gehenna, and

hell for the wicked." We do not, however, understand that "Abraham's bosom" refers to a place called heaven, nor that "Hades" refers to a place called hell. The Teller of this allegory, evidently, was striving to depict the two states of consciousness in which the higher and the lower principles of the sou find themselves after the death of the body."

• When man loses the material avenues of expression and has not developed the spiritual, he is in torment. Appetite longs for satisfaction, and in its anguished desire for the cooling draft, calls to its spiritual counterpart (Lazarus). But the body consciousness, the place of union between all the attributes of man, has been removed, producing in the life consciousness a great gulf or chasm that cannot be crossed, except by man's incarnation in another body.

• Then the sense man is contrite and would have his five brothers warned of the danger of sense life. These five brothers are the five senses. Abraham says: "They have Moses and the prophets; let them hear them"; that is, they understand the law (Moses) and they know what will follow its transgression (Prophets). The rich man rejoins: "Nay, father Abraham: but if one go to them from the dead, they will repents," "And he said unto him, If they hear not Moses and the prophets, neither will they be persuaded, if one rise from the dead." The personal consciousness, which has been formed through material attachments, can be reached only through its own plan of consciousness. The phenomenal manifestations of spiritualism do not cause people to repent of their sins.

• When one understands the disintegration that death produces in man this parable is perceived to be rich in description of that process and of the new relation of the segregated parts of the complete man.

935-936

Luke 17:5-10

And the apostles said unto the Lord, Increase our faith. And the Lord said, If ye had faith as a grain of mustard seed, ye would say unto this sycamine tree, Be thou rooted up, and be thou planted in the sea; and it would obey you. But who is there of you, having a servant plowing or keeping sheep, that will say unto him, when he is come in from the field, Come straightway and sit down to meat; and will not rather say unto him, Make ready wherewith I may sup, and gird thyself, and serve me, till I have eaten and drunken; and afterward thou shalt eat and drink? Doth he thank the servant because he did the things that were commanded? Even so ye also, when ye shall have done all the things that are commanded you, say, We are unprofitable servants; we have done that which it was our duty to do.

937

Interpretation

• Here Jesus is revealing the power of faith to remove any obstacle that hinders progress or has proved to be a burden. Faith removes mountains of error. Jesus was also endeavoring to teach His disciples that faithfully doing one's duty is always appreciated and rewarded by Almightiness.

938-939.

Luke 17:11-19

And it came to pass, as they were on the way to Jerusalem that he was passing along the borders of Samaria and Galilee. And as he entered into a certain village, there met him ten men that were lepers, who stood afar off: and they lifted up their voices, saying, Jesus, Master, have mercy on us. And when he saw them, he said unto them, Go and show yourselves unto the priests. And it came to pass, as they went, they were cleansed. And one of them when he saw that he was healed, turned back, with a loud voice glorifying God; and he fell upon his face at this feet, giving him thanks: and he was a Samaritan. And Jesus answering said, Were not the ten cleansed? But where are the nine? Were there none found that returned to give glory to God, save this stranger? And he said unto him, Arise, and go thy way: thy faith hath made thee whole.

940-943.

Interpretation

• We are all on the way to Jerusalem, the "city of peace." We are trying to reach it by our own road, but there is only one way: the way to a perfectly rounded character according to divine standard which we call the "Christ way."

• The I AM (Jesus) is on the way with His disciples, or faculties, to Jerusalem, and passes through the midst of Samaria and Galilee. Samaria means intellectual perception, and Galilee, life activity. The truth that there is but one Being and one Source of all that appears is first an intellectual perception in the realm of consciousness; then it is carried to the next plane of manifestation, which is the active life in the organism. Here are met "two men that were lepers, who stood afar off."

• The ten lepers represent the impure relation of life activities in one who has, by his error thoughts about life, separated from the great central life Source, that it has lost its vitality.

• The life in man finds expression through the avenue of the senses. Unless the senses are redeemed and uplifted there is a tendency to utilize the pure life of God in sense pleasure. An impure (leprous) condition in the organism is the result. When the new life rushes into consciousness and the inner man perceives its swift vibrations, he sometimes finds that these avenues of expression in the body are sadly deficient in life force. All this is changed when the I AM declares the law of omnipotent, omnipresent Life.

• The priests represent the connecting link between mortal man and God, and to "show yourselves unto the priests," means to make this connection absolute in consciousness. Then "as they went, they were cleansed." It is in the doing of these things that the healing is demonstrated externally. "Faith apart from works is dead."

• Everything resolves itself back to "one" as its starting point—the several avenues of expression are, after all, but one. All the avenues of expression in man are unified with God when one consciously lives in harmony with divine law. Thanksgiving follows in natural sequence.

944-945.

Luke 17:20-25

And being asked by the Pharisees, when the kingdom of God cometh, he answered them and said, The kingdom of God cometh not with observation: neither shall they say, Lo, here! or, There! for lo, the kingdom of God is within you.

And he said unto the disciples, The days will come, when ye shall desire to see one of the days of the Son of man, and ye shall not see it. And they shall say to you, Lo, there! Lo, here! Go not away, nor follow after them: for as the lightning, when it lighteneth out of the one part under the heaven, shineth unto the other part under the heaven; so shall the Son of man be in his day. But first must he suffer many things and be rejected of this generation.

946-951.

Interpretation

• The key to all Jesus' teaching about the kingdom of heaven is found in Luke 17: 20: "And being asked by the Pharisees, when the kingdom of God cometh, he answered them and said, The kingdom of God cometh not with observation: neither shall they say, Lo, here! or, Lo, There! for lo, the kingdom of God is within you." The Jews had no theory like the modern Christians, of a heaven somewhere in the skies. They looked forward to the setting up of a government on the earth, in which Jehovah should rule through the Messiah. When Jesus talked about the kingdom, they thought he meant this temporal government, but He had spiritual vision and saw that the kingdom of God had to be worked into the minds and bodies of the people before it could be set up in the earth. The people of His day could not be directly instructed in the metaphysical facts of the situation because they were crude and ignorant of that great mass of knowledge of the mind and its relation to the body, which has been acquired almost wholly in the last century. There have always been a select few who had understanding of the deep truths of existence, but there were no means of instructing the masses, such as we have today, and like Jesus, these wise ones all taught in parables.

• Jesus elaborated in His teachings on this point of the character of the kingdom more fully than any other. He never, in all His descriptions of the kingdom, gave it locality, except in the chapter in Luke above referred to. Do not go forth expecting to find the kingdom of God—you will be disappointed if you do. The teaching of Jesus is fully corroborated by the discoveries of modern science. Man cannot know, feel, or see anything which he has not first formed in his consciousness.

• With these facts before us we have no difficulty in determining who are going to heaven, or rather, who are on the way to heaven. It is those who have heaven within them, and none others. Man does not enter heaven, heaven enters him. When the seed ideas of the true character of God are planted in the mind, there begins a growth, the processes of which are beyond human ken. We know that ideas do grow in the mind similar to seeds in the ground, and that the growth of one is no more of a mystery than the growth of another.

• Modern science has failed to find the slightest explanation of what the life in a seed is or how it grows. But there is a steady progressive unfoldment in soul and body when one lets the true seed of Spirit take root in mind. It is often a very small seed-thought that starts this advance of the mind toward higher things. Every word of Truth that man utters may find soil fitted to its growth in some mind. The joy that comes to one who sees the harvest of such seed is greater by far than any earthly pleasure. If you want to taste the sweets of life in fullest measure plant good, true thoughts, in your own or another's mind, and then be at the harvest.

952-954.

Luke 17:26-37

And as it came to pass in the days of Noah, even so shall it be also in the days of the Son of man. They ate, they drank, they married, they were given in marriage, until the day that Noah entered into the ark, and the flood came, and destroyed them all. Likewise even as it came to pass in the days of Lot; they ate, they drank, they bought, they sold, they planted, they builded; but in the day that Lot went out from Sodom it rained fire and brimstone from heaven, and destroyed them all: after the same manner shall it be in the day that the Son of man is revealed. In that day, he that shall be on the housetop, and his goods in the house, let him not go down to take them away: and let him that is in the field likewise not return back. Remember Lot's wife. Whosoever shall seek to gain his life shall lose it: but whosoever shall lose his life shall preserve it. I say unto you, In that night there shall be two men on one bed; the one shall be taken and the other shall be left. There shall be two women grinding together; the one shall be taken, and the other shall be left. And they answering say unto him, Where, Lord? And he said unto them, Where the body is, thither will the eagles also be gathered together.

955-957.

Interpretation

• This Scripture is symbolical of the law of the Lord beginning to regulate the consciousness of man. The flood is representative of the baptism of Spirit, and is necessary in order to establish equilibrium in the three planes of mental activity.

- When the whole man (Noah and his family) has been washed in the regeneration, he takes refuge in the spiritual part of his consciousness (ark of the Lord), even in the midst of a flood of error.
- It is related in Genesis 19: 26 that when Lot's wife was fleeing from the destroyed cities of Sodom and Gomorrah, she looked back, and "became a pillar of salt." Salt is a preservative, corresponding to memory. When we remember the pleasures of the senses, and long for their return, we preserve the sense desire. This desire will manifest somewhere, sometime, unless the memory is dissolved through renunciation.
- "One man shall be taken, the other left;" "one woman shall be taken, the other left," pertains to the discriminating power of Spirit in activity.
- The eagle is of a destructive nature and is always on the look out for that upon which it may pray.

958-960

Luke 18:1-14

And he spoke a parable unto them to the end that they ought always to pray, and not to faint; saying, There was in a city a judge, who feared not God, and regarded not man: And there was a widow in that city; and she came oft unto him, saying, Avenge me of mine adversary. And he would not for a while: but afterward he said within himself, Though I fear not God, nor regard man; yet because this widow troubleth me, I will avenge her, lest she wear me out by her continual coming. And the Lord said, Hear what the unrighteous judge saith. And shall not God avenge his elect, that cry to him day and night, and yet he is long-suffering over them? I say unto you, that he will avenge them speedily. Nevertheless, when the Son of man cometh, shall he find faith on the earth?

And he spoke also this parable unto certain who trusted in themselves that they were righteous, and set all others at nought: Two men went up into the temple to pray; the one a Pharisee, and the other a publican. The Pharisee stood and prayed thus with himself, God, I thank thee, that I am not as the rest of men, extortioners, unjust, adulterers, or even as this publican. I fast twice in the week; I give tithes of all that I get. But the publican, standing afar off, would not lift up so much as his eyes unto heaven, but smote his breast, saying, God, be thou merciful to me a sinner. I say unto you, This man went down to his house justified rather than the other: for everyone that exalteth himself shall be humbled; but he that humbleth himself shall be exalted.

961-965

Interpretation

- Jesus illustrated the power of affirmative prayer or repeated silent demands for justice, by likening it to a widow, or one bereft of worldly protection and power. Under her persistence, even the ungodly judge succumbs. The unceasing prayer of faith is commanded in various places in the Scriptures.

• If a man's prayers are based upon the thought of his own righteousness and the sinfulness of others, he will not fulfill the law of true prayer. Self-righteousness is a thought of exclusiveness, and it closes the door to the great Father-love. We are not to justify ourselves in the sight of God; we are to let the Spirit of justice and righteousness do its perfect work through us.

• Undoubtedly the one thing that stands prominent in the teaching of Jesus Christ is the necessity of prayer. He prayed, or in some such manner invoked the presence of God, on the slightest pretext. He prayed over situations that most men would handle without the intervention of God. The skeptic often asks why, if He was verily God incarnate, did He so often appeal to an apparently higher one? To answer this intellectually and truly one must understand the constitution of man.

• There are always two men in each individual. The outer man is the picture which the inner man paints with his mind. Mind is the open door to the unlimited Principle of Being. When Jesus prayed He was setting into action these various departments of His individuality, in order to bring about certain results. Within, He was God-identity; without, He was human personality.

• The various mental attitudes included in the word prayer are not comprehended by those unfamiliar with the spiritual constitution of man. When the trained metaphysician speaks of his demonstrations through prayer he does not explain all the movements of his spirit and mind, because the outer consciousness has not the capacity to receive them.

• When we read of Jesus spending whole nights in prayer, the first thought is that He was asking and begging God for something. But we find prayer to be many-sided. It is not only asking, but it is receiving also. Pray believing that you shall receive. Prayer is also invocation and affirmation. Meditation, concentration, denials and affirmations in the silence, are forms of what is loosely termed "prayer."

• Jesus was demonstrating throughout the night over the error thoughts of mind. He was lifting the mortal mentality up to the plane of Spirit through some prayerful thought. The Son of man must be lifted up, and there is no way to do this except by prayer.

966-967.

Luke 19:1-10

And he entered and was passing through Jericho. And behold, a man called by name Zacchaeus; and he was a chief publican, and he was rich. And he sought to see Jesus who he was; and could not for the crowd, because he was little of stature. And he ran on before, and climbed up into a sycamore tree to see him: for he was to pass that way. And when Jesus came to the place, he looked up and said unto him, Zacchaeus, make hast, and come down; for today, I must abide at thy house. And he made haste, and came down; and received him joyfully. And when they saw it, they all murmured, saying, He is gone in to lodge with a man that is a sinner. And Zacchaeus stood, and said unto the Lord, Behold, Lord, the half of my goods I give to the poor; and if I have wrongfully exacted aught of any man, I restore fourfold. And Jesus said unto him, Today is salvation come to this house, forasmuch as he also is a son of Abraham. For the Son of man came to seek and to save that which was lost

968-97⁵

Interpretation

•   This Scripture covers the story of a chief publican who was rich. Zacchaeus, in common with all his fellow tax collectors, was permitted to gather for himself whatever sums he could over and above the legal amounts for which he was answerable to the Roman government. Apparently, he had lost no opportunity to enrich himself by using this privilege.

•   In a sense, Zacchaeus abides in each one of us. Each of us has an overweening desire to gain something. It may be money, power, influence, popularity, creature comforts, or the things that gratify the artistic sense. Our desires may rise higher and include the riches of the mind or of the spiritual kingdom.

•   It matters not how desirable may be the object of our acquisitive urge if we are seeking it for the natural self, which we have allowed to become strongly entrenched in the soul, we are still Zacchaeus up in the sycamore tree Such a tree produces fruit of very little value; and before we can gain a true consciousness of ourselves as spiritual beings fit to survive the exigencies of time and chance, we must come down from our false position and receive joyfully the royal guest, Truth. We must find out from infinite Mind the truth about this acquisitive urge in us, and make sure that it is centered in the universal self.

•   The universal self includes every living soul; in fact, all life. When we are centered in spiritual consciousness we shall realize our oneness with all life, and shall know that to extort from another money or anything else of value in order to increase our own fortune is really to impoverish our life. The divine law cannot be broken, and when we undertake to appropriate what is another's the law immediately balances accounts by taking out of our soul either character or other assets that are equivalent to what we have wrongfully exacted.

•   Zacchaeus climbed the sycamore tree out of curiosity about Jesus Christ, of whom he had heard startling reports. If he had had a sincere desire to meet Jesus and to learn of His teaching, he could have sent a messenger to invite Jesus into his home as a guest, since he himself was little of stature or could not push his way through the crowd. So our first desire to learn of Truth may arise out of curiosity.

•   The name Zacchaeus means "pure." We may be rich in intellectual accomplishments gathered at the expense of the other normal activities of life and yet our understanding of the realities of life may be so small as to be practically negligible. We shall gain an understanding of what life really is in its fullness only by receiving into our heart the Christ ideal of unselfishness. That ideal enables us to comprehend the law of restoration and fits us to receive eternal riches.

• We are not told what Jesus said in the home of Zacchaeus. Since Zacchaeus was a rich man and his occupation was well known in Jericho, Jesus evidently knew more of him than simply his name. The people murmured against Jesus for going to lodge with one whom they regarded as a sinner, whose sin lay not in legitimate tax collecting, but in the additional extortion. Everyone had unwillingly contributed to Zacchaeus's ill-gotten fortune and every one of course resented it. Jesus Christ doubtless went straight to the heart of the problem in His own kind but convincing fashion. He uttered, perhaps, a matchless parable on unselfish love—and the work was done. Zacchaeus's gold was melted by the Refiner's fire and flowed back into its rightful channels. Zacchaeus saw himself as incomparably small in the universal life. He was eager to turn back into the universal storehouse all that limited his capacity to receive the true riches of Spirit.

• To have faith in the spiritual values of life when we are awakened to their existence is to work out our own salvation. Every soul, when it actually grasps the higher law, hastens to turn back into the universal stream all accretion of substance that does not inhere in its own nature, that it may itself become aware of the transcendent quality of all.

• That which is converted from the universal into the concrete tends, unless the imbuing ray of Spirit infiltrates it, to disintegrate and slip back into the universal by the route of so-called material destruction. When the concrete is lifted up by the spiritualization of consciousness, it returns to the universal by way of obedience to the true law—all in one Spirit, and the same Spirit in and through all.

976-977.

Mat. 22:15-22

Then went the Pharisees, and took counsel how they might ensnare him in his talk. And they sent to him their disciples, with the Herodians, saying , Teacher, we know that thou art true, and teachest the way of God in truth, and carest not for any one: for thou regardest not the person of men. Tell us, therefore, What thinkest thou? Is it lawful to give tribute to Caesar, or not? But Jesus perceived their wickedness, and said, Why make ye trial of me, ye hypocrites? Show me the tribute money. And they brought unto him a denarius. And he saith unto them, Whose is this image and superscription? They say unto him, Caesar's. Then saith he unto them, Render therefore unto Caesar the things that are Caesar's; and unto God the things that are God's. And when they heard it, they marveled, and left him, and went away.

Interpretation

• The scribes and the chief priests sent out spies to catch some expression of Jesus in which they could find an excuse for handing Him over to the government of Caesar. Caesar was the Roman emperor; in consciousness he represents the tyrannical rule of the personal self-unmodified by spiritual love and mercy and justice. The government of the personal will has dominion over the intellectual religious beliefs. The consciousness of love and righteousness which has been established in the individual through the instruction and example of Jesus (the spiritual man), however, is outside the domain of Caesar, though seemingly at his mercy at times. In this instance, its wisdom is its protection.

• The outer man, as well as the inner, must be given of the substance of life. We even must make a certain agreement with the unenlightened human will, until the spiritual grows wise enough and loving enough and strong enough in our consciousness to take its rightful dominion throughout our entire being.

• The life of man flows out through countless avenues of expression. The heart, out of which come the issues of life, is the vast region of the subconscious mind. The soul is the emotional nature of man, packed with the rich fruitage of untold seasons of experience. The mind, commonly speaking, is the intellectual consciousness of the outer, every day life. The strength of man lies in his successful coordination of all these phases of his being, in his understanding the secret of drawing at will upon his boundless stores. It is easily seen that the question of temperance is one which applies to all these subdivisions of the individual. These subdivisions are not really separable into component parts, as an apple may be cut into pieces with a knife. Man is one and indivisible, and the various phases of his being cohere in the central unity which controls his life.

• The guarding of the thoughts of his mind with all the strength of his utmost earnestness is first essential in man's ascent to self-mastery and dominion. Jesus gives as the great and first commandment the charge to love the Lord God with all the heart, soul, and mind. Setting our thought upon the highest concept of the indwelling God lifts us into the realm of true thinking. In this realm the imagination reflect clearly all things as they are. No false images are created, no wrong concepts formed. We see and recognize the stamp of the worldly, or material, and we recognize the heavenly, or spiritual. We can give to Caesar what is Caesar's, and to God what is God's.

• Those who come into the spiritual understanding and practice of Truth outgrow their old Pharisaical beliefs that forms and ceremonies are fundamental in religious worship. But as the scribes and the chief priests and the Pharisees of the Jewish people ever sought to trap and destroy Jesus, so the old established religious thoughts of the intellect are always trying to find some discrepancy in the inspiration of the great Teacher within. The coldness and hardness of a formal religion would kill out the understanding of divine love and wisdom, if they could.

• That which is but a symbol of the true substance, the outer reasoning husk of the mortal thought of life and its resources, goes to Caesar. The real substance of life, love, understanding, and truth goes to build up and sustain the spiritual consciousness in our minds and bodies.

• The question of giving tribute is of importance to everyone. To what extent shall we recognize the demands of the worldly mind? What is our duty in fulfilling the desires of the outer, and what is its relation to the inner? To know the divine law and acknowledge its supremacy, and at the same time acquiesce in the exactions of human customs and pay the tax demanded by ruling Christian prudence and wisdom. Do not fall out with your environment, but make it serve you.

985-987.

Luke 20:27-40

And there came to him certain of the Sadducees, they that say that there is no resurrection; and they asked him, saying, Teacher, Moses wrote unto us, that if a man's brother die, having a wife, and he be childless, his brother should take the wife, and raise up seed unto his brother. There were therefore seven brethren: and the first took a wife, and died childless; and the second: and the third took her; and likewise the seven also left no children, and died. In the resurrection therefore whose wife of them shall she be? For the seven had her to wife. And Jesus said unto them, The sons of this world marry, and are given in marriage: but they that are accounted worthy to attain to that world, and the resurrection from the dead, neither marry nor are given in marriage: for neither can they die anymore: for they are equal to the angels; and are sons of God, being sons of the resurrection. But that the dead are raised, even Moses showed, in the place concerning the Bush, when he calleth the Lord the God of Abraham, and the God of Isaac, and the God of Jacob. Now he is not the God of the dead, but of the living: for all live unto him. And certain of the scribes answering him, said, Teacher, thou hast well said. For they durst not any more ask him any question.

988-990.

Interpretation

• The Sadducees who did not believe in a theory of resurrection after death sought to trap Jesus by asking Him who should have for wife in the resurrection the woman who had seven husbands? Jesus told them plainly that they did not understand the situation, either from Scripture or Divine Law—that in the true resurrection there is no marriage. Then He further elucidates the Truth by telling them that this resurrection is not a matter that has to do with physical death, that God does not recognize death—"God is not the God of the dead, but of the living."

• The intellectual man seems never to be silenced. At nearly every step in our spiritual unfoldment we find him questioning the I AM, as exemplified in the life of Jesus. He first wants to know how human entanglements will be adjusted in the resurrection. When he is informed that relations at the time of the resurrection are not based upon human standards, then he wants the "commandment," or the letter of the law. Jesus' reply will answer such questions for all time, as Truth stills the clamoring of the intellect.

• Physical death does not change the mind that is in error. The true resurrection is a coming forth into right understanding of and right relation to the one omnipresent Mind, and it begins and ends right where you are, regardless of time or geographical location.

991-992

Mark 12:22-34

And one of the scribes came, and heard them questioning together, and knowing that he had answered them well, asked him, What commandment is the first of all? Jesus answered, The first is, Hear, O Israel; The Lord our God, the Lord is one: and thou shalt love the Lord thy God with all thy heart, and with all thy soul, and with all thy mind, and with all thy strength. The second is this, Thou shalt love thy neighbor as thyself. There is none other commandment greater than these. And the scribe said unto him, Of a truth, Teacher, thou hast well said that he is one; and there is none other but he: and to love him with all the heart, and with all the understanding, and with all the strength, and to love his neighbor as himself, is much more than all burnt-offerings and sacrifices. And when Jesus saw that he answered discreetly, he said unto him, Thou art not far from the kingdom of God. And no man after that durst ask him any question.

993-999

Interpretation

• How to love God with the whole heart, soul, and mind is a problem which has engaged many an earnest seeker for the kingdom. Even after the new birth has taken place and man has become a citizen of the kingdom, the problem of whole-hearted devotion must be worked out before he can become fully master of himself. It is not enough to hold religious opinions and beliefs. Some of these may prove to be Pharisees seeking to entangle the I AM in a labyrinth of arguments about right and wrong. Innumerable arguments and mental wars over right have been made by man in his search for God. Not many of them bear the image of the heavenly Father. The Prince of Peace rules by the power of innate conviction, and all His thoughts harmonize. Man must seek and find for himself what is right.

• "God secludes Himself; but the thinker listens at the door." The body of man is the temple of God, and the door of this temple opens inward into the kingdom of heaven, on whose territory the temple stands. The door is the Christ consciousness—the Christ-like mind. Man listens at the door when he meditates on the highest truth that his mind can grasp, and reaches upward into the inner realm of peace toward the heights which his mind does not yet grasp, seeking more light. When he does this, he opens the door of his temple and the "light which lighteth every man, coming into the world," shines into his mind, into his body. Then intemperate thoughts, the product of lack of understanding, fall away from him.

• The student of Truth need have no doubt as to the character of thoughts that he entertains. Intemperate thoughts bear their own stamp; evil deeds no less, for the deed is but a thought put into action. Wicked thoughts, murders, adulteries, fornications, thefts, perjuries, blasphemies," all bear the unmistakable stamp of intemperance in thinking and living.

• As we gain calm, poise, self-control, we grow into clearer understanding of other minds, of other lives. As our consciousness of the one great animating Principle of the universe grows we see their problems as our own. Their interests and their aspirations stir in us the desire to add our efforts to the growth of a common understanding. We see in the life of every other man a replica of our own desires, our own problems, our own searching for light. Without the overlay of self, sometimes we see these desires and problems more clearly in our brother than in our self. Seeing oneness with the eye of mind brings oneness of heart—love of our neighbor as our self.

• Henry Drummond says that Paul wrote the greatest of all love poems, and his theme was the love of God. Jesus said that love toward God is the greatest commandment. Divine love is such a transcendent thing that words describing it seem flat and stale. But words used in right understanding quicken the soul, and we should not despise them. Affirming that we do love God with all our heart, with all our soul, with all our mind, and with all our might, will cause us to feel a love that we have never felt before. No better treatment for the realization of Divine Love can be given than that recommended by Jesus.

• It is found by metaphysicians that every question is sooner or later answered when we resolutely practice this development of Divine Love. Think love toward God with all your heart daily. Your heart is the symbol of all the vital issues that enter your life. Your soul is the realm of secret thought, and your mind is the outer consciousness. These are all to permeated with the thought of love to God. When this is done the love of neighbor will follow easily.

1000-1001.

Mark 12:35a

And Jesus answered and said, as he taught in the temple,

Mat. 22:42b-46

What think ye of the Christ? Whose son is He? They say unto him, The son of David. And he saith unto them, How then doth David in the Spirit call him Lord, saying, The Lord said unto my Lord, Sit thou on my right hand, Till I put thine enemies underneath thy feet? If David then calleth him Lord, how is he his son? And no one was able to answer him a word, neither durst any man from that day forth ask him any more questions.

1002-1003

Interpretation

• The I, the center in consciousness in each of us, and around which all states of consciousness revolve, cannot help but meditate upon and consider its own inner experience, and it says, "What think ye of the Christ? Whose son is he."

• The intellect, because of its limited range of perception, cannot conceive the formless, and it says this superior knowledge must have originated in some man, hence the Pharisee's reply, "The son of David." The difference between the divine and the human lineage of man is brought out in this question of the Sonship of Christ. Jesus did not give power to human heredity by tracing His descent through David, but showed that the Christ man, the Son of God, was the Higher Self, or Lord, of David, and that David so addressed Him: David called upon the universal Lord to give power to his lord (spiritual consciousness).

1004-1005

Mat. 23:1-12

Then spoke Jesus to the multitudes and to his disciples, saying, The scribes and the Pharisees sit on Moses' seat: all things therefore whatsoever they bid you, these do and observe: but do not ye after their works; for they say, and do not. Yea, they bind heavy burdens and grievous to be borne, and lay them on men's shoulders; but they themselves will not move them with their finger. But all their works they do to be seen of men: for they make broad their phylacteries, and enlarge the borders of their garments, and love the chief place at feasts, and the chief seats in the synagogues, and the salutations in the marketplaces, and to be called of men, Rabbi.

But be not ye called Rabbi; for one is your teacher, and all ye are brethren. And call no man your father on the earth: for one is your Father, even he who is in heaven. Neither be ye called masters: for one is your master, even the Christ. But he that is greatest among you shall be your servant. And whosoever shall exalt himself shall be humbled; and whosoever shall humble himself shall be exalted.

1006-1011

Interpretation

• This is a criticism of those who teach religion and do not practice it; they make religion a business and do not get at the real spiritual import. Today religion has become an industry and likewise a religion of outer forms and ceremonies, all without laying hold of the spiritual life.

- Truth teaches that the spiritual life comes first, and if there is any ceremony it is secondary. In this day people like to parade and light candles, etc. Let them first light the candle of Truth within their own souls. Then they will know what it is all about.
- Jesus , symbolizing the indwelling Christ, is talking to His multitude of receptive thoughts, (the multitude), and His spiritual helpers (the disciples).
- In referring to those who love the chief places at feasts and the chief seats in the synagogues, Jesus illustrated the effects of working in the outer instead of the within. The outer wants to be seen; to be honored in public; to be exalted in the eyes of others. The scribes and Pharisees loved to be honored, to be called, Rabbi—a title of respect and honor applied by the ancient Hebrews to their doctors and teachers. Jesus warned against thus receiving honor from men.
- We want continually to recognize the source from which we come and not be bound by any earthly ties in our spiritual unfoldment. "One is your Father, even God."
- We need to realize that we are all enrolled in Jesus Christ's school and that He is the Teacher. "One is your master, even Christ."
- Service and humility open the way to spiritual unfoldment. God (1010/ 1009) is the great Servitor, and the closer we live to Him and do His will the more we serve. If we are meek and lowly we unfold spiritually and develop, whereas if we exalt the personal ego, we fail.
- The scribes represent a faculty of mind that receives and transcribes upon the tablet of memory every wave of thought that touches the consciousness, whether from the flesh or from Spirit.
- The Pharisees were the religiously educated of Jesus' day, and to their minds all who claimed to do the work of the Lord were spurious unless they were members of the Pharisees cult. No matter how good the work of the outsider, the Pharisee always attributed it to an evil power.
- Moses represents the "thou shalt not" phase of the law. Jesus said to observe this, but He stressed the positive "thou shalt" rather than the negative.
- "They bind heavy burdens, grievous to be borne, and lay them on men's shoulders" means following the letter of the law without the illumination or quickening power of Spirit.
- Metaphysically interpreted, Rabbi represents a guiding, teaching thought in consciousness, of great prominence and influence, and belonging to the understanding faculty in man. One must be watchful that the thoughts belonging to the understanding faculty always recognize the true spiritual source of all wisdom and do not look to intellectual reasoning's for light on the various problems that are ever confronting one.

1012-1018.

Mat. 23:13-39

But woe unto you, scribes and Pharisees, hypocrites! because ye shut the kingdom of heaven against men: for ye enter not yourselves, neither suffer ye them that are entering to enter. Woe unto you, scribes and Pharisees, hypocrites! for ye devour widows' houses, even while for a pretense ye make long prayers: therefore ye shall receive greater condemnation.

Woe unto you, scribes and Pharisees, hypocrites! for ye compass sea and land to make one proselyte; and when he is become so, ye make him twofold more a son of hell than yourselves.

Woe unto you, ye blind guides, that say, Whosoever shall swear by the gold of the temple, he is a debter. Ye fools and bind: for which is greater, the gold or the temple that hath sanctified the gold? And, whosoever shall swear by the altar, it is nothing; but whosoever shall swear by the gift that is upon it, he is a debtor. Ye blind: for which is greater, the gift, or the altar that sanctifieth the gift? Ye therefore that sweareth by the altar, sweareth by it, and by all things thereon. And he that sweareth by the temple, sweareth by it, and by him that dwelleth therein. And he that sweareth by the throne of God, swear by the throne of God, and by him that sitteth thereon.

Woe unto you, scribes and Pharisees, hypocrites! for ye tithe mind and anise and cumin, and have left undone the weightier matters of the law, justice, and mercy, and faith: but those ye ought to have done, and not to have left the other undone. Ye blind, guides, that strain out the gnat, and swallow the camel!

Woe unto you, scribes and Pharisees, hypocrites! for ye cleanse the outside of the cup and of the platter, but within they are full from extortion and excess. Thou blind, Pharisee, cleanse first the inside of the cup and of the platter, that the outside thereof may become clean also.

Woe unto you, scribes and Pharisees, hypocrites! for ye are like unto whited sepulchers, which outwardly appear beautiful, but inwardly are full of dead men's bones, and of all uncleanness. Even so ye also outwardly appear righteous unto men, but inwardly ye are full of hypocrisy and iniquity. Woe unto you, scribes and Pharisees, hypocrites! for ye build the sepulchers of the prophets, and garnish the tombs of the righteous, and say, If we had been in the days of our fathers, we should not have been partakers with them in the blood of the prophets. Wherefore, ye witness to yourselves, that ye are sons of them that slew the prophets. Fill ye up them the measure of your fathers. Ye serpents, ye offspring of vipers, how shall ye escape the judgment of hell! Therefore, behold, I send unto you prophets, and wise men, and scribes: some of them shall ye kill and crucify; and some of them shall ye scourge in your synagogues, and persecute from city to city: that upon you may come all the righteous blood shed on the earth, from the blood of Abel the righteous unto the blood of Zachariah son of Harachiah, whom ye slew between the sanctuary and the altar. Verily I say unto you, All these things shall come upon this generation.

O Jerusalem, Jerusalem that killeth the prophets, and stoneth them that are sent unto her! How often would I have gathered thy children together, even as a hen gathereth her chickens under her wings, and ye would not! Behold, your house is left unto you desolate. For I say unto you, Ye shall not see me henceforth, till ye shall say, Blessed is he that cometh in the name of the Lord.

1019-1024.

Interpretation

• In this Scripture Jesus is pronouncing the penalty on one who is not complying with the spiritual law. He is making very clear that we reap as we sow. He is calling the attention of the Pharisees and the lawyers to the result of broken law. He is explaining that all in-harmonies and seeming limitations in the world are the result of man's error thinking, usually caused by personal dominance, selfishness, and greed.

• No doubt in the beginning the Pharisaical mind was endeavoring to follow the laws of Moses, but as this state of mind proceeds it makes the old laws become contaminated with personal ambitions until spiritual law is utterly ignored.

• In the seven woes Jesus refers to outer religious practices of His day. We have nothing today to compare with them. The people were hypnotized by outer forms and ceremonies and overlooked the real. They strained out the gnat, and swallowed the camel.

• Jesus called the scribes and Pharisees hypocrites because they thought their observance of ceremonies and rituals fulfilled the law.

• Jesus showed that those who follow the letter of the law shut the door to spiritual unfoldment. Those who practice the letter of religion set up standards and try to make others conform to them. This prevents the natural inflow of Spirit.

• In the Temple, there was first the court of the Gentiles, the outer court where people of every nation could gather and be in touch with spiritual life; but the Gentiles were not allowed to enter the inner court. Only those were permitted there who took religious vows. These two courts are representative of two states of mind.

• In orderly process of man's development there are certain conditions to be observed. The rabble from the outer court cannot enter the inner without purification. People who strive to enter without a mental cleansing, a change of mind, meet conditions worse than they had before.

• The ones who follow the letter of the law do not show mercy. They are hidebound, self-righteous, believing that they fulfill the law when they conform to outer practices such as tithing. They need to live the spiritual life and then the outer will take care of itself. Jesus was warning them of the many woes and sorrows that would come to them if they persisted in living the outward life and continued to turn a deaf ear to the inspiration of Spirit. Jesus wept because Jerusalem should have been a city of perfect peace instead of being infested with such thoughts.

• An altar represents the place in consciousness where we are willing to give up the lower to the higher, the personal to the impersonal, the animal to the divine. The true altar is the consciousness of the quickening of Spirit. It calls the attention to something that occurred two thousand years ago, and directs the mind from the true blessing. Proselytizing means to try to force your religion on other people. We know that people cannot be forced into accepting Truth. The soul has to unfold and lay hold of it.

1025

Mark 12:41-44

And he sat down over against the treasury, and beheld how the multitude cast money into the treasury; and many that were rich cast in much. And there came a poor widow, and she cast in two mites, which make a farthing.

And he called unto him his disciples, and said unto them Verily I say unto you, This poor widow cast in more than all they that are casting into the treasury: for they all did cast in of their superfluity; but she of her want did cast in all that she had, even all her living.

1026-1028

Interpretation

• The intellectually wise and intellectually rich thoughts in us like to make a show of giving. They may seem, through their arguments and reasoning's to impart much toward the maintenance of the body temple and the mentality's religious worship. But until the intellect is quickening by Spirit and comes under the instruction of true wisdom, its gifts do not really count for much.

• The affectional intuitive soul of the individual the woman is kept widowed and impoverished until divine wisdom in consciousness is unified with love. Then it gives according to the law of true giving. "She of her want did cast in all that she had, even all her living." She imparts all the substance of her love and her life; thus, her gift is made great, and it does much to enrich the entire man.

• It is also shown here that a gift is not measured by its amount or by its cost in money; it is measured by what it means to the one who gives it, by the love and substance and faith he puts into it. "Who gives himself with his alms feed three, Himself, his hungering neighbor, and me," is founded on the teaching of Christ.

1029-1034

Luke 21:2, 6

And as some spoke of the temple, how it was adorned with goodly stones and offerings, he said, As for these things which ye behold, the days shall come in which there shall not be left one stone upon another, that shall not be thrown down.

Mark 13:3-6

And as he sat on the mount of Olives over against the temple, Peter and James and John and Andrew asked him privately, Tell us, when shall these things be? And what shall be the sign when these things are all about to be accomplished? And Jesus began to say to them, Take heed that no man lead you astray. Many shall come in my name, saying, I am he; and shall lead them astray.

Luke 21:9-20

And when ye shall hear of wars and tumults, be not terrified; for these things must needs come to pass first; but the end is not immediately.

Then said he unto them, Nation shall rise against nation, and kingdom against kingdom; and there shall be great earthquakes, and in divers places famines and pestilences; and there shall be terrors and great signs from heaven. But before all these things, they shall lay hands on you, and shall persecute you, delivering you up to the synagogues and prisons, bringing you before kings and governors for my name's sake.

It shall turn out unto you for a testimony. Settle it therefore in your hearts, not to meditate beforehand how to answer: for I will give you a mouth and wisdom which all your adversaries shall not be able to withstand or to gainsay. But ye shall be delivered up even by parents, and brethren, and kinsfolk, and friends; and some of you shall they cause to be put to death. And ye shall be hated of all men for my name's sake. And not a hair of your head shall perish. In your patience ye shall win your souls. But when ye see Jerusalem compassed with armies, then know that her desolation is at hand.

Mark 13:14-27

But when ye see the abomination of desolation standing where he ought not let him that readeth understand, then let them that are in Judea flee unto the mountains: and let him that is on the housetop not go down, nor enter in, to take anything out of his house: and let him that is in the field not return back to take his cloak. But woe unto them that are with child and to them that give suck in those days! And pray that it be not in the winter. For those days shall be tribulation, such as there hath not been the like from the beginning of the creation which God created until now, and never shall be. And except the Lord had shortened the days, no flesh would have been saved; but for the elect's sake, whom he chose, he shortened the days. And then if any man shall say unto you, Lo, here is the Christ; or lo, there; believe it not: for there shall arise false Christ's and false prophets, and shall show signs and wonders, that they may lead astray, if possible, the elect. But take ye heed: behold, I have told you all things beforehand.

Mark 13:24-27

But in those days, after that tribulation, the sun shall be darkened, and the moon shall not give her light, and the stars shall be falling from heaven, and the powers that are in the heavens shall be shaken. And then shall they see the Son of man coming in the clouds with great power and glory. And then shall he send forth the angels, and shall gather together his elect from the four winds, from the uttermost part of the earth to the uttermost part of heaven.

1035-104?

Interpretation

• We look to this chapter both as a prophecy and symbology. The old is passing away and the new is being ushered in. Interpreted within ourselves a temple, as here referred to, represents material conditions, which Jesus taught would dissolve and disappear like a dream at the end of the age. No doubt today is the time to which He was looking forward. This whole chapter (Mark 13) refers to regeneration. At the same time it has its outer manifestation. Everything that takes place in the mind also expresses itself in outer changes. It pictures man in his many experiences on the journey from the human to the divine consciousness.

• Christ is Spirit and Christ is universal. Yet people are looking to the without, expecting the Christ to come again in a flesh-and-blood body. The truth is Christ is already here, seeking expression through man. It has taken 2000 years for man to begin to awaken to this truth and to lay hold of it. Until man does awaken there shall be wars and rumors of wars, nation shall rise against nation, and kingdom against kingdom, and there shall be famines and pestilences

• "Woe unto them that are with child and to them that give suck in those days!" refers to those who live under the law of generation. Anyone living under this law will meet with hazardous conditions. This is the age of regeneration.

• Spiritually interpreted, "those days" do not refer to some far off future date, but to man's own consciousness. When we are awakened to the truth about God and man, and begin to practice that truth, then our material consciousness is nearing its last days of existence. Every day is the "last day" of the old way of thinking and the "beginning" of the new day.

• It is up to us to see that we do not give birth to material thoughts, words, and actions. If we continue to "give suck" to grudges, fears, grief's, or inharmony of any kind, we are depriving ourselves of the infinite blessings which each day holds forth to us. We cannot enjoy its blessings unless we stop generating negative thoughts and beliefs, and instead regenerate ourselves in the way of Spirit.

• "And pray ye that it be not in the winter." Winter is a season of rest. At the time Jesus refers to we must be up and doing and not resting. There must be activity.

• "Great tribulation" means sacrifice, giving up things. Changes must take place in this present day. The old is passing away and the new coming in

- The "low here" and "low there" refers to the belief that the Christ will be found in this personality or that personality. The truth is that Christ must be found in you, and must be formed in humanity.
- When we have the power to keep the mind on Principle, refusing to be influenced by outer conditions then shall come the end.
- In order to discern that which is true from that which is false, we must live very close to Spirit, and seek the guidance of the Spirit of Truth moment by moment.
- "And except the Lord had shortened the days, no flesh would have been saved; but for the elect's sake, whom he chose, he shortened the days." We should deny time; realize that we must change our mind and work with the condition. We shorten the time by the realization that there is no reality in time, that all is in mind. Now is the time of salvation—that idea will hasten the salvation.
- "There shall arise false Christ's and false prophets, and shall show signs and wonders, that they may lead astray,, if possible, the elect." False Christ represent ideas in individual consciousness—ideas that are not true to principle, a mixture of Spirit with matter. These ideas endeavor to deceive our most elect thoughts. We have to take it under the light of Spirit and determine that which is true. The light of Spirit manifests as new light and new life.
- "The sun shall be darkened and the moon shall not give her light...and then shall they see the Son of man coming in clouds of great power and glory." This refers no doubt to the various experiences one goes through in regeneration. In passing from one step to another, the spiritual consciousness is darkened. The reason is that hitherto we have lived in our personal expression with Spirit and at this point there is an inrush of universal consciousness. This darkens the consciousness of even the spiritual person for a season. Eventually the spiritual man must come into consciousness and the person must be raised up.
- The Son of man is the spiritual presence, not personality. Jesus translated His body into spiritual substance and that spiritual substance is, in the regeneration, become like unto even a finer expression of life than electricity.
- "Then shall he send forth the angels, and shall gather together his elect from the four winds." Angels symbolize the universal spiritual thoughts; thoughts direct from Divine Mind whose nature draw to it the elect our chosen, spiritual thoughts. Where heretofore we have been getting spiritual information filtering through sense consciousness, now we will get it direct from God, as angels of light. Being gathered together "from the four winds" means from every direction. The east represents the within; the west, the manifest; the north, the cold intellect without the warmth of Spirit; and the south, life on the natural plane.
- Regeneration is the resurrection of the whole man, spirit, soul, and body, into the Christ consciousness. This is accomplished by the quickening power of the Holy Spirit. Those who are being raised in the Christ consciousness will gradually, as their growth in understanding makes it

possible, let go of all that is selfish and personal in their relationships and come into the larger love, the universal love, where all who do the will of God are love universal.

1046-1050.

Mark 13:28-37

Now from the fig tree learn her parable: when her branch is now become tender, and putteth forth its leaves, ye know that the summer is nigh; even so ye also, when ye see these things coming to pass, know ye that is nigh, even at the doors. Verily I say unto you, This generation shall not pass away, until all these things are accomplished. Heaven and earth shall pass away: but my words shall not pass away. But of that day or that hour knoweth no one, not even the angels in heaven, neither the Son, but the Father. Take ye heed, and pray: for ye know not when the time is. It is as when a man, sojourning in another country, having left his house, and given authority to his servants, to each one his work, commanded also the porter to watch. Watch therefore: for ye know not when the Lord of the house cometh, whether at even, or at midnight, or at cockcrowing, or in the morning; lest coming suddenly he find you sleeping. And what I say unto all, Watch.

Mat. 24:37-51

And as were the days of Noah, so shall be the coming of the Son of man. For as in those days which were before the flood they were eating and drinking, marrying and giving in marriage, until the day that Noah entered into the ark, and they knew not until the flood came and took them all away; so shall be the coming of the Son of man. Then shall two men be in the field; one is taken, and one is left: two women shall be grinding at the mill; one is taken, and one is left. Watch therefore: for ye know not on what day your Lord cometh. But know this, that if the master of the house had known in what watch the thief was coming, he would have watched, and would not have suffered his house to be broken through. Therefore be ye also ready; for in an hour that ye think not the Son of man cometh.

Who then is the faithful and wise servant, whom his Lord hath set over his household, to give them their food in due season? Blessed is that servant, whom his lord when he cometh shall find so doing. Verily I say unto you, that he will set him over all that he hath. But if that evil servant shall say in his heart, My lord tarrieth; and shall begin to beat his fellow-servants, and shall eat and drink with the drunken; the lord of that servant shall come in a day when he expecteth not, and in an hour when he knoweth not, and shall cut him asunder, and appoint his portion with the hypocrites: there shall be the weeping and gnashing of teeth.

Interpretation

•   Summer is a time of activity and growth. The "tender leaves of the fig tree" symbolize entering a new life consciousness. Outer activities that man has accounted so great are falling away. We come to know that the great change ahead of us is entering this new life consciousness.

•   Many changes are being brought about through the power of prayer, and each change is a decisive step in soul unfoldment from the mental to the divine plane of consciousness. This generation shall not pass away, until all these things be accomplished." A generation is a dispensation of spiritual power. Today we are approaching the end of the age or the end of a generation as Spirit measures a generation—which has nothing to do with a man's conception of time.

•   Through scientifically working with the law as Jesus did, man can make perfect union with God Mind. Then realizations are eternal. Jesus said His Word is from everlasting to everlasting. "Heaven and earth shall pass away, but my words shall not pass away."

•   The Lord is carrying forth His mighty work and He desires the perfect instrument through which to operate. Those who pray most, those who are established in spiritual consciousness, those who work from principle, are those who can demonstrate the power of the Word, and those who are going to be called upon to govern. They will be trusted to do the Lord's will and achieve spiritually. "Watch therefore: for ye know not when the Lord of the house cometh" and "find you sleeping." Some souls have attained a greater degree of unfoldment than others. Through man the Lord is continually sifting through all the nations of the earth, selecting choice seed for His planting, or for souls whom he can trust to carry forward His work. "Two men shall be in a field; one is taken, and one is left: two women shall be grinding at the mill; one is taken, and one is left."

1055-1056.

Mat. 25:1-13

Then shall the kingdom of heaven be likened unto ten virgins, who took their lamps, and went forth to meet the bridegroom. And five of them were foolish, and five were wise. For the foolish, when they took their lamps, took no oil with them: but the wise took oil in their vessels with their lamps. Now while the bridegroom tarried, they all slumbered and slept. But at midnight there is a cry, Behold, the bridegroom! Come ye forth to meet him.

Then all those virgins arose, and trimmed their lamps. And the foolish said unto the wise. Give us of your oil; for our lamps are going out. But the wise answered, saying, Peradventure there will not be enough for us, and you: go ye rather to them that sell, and buy for yourselves. And while they went away to buy, the bridegroom came; and they that were ready went in with him to the marriage feast: and the door was shut. Afterward came also the other virgins, saying, Lord, Lord, open to us. But he answered and said, Verily I say unto you, I know you not. Watch therefore, for ye know not the day nor the hour.

1057-1062

Interpretation

• The kingdom of heaven is a state of consciousness in which soul and body are in harmony with Divine Mind. This requires a building up of man along several lines; so Jesus brings many comparisons in his parables representing the kingdom of heaven.

• Those who have persistently looked for an outer coming, not having perceived His presence within themselves, and who have not gone through the inner preparation for the outer change, are likened to the foolish virgins who, when the bridegroom came, had no oil in their vessels for their lamps, so were not ready to go with him to the marriage feast.

• The ten virgins represent the senses. They are five in number, but they have a twofold action—five within and five without. The outer are connected with the inner, and both draw their supply from the same source. The eye has an inner eye, and the ear an inner ear. So feeling in the surface nerves is dependent upon centers of consciousness within. The supply of nerve force at the surface is proportioned to the completeness of contact with the inner center. This contact is made through consciousness, on the part of the individual, with the source of life and sensation. If we are not spiritually alert, the contact is broken and the oil in the outer lamp the eye, for example runs low and finally goes out. If this is extended to the whole five senses, there is a break all along the line, and when the Higher Consciousness seeks to make a union with the lower, there is nothing but darkness and dismay.

• To be prepared for this hour of union marriage, which may be consummated when we are consciously unaware of it, we should be on the watch and see to it that our lamps are being constantly supplied with oil. The coming of the bridegroom, which is the subtle joining of spirit, soul, and body is so deep in consciousness that we do not know when it takes place. We feel the result in a greater satisfaction and harmony, when we have been true in thought to the Spirit, and this is in reality the forming in us of the kingdom of heaven. This kingdom is built up in human consciousness day by day, or rather, degree by degree. Time is not a factor, but the right adjustment of thought and act to the Divine Law.

• The way to supply oil in the lamps of the foolish virgins is to affirm that the life source of Spirit in seeing, hearing, smelling, feeling, and tasting is not in material, but in spiritual understanding. This is absolute Truth which can be proved from even a so-called physical standpoint. The eye cannot see without the conscious comparison in thought of the images reflected into it. Thus sight is really mental, which is but another name for spiritual. The more fully we realize this, the better fed the eye is with that life force necessary to strong, clear sight. When we, through concentration on Spirit, make the union between each of the senses by which they are constantly supplied with the

Universal Life, our kingdom of heaven is established in that degree of unfoldment, and from this we go on to other and higher attainments.

1063-1066.

Mat. 25:14-30

For it is as when a man, going into another country, called his own servants, and delivered unto them this goods. And unto one he gave five talents, to another two, to another one; to each according to his several ability; and he went on his journey. Straightway he that received the five talents went and traded with them, and made other five talents. In like manner he also that received the two gained other two. But he that received the one went away and digged in the earth, and hid his lord's money. Now after a long time the lord of those servants cometh, and maketh a reckoning with them. And he that received the five talents came and brought other five talents, saying, Lord, thou deliveredest unto me five talents: Lo, I have gained other five talents. His lord said unto him, Well done, good and faithful servant: thou hast been faithful over a few things, I will set thee over many things; enter thou into the joy of thy lord. And he also that had received the one talent came and said, Lord, I knew that thou art a hard man, reaping where thou didst not sow, and gathering where thou didst not scatter; and I was afraid, and went away and hid thy talents in the earth; lo, thou hast thine own. But his lord answered and said unto him, Thou wicked and slothful servant, thou knewest that I reap where I sowed not, and gather where I did not scatter; thou oughtest therefore to have put my money to the bankers, and at my coming I should have received back mine own with interest. Take ye away therefore the talent from him, and give it unto him that hath the ten talents. For unto every one that hath shall be given, and he shall have abundance; but from him that hath not, even that which he hath shall be taken away. And cast ye out the unprofitable servant into the outer darkness: there shall be the weeping and the gnashing of teeth.

1067-1071.

Interpretation

•	This Scripture shows how the soul increases its capacity to know Divine Mind. We are the offspring of that Mind, but we must acquire self-consciousness, with all that it implies.

•	Involved in us is the capacity to evolve or bring forth divinity. This Divine Mind is the man who delivered his goods unto his servants and went into a "far country." The talents are capacities and evolution is their increase.

•	The five talents also represent the five senses. The senses are fundamentally spiritual, and the increase is the realization of this in consciousness. Before we can see truly, our sight must be increased until spiritual perception is developed. Then our sight is established. This is true of hearing, feeling, tasting, and smelling. The five avenues of expression are to be under the dominion of Divine Mind, and their reality proven and demonstrated.

• It is a fact that the unregenerate man or woman is ignorant of the rea character of the senses. To such the eye is a telescope and the ear a telephone Explain that it is the mind that hears and sees, and they are the incredulous. In the regeneration these facts are made plain to the individual and he learns the law of mind increase. This is the gain in the talents, which was commended by the Lord.

• Those who do not understand how to increase their mental and spiritual capacity through right thought are in danger of timidity and cautiousness.

• The fear that they will do wrong has made cowards and incompetents of millions. It is better to make mistakes than to remain inactive. The world full of people who have carefully put their talent in a napkin and buried it. They are more or less bitter because others have succeeded while they have failed. The cause of failure is not incapacity, but comes from failure to use the capacity one has. Potential capacity is really all that man possesses, until he has made his talents his very own by opening up their inner side. This is the increase that pleases the Lord, and that servant is put at the right hand.

• It looks like a hard law that would take away from a man that which he seems to have, because he fails to increase it. But such must be the condition of the slothful servant. If the potential talents are not regenerated by the individual, they are lost to consciousness. Thus the Lord takes away from the fearfully cautious servant the potential seeing or hearing, and he is left in total darkness.

1072-107!

Mat. 25:31-46

But when the Son of man shall come in his glory, and all the angels with him, then shall he sit on the throne of glory: and before him shall be gathered all the nations: and he shall separate them one from another, as the shepherd separateth the sheep from the goats; and he shall set the sheep on his right hand, but the goats on his left. Then shall the King say unto them or his right hand, Come, ye blessed of my Father, inherit the kingdom prepared for you from the foundation of the world: for I was hungry, and ye gave me to eat; I was thirsty, and ye gave me to drink; I was a stranger, and ye took me in; naked, and ye clothed me; I was sick, and ye visited me; I was in prison, and ye came unto me.

Then shall the righteous answer him, saying, Lord, when saw we thee hungry, and fed thee? or athirst, and gave thee drink? or naked, and clothed thee? and when saw we thee sick, or in prison, and came unto thee? And the King shall answer and say un to them, Verily I say unto you, Inasmuch as ye did it unto one of these my brethren, even these least, ye did it unto me. Ther shall he say also unto them on the left hand, Depart from me, ye cursed, into the eternal fire which is prepared for the devil and his angels: for I was hungry, and ye did not give me to eat; I was thirsty, and ye gave me no drink;

was a stranger, and ye took me not in; naked, and ye clothed me not; sick, and in prison, and ye visited me not.

Then shall they also answer, saying, Lord, when saw we thee not. Then shall they also answer, saying Lord, when saw we thee hungry, or athirst, or a stranger, or naked, or sick, or in prison, and did not minister unto thee? Then shall he answer them, saying, Verily I say unto you, Inasmuch as ye did it not unto one of these least, ye did it not unto me. And these shall go away into eternal punishment: but the righteous into eternal life.

Luke 21:37-38

And every day he was teaching in the temple; and every night he went out, and lodged in the mount that is called Olivet. And all the people came early in the morning to him in the temple, to hear him.

1076-1081.

Interpretation

• The Son of God is Christ, the Divine Idea Man. The Son of man is Adam, the manifestation of Christ, the Lord God. When it dawns upon the Son of man that he is in reality the Son of God, a higher consciousness is born in him; he rules instead of being ruled. This symbolically pictured: "the Son of man shall sit on the throne of his glory."

• When the light of divine understanding begins to shine in consciousness the "glory" causes a quickening of the discrimination. The Truth is the standard and all motives, thoughts, and acts that do not chord therewith are denied, and those that do, affirmed. This is the separation symbolized by the division of sheep and goats.

• The belief that a great day of judgment at some future time was here prophesied by the Lord, still holds with many Christians, but one of the foremost orthodox Bible commentators says in a recent work, "That there is a day of judgment is a fact, but it is difficult, and not so important, to decide the exact nature or time of the coming of the Lord to judgment." It is said Matt. 24 that "This generation shall not pass away till all these things be accomplished," and it is not profitable to discuss for a moment any other meaning. The kingdom inherited from the foundation of the world is the kingdom within, which Jesus referred to when he located heaven.

• Jesus taught that service was the test of value. "He that is greatest among you, let him serve." In every department of life we find that the things that best serve us are considered most valuable. This is true in the mechanical, the moral, and the intellectual world. In choosing between the emotions and thoughts upon which human consciousness, and all that comes out of it, is founded, we should make service the standard.

• First of all, man should not be servant of appetite, passion, or thought, but these should all serve him and minister to him. The righteous servants of mind and body should be given greater power, because they minister in all ways to man while he is yet bound in sense consciousness. The body is built and sustained by the serving forces of nature, and in every function of the organism they are clothing, feeding, healing, and giving life and strength to mind and body. All this is being done without thought that they are building a temple for the soul. When the Higher Self comes into dominion and recognizes the service of these silent workers, they are surprised at being set at the right hand, and are told that when they served the body, which is brother of the mind, they were at the same time serving the Christ.

• The goats, the adverse states of thought, are sent into the "age-abiding fire," as translated by Rotherham. This implies purification, but not necessarily punishment. But there is disappointment, and to the "unprofitable servant," "wailing and gnashing of teeth."

1082.

Mat. 26:1-5

And it came to pass, when Jesus had finished all these words, he said unto his disciples, Ye know that after two days the passover cometh , and the Son of man is delivered up to be crucified. Then were gathered together the chief priests, and the elders of the people, unto the court, of the high priest, who was called Caiaphas; and they took counsel together that they might take Jesus by subtlety, and kill him. But they said, Not during the feast, lest a tumult arise among the people.

1083.

Interpretation

• The Passover symbolizes the passing over from one state of consciousness to another, preparing for a great awakening. Formerly in the Passover feast a lamb was offered up as a sacrifice. In this Scripture we readily recognize that Jesus Himself is the great sacrifice.
• When a new spiritual unfoldment, here represented by the Christ, takes the higher intellectual consciousness, symbolized by Caiaphas and his followers, plot to do away with this spiritual power.

1084-1085.

Mark 14:3-9

And while he was in Bethany in the house of Simon the leper, as he sat at meat, there came a woman having an alabaster cruse of ointment of nard very costly; and she brake the cruse, and poured it over his head. But there were some that had indignation among themselves, saying, To what purpose hath this waste of the ointment been made? For this ointment might have been sold for above three hundred shillings, and given to the poor. And they murmured against her.

But Jesus said, Let her alone; why trouble ye her? She hath wrought a good work on me. For ye have the poor always with you , and whenever ye will ye can do them good: but me ye have not always. She hath done what she could; she hath anointed my body beforehand for burying. And verily I say unto you, Wheresoever the gospel shall be preached throughout the whole world, that also which this woman hath done shall be spoken of for a memorial for her.

1086.

Interpretation

• The substance of Love's sympathy infuses hope and faith into the discouraged soul. Understanding alone is cold and indifferent. It must have the precious, fragrant ointment of love poured out upon it.

• When Jesus went to Bethany He realized the fruit or effect of raising Lazarus--that is, quickening certain sleeping energies in his subconsciousness *(subconscious – Ed.)*. This realization is a feast to the soul—a filling of the whole man with a sense of satisfaction.

• The anointing of Jesus' feet by "the woman having an alabaster cruse of ointment of pure nard" represents the willingness of love to serve. This is a lesson of great import to metaphysicians because the tendency is to concentrate upon the understanding and count its logic and cold reason as fulfilling the law. But we learn by experience that the cold science of mind, without the warmth of the heart, is a very chilly doctrine.

• An eminent metaphysician once said that she observed in her experience of fifteen years among those who were putting the doctrine into practice, that those who were self-sufficient and exacting, those who were narrow and bigoted, those who were penurious and stingy, those who were cold and indifferent to the needs of their fellows, those who were critical and condemnatory—all of them became more so where they cultivated the science as a doctrine based upon understanding alone. The flood gates of love must be opened in the soul and its precious, fragrant ointment poured out upon the understanding. This fills the whole house, or body, with a balm and odor that heals and blesses all.

1089.

Luke 22:3-4a,b

And Satan entered into Judas who was called Iscariot, being of the number of the twelve. And he went away, and communed with the chief priests and captains, and said, What are ye willing to give me, and I will deliver him unto you? And they weighed unto him thirty pieces of silver. And from that time he sought opportunity to deliver him unto them.

Interpretation

•   Among our disciples, or faculties, is one whose tendency is such that through it we are brought into condemnation and suffering. This one is known from the first; it is Judas—self-appropriation.

•   Judas was the treasurer of the disciples of Jesus, but he became covetous Satan entered into him and his sin brought tragedy. Judas represents the unredeemed life forces which are a thief and a destroyer and a betrayer. They deliver up Jesus for gratification of flesh desire thirty pieces of silver. As in the days of Jesus, so it is today—misuse of the life faculty is deceiving the whole world and even metaphysicians who are free in every other way are bound by its false reasoning.

Luke 22:7-13

And the day of unleavened bread came on which the Passover must be sacrificed. And he sent Peter and John, saying, Go and make ready for us the Passover, that we may eat. And they said unto him, Where wilt thou that we make ready? And he said unto them, Behold, when ye are entered into the city, there shall meet you a man bearing a pitcher of water; follow him into the house where into he goeth. And ye shall say unto the master of the house, The Teacher saith unto thee, Where is the guest-chamber, where I shall eat the passover with my disciples? And he will show you a large upper room furnished: there make ready. And they went, and found as he had said unto them: and they made ready the passover.

Interpretation

•   The feast of unleavened bread, or the passover, was in commemoration of the escape of the first born of Israel, when the angel of death passed over. The door-posts had blood sprinkled on them, which sign the Lord saw and passed them by.

•   The "first born" in consciousness is I—self-identity. In its ignorance Egypt, it does not know that it is immortal, and seems to go down when the thought, or angel, of death passes over. In the Is real state it proclaims life—sprinkles blood on its doorposts.

•   Jesus came to proclaim a new and stronger influx of life: "I am come that ye might have life, and have it more abundantly." Sin is "missing the mark," falling short in expressing God's ideas of ourselves. If death and suffering are part of our experience, it is self-evident that we have not eaten the passover with Jesus.

•   The metaphysician always remembers that the passover represents an overcoming or a passing over from one state of consciousness to another. In the experiences of Jesus and His disciples the passover had to do with an outpouring of the Holy Spirit, and where they attained a high state of mind by concentrating continually upon spiritual things. After a feast of this character, the mind and the heart reach out only for heavenly things and we realize that God is truly the one and the only power.

•   The man with the pitcher of water symbolizes the sign whereby the disciples were to know they had contacted the spiritual power that would guide them to the upper room furnished which Jesus had ordered made ready for the Holy Communion.

1098.

Luke 22:14-16

And when the hour was come, he sat down, and the apostles with him. And he said unto them, With desire I have desired to eat this passover with you before I suffer; for I say unto you, I shall not eat it, until it be fulfilled in the kingdom of God. And as they were eating, he said, Verily I say unto you, that one of you shall betray me. And they were exceeding sorrowful, and began to say unto very one, Is it I, Lord? And he answered and said, He that dipped his hand with me in the dish, the same shall betray me. The son of man goeth, even as it is written of him: but woe unto that man through whom the Son of man is betrayed! Good were it for that man if he had not been born. And Judas, who betrayed him, answered and said, Is it I, Rabbi? He saith unto him, Thou hast said.

1100-1101.

Interpretation

•   "The hand of him that betrayeth me is one the table" refers to Judas, the custodian of life. He represents the unredeemed life forces. He also typifies that in humanity which, though it has caught the higher vision of life, still resorts to underhanded methods in order to meet its obligations.

•   In its highest office the life faculty is spiritual; introverted in human consciousness it becomes acquisitiveness Judas. It is through the exercise of this faculty that suffering and crucifixion are brought about. It is the faculty that draws to us the substance of things. In essence it is good, but in its personal sense "it had been good for that man if he had not been born."

•   In our present state, Judas could not be excluded from the twelve. He carries the bag, he is the treasurer of our system, a thief also. He is selfish, proud, ambitious, tyrannical. But he cannot be spared. The secret of overcoming his faults is to first point them out fearlessly—"Is it I?" "It is one of the twelve, he that dippeth with me in the dish."

Mat. 26:26a

And as they were eating, Jesus took bread, and blessed, and brake it; and he gave to the disciples, and said, Take, eat;

Luke 22:19b

This is the body which is given for you: this do in remembrance of me.

Mat. 26:27-29

And he took a cup, and gave thanks, and gave to them, saying, Drink ye all of it; for this is my blood of the covenant, which is poured out for many unto remission of sins. But I say unto you, I shall not drink henceforth of this fruit of the vine, until that day when I drink it new with you in my Father's kingdom.

Interpretation

• The orthodox church celebrates the "Holy Communion" by taking a wafer and a sip of wine. This outer service affirms they have drunk of the blood and have eaten of the body of Jesus. To the spiritual metaphysician communion is a far more intricate procedure. The first step in drinking of the blood and eating of the body of Jesus is to resolve this whole Scripture back into the primal ideas. The blood has back of it the idea of life, and the body has back of it the idea of substance.

• The only way to appropriate these ideas is through the very highest activity of the mind. As a race, we have settled down until we have become crystallized, until out flesh is a mere crust. We should have electrical bodies, fluid bodies, bodies of radiant substance.

• Through spiritual realization, through spiritual regeneration, and through scientific prayer Jesus Christ attained this. Through this process He was constantly renewed by the renewing of the mind. Through Jesus' experience on the cross where His precious blood was spilled, He lowered His body to that of the race, thereby enabling Him to administer to the race a blood transfusion, to implant in both soul and body the seed of life eternal here and now, the seed of divine substance.

• Jesus Christ broadcast the electrons of His blood, also the electrons of His body, into the whole race thought- atmosphere, and today they may be apprehended by all seeking souls, by all those who have faith in Jesus Christ.

• Today in all of those who are appropriating these electrons they are becoming centers of energy and substance. Through silent realization we are laying hold of a new life germ and a new substance germ which gives to the blood a new energy and to the body a new radiation. Thus we are beginning t lay hold of the definite idea of a radiant body-temple composed of the pure substance of Spirit. In order to drink of the blood and eat of the body of Jesus Christ we must take the idea of blood, which is life, and the idea of the body, which is substance, into the silence and clothe these ideas with realizations of life and substance. We must realize that each of these ideas is a magnet functioning in omnipresence, which we may appropriate to our heart's content.

• Let go of the idea that you can personally possess even the life and substance of your organism. They are of the universal, and must be given up "for the remission of sins." When this place of absolute renunciation of all is attained there rushes into consciousness a new relation; the fruit of the vine of infinite life is drunk anew in every faculty "in my Father's kingdom."

1109-1110.

Luke 22:24-30

And there arose also a contention among them, which of them was accounted to be greatest. And he said unto them, The kings of the Gentiles have lordship over them; and they that have authority over them are called Benefactors. But ye shall not be so: but he that is the greater among you, let him become as the younger; and he that is chief, as he that doth serve. For which is greater, he that sitteth at meat, or he that serveth? is not he that sitteth at meat? But I am in the midst of you as he that serveth. But ye are they that have continued with me in my temptations; and I appoint unto you a kingdom, even as my Father appointed unto me, that ye may eat and drink at my table in my kingdom; and ye shall sit on thrones judging the twelve tribes of Israel.

1111-1112.

Interpretation

• The disciples had gone a long way in spiritual unfoldment, but the personal ego had not been fully redeemed. This is proved by the contention among them as to who was the greatest. The wise metaphysician recognizes God as the great Servitor and that man is great only as he opens his soul to Spirit and takes on spiritual qualities. Gradually he comes to know that the disciple who frees himself from the limitations of the mortal and allows the unselfishness and the beauty of Christ to express freely is greatest in the kingdom. Jesus who became the Christ expressed perfectly God Mind. The twelve tribes of Israel always refer to the twelve faculties established on the throne of dominion, which proves fulfillment of spiritual law.

1113-1114.

Mark 14:26-30a

And when they had sung a hymn, they went out unto the Mount of Olives. And Jesus saith unto them, All ye shall be offended: for it is Written, I will smite the shepherd, and the sheep shall be scattered abroad. How be it, after I am raised up, I will go before you into Galilee. But Peter said unto him, Although all shall be offended, yet will not I. And Jesus saith unto him,

Luke 22:31-34

Simon, Simon, behold, Satan asked to have you, that he might sift you as wheat: but I made supplication for thee, that thy faith fail not; and do thou, when once thou hast turned again, establish they brethren. And he said unto him, Lord, with thee I am ready to go both to prison and to death. And he said, I tell thee, Peter, the cock shall not crow this day, until thou shalt thrice deny that thou knowest me.

1115-1116.

Interpretation

• The development of faith (Peter) is portrayed in the life of Jesus in conjunction with all the other faculties (disciples). All the faculties are bound together, and when one ails there is uncertainty and weakness in all. When the conservator of life (Judas) proves disloyal, the whole body is weakened. The context recites that all the disciples fell away after the arrest of Jesus. The life center sustains the substance, which permeates the spinal cord like a column of mercury in a tube.

• When the sustaining support in the life center is withdrawn the sustenance of every faculty is weakened. This is especially true of faith, whose center of action is in the head. The central I AM, (Jesus) sees this and is prepared for the confusion and scattering of His disciples; hence His statement to Peter that he would deny Him three times before the cock crew.

1117.

Luke 22:35-38

And he said unto them, When I sent you forth without purse, and wallet, and shoes, lacked ye anything? And they said, nothing. And he said unto them, But now, he that hath a purse, let him take it, and likewise a wallet; and he that hath none, let him sell his cloak, and buy a sword. For I say unto you, that this which is written must be fulfilled in me, And he was reckoned with transgressors: for that which concerneth me hath fulfillment. And they said, Lord, is enough.

1118-1119.

Interpretation

• You will observe that this chapter is a direct contradiction of the tenth chapter of Matthew, in which Jesus sent forth His disciples without purse, or script or wallet or shoes or anything except the word of God, and we wonder why this paradox. Why didn't He send out representatives with supreme faith in the power of the Spirit instead of telling them to arm themselves, to take shoes and wallet and even two swords? Why this contradiction?

• We are told that circumstances alter cases. Jesus didn't base His doctrine on circumstances. He based it on states of mind. As we study the situation, we find that there is an entirely different mental attitude on the part of those disciples when he sent them forth in faith and in spiritual understanding. This episode immediately followed James' and John' quarrel as to who should be first in the kingdom of Jesus. A warring spirit is met with a warring spirit in the world; therefore Jesus took two different attitudes for demonstrating, depending upon the states of mind of His representatives.

CHAPTER 5

GETHSEMANE

1120-1122.

Mark 14:32-40

And they come unto a place which was named Gethsemane: and he saith unto his disciples, Sit ye here, while I pray. And he taketh with him Peter and James and John, and began to be greatly amazed, and sore troubled. And he saith unto them, My soul is exceeding sorrowful even unto death: abide ye here, and watch. And he went forward a little, and fell on the ground, and prayed that, if it were possible, the hour might pass away from him. And he said, Abba, Father, all things are possible unto thee; remove this cup from me: howbeit Not what I will, but what thou wilt. And he cometh, and findeth them sleeping, and saith unto Peter, Simon, sleepest thou? couldest thou not watch one hour? Watch and pray, that ye enter not into temptation: the spirit indeed is willing, but the flesh is weak. And again he went away, and prayed, saying the same words. And again he came, and found them sleeping, for their eyes were heavy; and they knew not what to answer him.

Luke 22:43-44

And there appeared unto him an angel from heaven, strengthening him. And being in an agony he prayer more earnestly; and his sweat became as it were great drops of blood falling down upon the ground.

Mark 14:41-42

And he cometh the third time, and saith unto them, Sleep on now, and take your rest: it is enough; the hour is come; behold, the Son of man is betrayed into the hands of sinners. Arise, let us be going: behold, he that betrayeth me is at hand.

1123-1125.

Interpretation

• The name Gethsemane means "oil press," "press for extracting unguents and ointments." A press is an emblem of trial, distress, agony, while oil points to Spirit and illumination. Gethsemane represents the struggle of the soul when it recognizes that God is all, and man must be willing to sacrifice all for God.

• The Christ consciousness meets much opposition in its attempt to incorporate itself in human mentality. The body and its thoughts are very material and have but slight concept of spiritual things. The task of lifting up the soul that is sunk in sense is prodigious, and the Christ mind realizes this fact.

• The disciples of Jesus who followed Him represent the various faculties of mind—faith, judgment, and love not yet awakened to the presence of the higher self. This quickening Spirit is active while the man of sense sleeps, but there would be much more rapid development if the mind of the personal man could be kept awake. In this sleep of sense, the soul and body are negative and they absorb all kinds of error thoughts. Hence the words of Jesus: "Why sleep ye? rise and pray, that ye enter not into temptation."

• The various experiences which Jesus had represent the phases of mind through which every man passes who puts on Christ. These experiences may be repeated daily for years; they will be repeated until the mortal consciousness is completely regenerated.

1126-112?

Mark 14:43-44

And straightway, while he yet spoke, cometh Judas, one of the twelve and with him a multitude with swords and staves, from the chief priests and the scribes and the elders. Now he that betrayed him had given them a token saying, Whomsoever I shall kiss, that is he; take him, and lead him away safely.

Mat. 26:49-55a

And straightway he came to Jesus and said, Hail, Rabbi; and kissed him. And Jesus said unto him, Friend, do that for which thou art come. Then they came and laid hands on Jesus, and took him. And behold, one of them that were with him stretched out his hand, and drew his sword, and smote the servant of the high priest, and struck off his ear. Then saith Jesus unto him, Put up again thy sword into its place: for all they that take the sword shall perish with the sword. Or thinkest thou that I cannot beseech my Father, and he shall even now send me more than twelve legions of angels? How then should the scriptures be fulfilled, that thus it must be? In that hour said Jesu to the multitudes, Are ye come out as against a robber with swords and staves to seize me?

Luke 22:53

When I was daily with you in the temple, ye stretched not forth your hands against me: but this is your hour, and the power of darkness.

Mat. 26:56

but all this is come to pass, that the scriptures of the prophets might be fulfilled. Then all the disciples left him and fled.

1129-113?

Interpretation

• This Scripture instructs us in two ways: First, as an illustration of the action and reaction of mind and body; and second, as the cause of lapse of faith.

- The "certain one" who struck off the ear of the servant of the high priest is identified as Peter in John 18:10. Your faith Peter in the righteousness of your cause may lead you to combat the thoughts of the ruling religious powers, and in your impetuosity you resent their counsel and deny their capacity to receive Truth cut off the right ear, but good judgment and the broad comprehension of the divine overcoming through which you are passing will cause you to adopt pacific means.
- Regeneration is an educational process. The faculties are like children at school. The head instructor is I'AM, represented by Jesus. He cannot force this faculties to conform to the divine law, but through a process of thought culture he can make them wise and powerful. Jesus would not through sheer will make Judas do right, because he knew that was not the true way to develop His powers. Man must understand the law, then he will always keep it.
- A propensity is bound by the will and forced into certain channels, it will eventually break out and go wild, because it has no foundation in understanding. This explains why Jesus allowed His disciples to do many unrighteous things which, with
- The soul suffers and struggles when it sees the necessity of giving up its human ambitions, its hates, and its desire for revenge, as well as human idols. There are deeply rooted thoughts stored away in the subconsciousness *(subconscious – Ed.)* and on their own they come forward to crucify the new unknown power, the so-called imposter, the indwelling Christ.
- The Christ is captured by these forces which proceed to carry out the process in the darkness of the subconscious mind. This is the betrayal that leads to mental and physical crucifixion. When man allows sense selfishness to rule in the body, the door is opened to enemies of many kinds and the life essence of the organism is dissipated. When this occurs there is lack of nerve force, and confusion ensues. Faith is not at heart recreant or disloyal to the Christ, but lapses from its fount of expression because of lack of substance. The Christ may be held in obscurity for a while, but it cannot be done away with. That which died on the cross when Jesus was crucified was personality— the Christ resurrects itself from the very depths of the subconsciousness *(subconscious – Ed.).*
- The betrayal of Jesus into the hands of the multitude is a picture of the way in which the spiritual life imparted by the higher self is captured by the lower forces and subjected to indignities foreign to its nature. But as long as the predominating desires of the soul are on the sense plane, the betrayal of Jesus will follow every descent of His Spirit into consciousness. Thus the experience in Gethsemane may take place again and again. Every time we allow the life and the substance which we have received Spirit to be pressed into sense ideas and used on the material plane, we are giving Jesus into the hands of his enemies.
- Mind and body being one in essence, man must be considered as a unit. Mind acts upon body, and body reacts upon mind. Body must therefore

do its part in sustaining the unity of the law. If it falls in any particular it is untrue to its Higher Self, the Christ.

•   The remedy is: Declare that the Spirit of the Christ in you is not subject to the law of the flesh, but to the law of God. This attitude if maintained, will keep spiritual life and substance inviolate.

1136.

Mark 14:51-52

And a certain young man followed with him, having a linen cloth cast about him, over his naked body: and they lay hold on him; but he left the linen cloth, and fled naked.

1137.

Interpretation

•   The certain young man referred to here symbolizes a spiritual thought that would show grace and mercy toward all, but which does not prove stable in the face of the great overcoming.

1138-1139.

Mat. 26:57-64

And they that had taken Jesus led him away to the house of Caiaphas the high priest, where the scribes and the elders were gathered together. But Peter followed him afar off, unto the court of the high priest, and entered, and sat with the officers, to see the end. Now the chief priests and the whole council sought false witness against Jesus, that they might put him to death; and they found it not, though many false witnesses came. But afterward came two, and said, This man said, I am able to destroy the temple of God, and to build it in three days.

And the high priest stood up, and said unto him, Answerest thou nothing? what is it which these witness against thee? But Jesus held his peace. And the high priest said unto him, I adjure thee by the living God, that thou tell us whether thou art the Christ, the Son of God. Jesus saith unto him, Thou hast said: nevertheless I say unto you, Henceforth ye shall see the Son of man sitting at the right hand of Power, and coming on the clouds of heaven.

1140-1143.

Interpretation

•   The priests, the scribes, and the elders represent the highest intellectual thoughts in man's consciousness. They are the originators of all creeds and dogmas, and strictly follow the letter of the law. Since the intellectual plane of consciousness thinks it is the highest it is jealous of any force that threatens to uproot it or to hinder it in any way. Hence they would kill out spiritual consciousness represented by Jesus. The multitude symbolizes the mob thought on the intellectual plane.

•   It is necessary that the Christ be tested and tried in every department of the Mind. He is a new life essence, which includes all that goes to make a new man, a new body. The old religious thought has been that the body must die, and when a "new commandment" is given it is resisted. The temple represents the consciousness of body, and the three days represent three unfoldments in mind power. The body is made and sustained by the mind—it is ideas pressed into visibility. These ideas are established in subconsciousness *(subconscious – Ed.)*, and have to be met and changed by the Christ before the work can be done. The proposition that the body can be destroyed and again rebuilt in three days, seems, to the thoughts that have seen it so long in the clutches of the material law, absurd and preposterous.

•   The two false witnesses that are finally produced are not here identified, but we who have had experience readily locate them as external sight and feeling. These both deceive us into believing that material things are real and spiritual things intangible. We find ourselves almost unconsciously doubting the ability of the new life in Christ to build a new body.

•   This all means that our religious thoughts and opinions try the Christ consciousness, and certain opposition exists, which seeks to kill the new life, even though it be done through false charges.

1144.

Mat. 26:65-68

Then the high priest rent his garment, saying, He hath spoken blasphemy: what further need have we of witnesses? Behold, now ye have heard the blasphemy: what think ye? They answered and said, He is worth of death.

Then did they spit in his face and buffet him: and some smote him with the palms of their hands, saying, Prophesy unto us, thou Christ: who is he that struck thee.

1145-1146.

Interpretation

•   The high intellectual thoughts symbolized by the high priests claim to be Truth. We may know a great deal about Truth with our intellects , but when something comes that is beyond our understanding and we have to accept it on faith, we often put aside Truth. Spitting in Jesus' face and buffeting Him symbolizes utter disapproval and contempt of the spiritual man.

•   When a purely spiritual thought is trying to replace an intellectual thought, it meets opposition on some ground or other. A leading significance of blasphemy is a tendency to think we can go too far in spiritualizing our thoughts and their environment.

Mark 14:66-68

And as Peter was beneath in the court, thee cometh one of the maids of the high priest; and seeing Peter warming himself, she looked upon him, and saith, Thou also was with the Nazarene, even Jesus. But he denied, sayin I neither know, nor understand what thou sayest: and he went out into the porch; and the cock crew.

Mat. 26:71-74

And when he was gone out into the porch, another maid saw him, an saith unto them that were there, This man also was with Jesus of Nazarath. And again he denied with an oath, I know not the man. And after a little whil they that stood by came and said to Peter, Of a truth thou also art one of them; for thy speech maketh thee known. Then began he to curse and to swear, I know not the man. And straightway the cock crew.

Luke 22:61-62

And the Lord turned, and looked upon Peter. And Peter Remembere the word of the Lord, how that he said unto him, Before the cock crow this da thou shalt deny me thrice. And he went out, and wept bitterly.

1149-1150

Interpretation

• Changeable faith is the leading characteristic of Peter, before he is firmly established in spiritual consciousness. When our faith is not yet established so that we hold firmly to Truth in the face of great opposition, we fall from our high standard. Everything at the moment indicated that Jesus was a failure and a fraud. Peter's action revealed how our faith is often tempted to waver when we face alarming situations, adversity, and persecutions. We go along with the popular trend instead of being faithful to the Christ.

• Until faith within us is identified with the Christ, we find that it is extremely vacillating. It will in all sincerity affirm its allegiance to Spirit, and in the hour of adversity will deny that it ever knew Spirit. As a result many times we weep bitterly.

1151-1152

Mat. 27:3-10

Then Judas, who betrayed him, when he saw that he was condemned repented himself, and brought back the thirty pieces of silver to the chief priests and elders, saying, I have sinned in that I betrayed innocent blood. Bu they said, What is that to us? see thou to it. And he cast down the pieces of silver into the sanctuary, and departed: and he went away and hanged himself.

And the chief priests took the pieces of silver, and said, It is not lawful to put them into the treasury, since it is the price of blood. And they took counsel, and bought with them the potter's field, to bury strangers in. Wherefore that field was called, The field of blood, unto this day. Then was fulfilled that which was spoken through Jeremiah the prophet, saying, And they took the thirty pieces of silver, the price of him that was priced, whom certain of the children of Israel did price; and they gave them for the potter's field, as the Lord appointed me.

1153-1155.

Interpretation

• Judas, the last disciple Jesus called, symbolizes desire, appropriation, acquisitiveness. Exercised in its natural realm the free essence of being, it draws to man the supplies of the universe, and through it man enters into permanent possession. But when under the dominion of the intellect it oversteps the law, it becomes a destroyer. This brings about tragedy. Judas killed himself.

• The potter's field was called "the field of blood" because it was bought with the money of betrayal, which led to the shedding of Jesus' precious blood. The potter's field represents the place in consciousness where we bury all dead, negative, impoverished thought forces.

• The potter's field also pertains to the redeeming blood of Jesus Christ. Jesus lowered His consciousness to that of the race and spilled His blood in order to sow the seed of eternal life into the race consciousness.

• The thirty pieces of silver represent the negative side—a bribe—a price that was paid to influence Judas to corruption. In this instance, the intellectual thoughts in authority, are attempting to get into their power the spiritual forces in order to destroy them.

• Jeremiah always looked on the dark side of things. This also represents negation—that which is not true. Part of the time the natural man ridicules this side of consciousness and again he thinks it is real.

CHAPTER 6

CRUCIFIXION

1156-1158.

Mat. 27:1-2

Now when morning was come, all the chief priests and the elders of the people took counsel against Jesus to put him to death: And they bound him, and led him away, and delivered him up to Pilate the governor.

Luke 23:2-12

And they begin to accuse him, saying, We found this man perverting our nation, and forbidding to give tribute to Caesar, and saying that he is Christ a king. And Pilate asked him, saying, Art thou the king of the Jews? And he answered him and said, Thou sayest. And Pilate said unto the chief priests and the multitudes, I find no fault in this man. But they were more urgent, saying, He stirreth up the people, teaching throughout all Judaea, and beginning from Galilee even unto this place. But when Pilate heard it, he asked whether the man were a Galilean. And when he heard that he was of Herod's jurisdiction, he sent him unto Herod, who himself also was at Jerusalem in these days.

Now when Herod saw Jesus, he was exceeding glad: for he was of a long time desirous to see him, because he had heard concerning him; and he hoped to see some miracle done by him. And he questioned him in many words; but he answered him nothing. And the chief priests and the scribes stood, vehemently accusing him. And Herod with his soldiers set him at naught, and mocked him, and arraying him in gorgeous apparel sent him back to Pilate. And Herod and Pilate became friends with each other that very day: for before they were at enmity between themselves.

1159-1162.

Interpretation

• Though it was morning symbolizing the dawn of new light Jesus' accusers were so steeped in intellectuality that they were unable to lay hold of a new inspiration but continued opposing the Christ.

• The activity of the chief priests and elders of the church symbolize intellectual quibbling bent on the destruction of Truth but at the same time trying to justify themselves.

• Pilate symbolizes the carnal will, the ruling principle over the sense plane. He represents that in individual consciousness which has not caught the light sufficiently to depend wholly upon the Spirit, but works to retain its worldly prestige. It questions, "Is there a ruling will over my religious nature?" I AM does not need to resort to outer methods of defending itself. It is Truth, and Truth abides. "And he questioned him in many words; but he answered him nothing."

• The personal will has no concept of the factors of that inner religious realm, and believes it is the ruler of the whole man. It is jealous of any attempt to usurp its power, but when it is assured that the kingdom which the higher self would rule is "not of this world." John 18: 36 it finds "in him no fault."

• Though Pilate cannot understand the case, he feels that Jesus I AM Presence and power should not be denied or put away killed. He seeks to set it free. He shifts the burden and turns Jesus over to Herod the ruling ego in sense consciousness.

• "And Pilate and Herod became friends with each other that very day." The personal will and sense consciousness have much in common, and are practically on the same plane of expression. They become friendly as like attracts like.

1163-1167.

Mat. 27:15-23

Now at the feast the governor was wont to release unto the multitude one prisoner, who they would. And they had there a notable prisoner called Barabbas. When therefore they were gathered together, Pilate said unto them, Whom will ye that I release unto you? Barabbas, or Jesus who is called Christ? For he knew that for envy they had delivered him up. And while he was sitting on the judgment seat, his wife sent unto him, saying, Have thou nothing to do with that righteous man; for I have suffered many things this day in a dream because of him. Now the chief priests and the elders persuaded the multitudes that they should ask for Barabbas, and destroy Jesus. But the governor answered and said unto them, Which of the two will ye that I release unto you? And they said, Barabbas. Pilate saith unto them, What then shall I do unto Jesus, who is called Christ? They all say, Let him be crucified. And he said, Why, what hath he done?

Luke 23:14b-23

Ye brought unto me this man, as one that perverteth the people: and behold, I, having examined him before you, found no fault in this man touching these things whereof ye accuse him: no, nor yet Herod: for he sent him back to us; and behold, nothing worthy hath been done by him. I will therefore chastise him, and release him. Now he must needs release unto them at the feast one prisoner. But they cried out altogether, saying, Away with this man, and release unto us Barabbas: one who for a certain insurrection made in the city, and for murder, was cast into prison. And Pilate spoke unto them again, desiring to release Jesus; but they shouted saying, Crucify him, crucify him. And he said unto them the third time, Why, what evil hath this man done? I have found no cause of death in him: I will therefore chastise him and release him. But they were urgent with loud voices, asking that he might be crucified. And their voices prevailed.

Mat. 27:24-25

So when Pilate say that he prevailed nothing, but rather that a tumult was arising, he took water, and washed his hands before the multitude, saying, I am innocent of the blood of this righteous man; see ye to it. And all the people answered and said, His blood be on us, and on our children.

Luke 23:24-25a

And Pilate gave sentence that what they asked for should be done. And he released him that for insurrection and murder had been cast into prison, whom they asked for;

Mat. 27:26b

but Jesus he scourged and delivered to be crucified.

1168-1170.

Interpretation

• The most powerful thought is that pertaining to religion. This is because it relates to that which is nearest to the source of being. A close analysis of the whole range of human life will reveal that religious convictions instigate and shape almost every act, for under the head of religion may be classed everything of a moral character.
• The I AM cannot be crucified or killed, but the consciousness that will not accept or advance to its higher concepts forces a temporary separation between itself and the I AM. But the mortal will Pilate having no inherent religious convictions, is loath to act upon the priestly promptings. It would stand aloof from all religious questions with the oft repeated assertion that civil law has nothing to do with religion.
• Pilate's wife represents that in consciousness that has in a measure received spiritual quickening, and seeks to protect spiritual man, or the Christ within, as best it can. "Have then nothing to do with that righteous man; for I have suffered many things this day in a dream because of him." The psychical nature may be spiritually awakened so that flashes of truth are revealed in dreams and visions, but have no enduring influence in consciousness.
• The intellectual man would rather let the lower forces of being Barabbas go free. He simply washes his hands of the whole affair. We know that Truth is the right way and like Pilate we say, "I find no cause of death in him;" but still we let the voice of the mob prevail and crucify our highest aspirations. But strive as we may, we cannot separate our acts from the promptings of spiritual thought. We are forced eventually to carry out in act the word of the I AM.

Mat. 27:27-31

Then the soldiers of the governor took Jesus into the Praetorium, and gathered unto him the whole band. And they stripped him, and put on him a scarlet robe. And they platted a crown of thorns and put it upon his head, and a reed in his right hand; and they kneeled down before him, and mocked him, saying, Hail, King of the Jews! And they spat upon him, and took the reed and smoot him on the head. And when they mocked him, they took off from him the robe, and put on him his garments, and led him away to crucify him.

Mark 15:21

And they compel one passing by, Simon of Cyrene, coming from the country, the father of Alexander and Rufus, to go with them, that he might bear his cross.

Interpretation

• Jesus had come into that place where He was to relinquish the old an enter into the kingdom of the heavens. This is accomplished not through dying but by becoming more and more alive, which is the last step in regeneration. The crucifixion is not a destructive process but a transforming process. The personal man Jesus has to give up entirely to the spiritual man Christ. The crucifixion is a great victory instead of a tragedy. The Adam man in Jesus was transformed into the Christ man, which made Jesus immortal. Before this He was still mortal man who had not attained immortality.

• Today those spiritually quickened souls who are working to lift up the Adam into spiritual consciousness come into trying experiences. But by faith and continuous application of the spiritual law, step by step they are gaining the mastery.

• As the mind is raised in power the body is also elevated and all the cells are quickened. The acceleration continues throughout the whole organism and the new man comes forth.

• When ice is melted into water the form changes but the essential elements are preserved. When water is changed is changed into steam nothing is lost but the power is much increased. By this same token each change that takes place in man's unfoldment is a forward step until the spiritual man comes forth in all his glory.

• Simon of Cyrene bore Jesus' cross for him. Cyrene refers to fixed states of thought in the realm of sense, and yet are illumined to the measure that they represent what we hope for and mentally see as possibilities in our lives. These thoughts in some degree help to relieve the pressure brought to bear by the intellectual man.

Luke 23:27-31

And there followed him a great multitude of the people, and of women who bewailed and lamented him. But Jesus turning unto them, said, Daughters of Jerusalem, weep not for me, but weep for yourselves, and for your children. For behold, the days are coming, in which they shall say, Blessed are the barren, and the wombs that never bare, and the breasts that never gave suck. Then shall they begin to say to the mountains, Fall on us; and to the hills, Cover us. For if they do these things in the green tree, what shall be done in the dry?

1176a,b-1177.

Interpretation

• In this scripture Jesus saw the effects that would follow when the spiritual life was killed about 500 years A. D.
• We point to the dark ages as that period in which the spiritual was obscured and
Jesus' followers persecuted, imprisoned, burned at the stake, destroyed in many ways.
• Just as the Christ was persecuted by the Jews, so the real Christians were persecuted by those who claimed to represent Christianity but were really barbarians.
• Metaphysically interpreted, this Scripture describes the experience of an individual who refuses to follow the inspiration and guidance of Spirit; a period of darkness overtakes him, and his spiritual nature suffers greatly as the result. The finer forces of soul are killed out.
• The great multitude of people who followed Jesus and the women who bewailed and lamented His situation symbolize a multitude of thoughts who bewail prevailing conditions but are not able to do anything about them. This state of consciousness naturally has many crosses to bear because it is not open and receptive to the working power of God's word.

1178-1181.

Mat. 27:33-34

And when they were come unto a place called Golgotha, that is to say, The place of a skull, they gave him wine to drink mingled with gall; and when he had tasted it, he would not drink.

Mark 15:25

And it was the third hour, and they crucified him.

Mat. 27:35-38

And when they had crucified him, they parted his garments among them, casting lots; and they sat and watched him there. And they set up over

his head his accusation written, THIS IS THE KING OF THE JEWS. Then ar
there crucified with him two robbers, one on the right hand, and one on the
left.

Luke 23:34a

And Jesus said, Father, forgive them; for they know not what they do

Mat. 27:39-43

And they that passed by railed on him, wagging their heads, and
saying, Thou that destroyest the temple, and buildest it in three days, save
thyself: if thou art the Son of God, come down from the cross. In like manne
also the chief priests mocking him, with the scribes and elders, said, He saved
others, himself he cannot save. He is the King of Israel. Let him now come
down from the cross, and we will believe on him. He trusteth on God; let him
deliver him now, if he desireth him: for he said, I am the Son of God.

Luke 23:39-43

And one of the malefactors that were hanged railed on him, saying,
Art thou not the Christ: save thyself and us. But the other answered, and
rebuking him said, Dost thou no even fear God, seeing thou art in the same
condamnation? And we indeed justly; for we receive the due reward of our
deeds: but this man hath done nothing amiss. And he said, Jesus, remember
me when thou comest in the kingdom. And he said unto him, Verily I say
unto the, Today shalt be with me in Paradise.

1182-118

Interpretation

•   The crucifixion represents the final erasure of error from
consciousness. Every time we give up an error, there is a crucifixion. When w
are willing to surrender all evil and retain only the good, the death on the
cross is accomplished. In consciously giving up the whole error mentality, ma
does not die, but the false ego adversity that has entered the human and
become part of the consciousness is fully eradicated.
•   Golgotha is a place just outside of Jerusalem, a hill, where Jesus was
crucified. It is also called Calvary. The name Golgotha in the Aramaic-Jewish
language, means "place of the skull." This is suggestive of the place where
intellect is crossed out, that Spirit man win an eternal ascendancy. Jesus the
intellectual was crucified at the place of the skull, that Christ Truth might
become all in all.
•   The seamless robe represents Truth in its harmonious expression and
unchangeable perfection. The superscription written over Jesus in three
languages, "THIS IS THE KING OF THE JEWS," is indicative of the ruling
power of the principles enunciated by this great King of men. Greek was the
language of literature and of culture; Latin was the language of the soldiers
and officers of Rome; Hebrew was the language of the Jews, or religion. The

use of these three languages indicates the universality of the Word of the Great One, which goes forth to the world and reaches people in Spirit, soul, and body.

• Those that passed by railed at Jesus, saying, "Thou that destroyeth the temple, and buildest it in three days, save thyself, and come down from the cross." They did not know that He was talking about His body-temple instead of the temple of Jerusalem. He knew of a way of restoring life which others in His day did not know, and He tried to explain it to them, but they did not understand.

• The two malefactors crucified with Him, represent the past and the future. The past is full of regrets and accusations, but the future is hopeful and sees good ahead in spite of the great trial at hand. This is commended by the Christ and promise of reward is made.

1186-1188.

Luke 23: 44-45a

And it was now about the sixth hour, and a darkness came over the whole land until the ninth hour, the sun's light failing:

Mat. 27: 46-50

And about the ninth hour Jesus cried with a loud voice, saying, Eli, Eli, lama sabachthani? that is, My God, my God, why hast thou forsaken me? And some of them that stood there, when they heard it, said, This man calleth Elijah. And straightway one of them ran, and took a sponge, and filled it with vinegar, and put it on a reed, and gave him to drink. And the rest said, Let be; let us see whether Elijah cometh to save him. And Jesus cried again with a loud voice, and yielded up his spirit.

Mat. 27:51-54

And behold, the veil of the temple was rent in two from the top to the bottom; and the earth did quake; and the rocks were rent; and the tombs were opened; and many bodies of the saints that had fallen asleep were raised; and the coming forth out of the tombs after his resurrection they entered into the holy city and appeared unto many. Now the centurion, and they that were with him watching Jesus, when they saw the earthquake, and the things that were done, feared exceedingly, saying, Truly this was the Son of God.

Mark 15:40-41

And there were also women beholding from afar: among whom were both Mary Magdalene, and Mary the mother of James the less and of Joses, and Salome; who, when he was in Galilee, followed him, and ministered unto him; and many other women that came up with him from Jerusalem.

Interpretation

• Like all the other allegories of Jesus' life, the death on the cross is less important as a historical event than it is as the demonstration of an experience common to all men who are passing from the human to the divine. We have our crucifixions, deaths, and burials, yet none of them is real when we believe in the power of the one life to save up to the uttermost.

• Jesus' words, "My God, my God, why hast thou forsaken me?" symbolize the struggle and the passing away of the very last of the natural state of consciousness in Jesus.

• After Jesus was resurrected, all these sleeping thoughts were also resurrected with Him. In individual consciousness we have buried away in the subconscious mind saintly thoughts. When the Christ is in authority there is a general illumination and the resurrection of spiritual thoughts takes place. These saintly thoughts symbolize in the newly resurrected man the abiding consciousness of spiritual peace, which is the result of continuous realizations of spiritual power and confidence tempered with spiritual poise and peace.

• The darkness and the rending of the temple veil represent the failure in understanding that sweeps over the soul in times of great trial, and the letting go of the idea of the reality of material consciousness. The relinquishment of the soul to God is the final giving up of all human ambitions and aims. When this point is reached, the soul enters into glory.

• The "women beholding from afar" symbolize witnesses who on future occasions would be able to testify to the validity of Jesus' apparent death and His resurrection.

Mark 15:42-43a

And when even was now come because it was the Preparation, that is, the day before the Sabbath, there came Joseph of Arimathaea, a councilor of honorable estate:

Mat. 27:57b

who also himself was Jesus' disciple,

Mark 15:43b-46a

looking for the kingdom of God; and he boldly went in unto Pilate, and asked for the body of Jesus.

Mark 15:44-46

And Pilate marveled if he were already dead: and calling unto him the centurion, he asked him whether he had been any while dead. And when he learned it of the centurion, he granted the corpse to Joseph. And he bought a linen cloth, and taking him down, wound him in the linen cloth,

Luke 23:53b

and laid him in a tomb that was hewn in stone, where never Man had yet lain.

Mat. 27:60b-61

and he rolled a great stone to the door of the tomb, and departed. And Mary Magdalene was there, and the other Mary, sitting over against the sepulcher.

1194-1195.

Interpretation

• The Preparation refers to the observances preliminary to the celebration of the Jewish Sabbath, or to the festival, the day before the Sabbath. Among the Jews there was a law to the effect that the lifeless body should not remain upon the cross on the Sabbath, as this was a day set aside for rest and freedom from all troubled or contentious thoughts. Therefore, when the centurion assured Pilate that Jesus had been a while dead, "he granted the corpse to Joseph."

• Joseph of Arimathaea symbolizes a high lofty state of consciousness that recognizes the Christ. His tomb represents an elevated, peaceful state of consciousness in which Jesus rested the three days previous to His resurrection.

• The stone was rolled against the door of the tomb to insure against all disturbing outer powers.

1196-1197.

Mat. 27:62-66

Now on the morrow, which is the day after the preparation, the chief priests and the Pharisees were gathered together unto Pilate, saying, Sir, we remember that that deceiver said while he was yet alive, After three days I rise again. Command therefore that the sepulchre be made sure until the third day, lest haply his disciples come and steal him away, and say unto the people, He is risen from the dead: and the last error will be worse than the first. Pilate said unto them, Ye have a guard: go, make it as sure as ye can. So they went, and made the sepulcher sure, sealing the stone, the guard being with them.

The reasoning, intellectual man always endeavors to make sureness doubly sure. The tomb was sealed to guard against fraudulent methods to satisfy their distrustful nature.

CHAPTER 7

RESURRECTION-ASCENSION

1198-1201.

Mat. 28:2-3

And behold, there was a great earthquake; for an angel of the Lord descended from heaven, and came and rolled away the stone, and sat upon it. His appearance was as lightning, and his raiment white as snow:

Mark 16:1-4

And when the Sabbath was past, Mary Magdalene, and Mary the mother of James, and Salome, bought spices, that they might come and anoint him. And very early on the first day of the week, they come to the tomb when the sun was risen. And they were saying among themselves, Who shall roll us away the stone from the door of the tomb? And looking up, they see that the stone is rolled back; for it was exceeding great.

Luke 24:3-7

And they entered in, and found not a body of the Lord Jesus. And it came to pass, while they were perplexed thereabout, behold, two men stood by them in dazzling apparel: and as they were affrighted and bowed down their faces to the earth, they said unto them, Why seek ye the living among the dead? He is not here, but is risen: remember how he spoke unto you when he was yet in Galilee, saying that the Son of man must be delivered up into the hands of sinful Men, and be crucified, and the third day rise again.

Mat. 28:7b-10

go quickly, and tell his disciples, He is risen from the dead; and lo, he goeth before you into Galilee; there shall ye see him: lo, I have told you. And they departed quickly from the tomb with fear and great joy, and ran to bring his disciples word. And behold, Jesus met them, saying, All hail. And they came and took hold of his feet, and worshiped him. Then saith Jesus unto them, Fear not; go tell my brethren that they depart into Galilee, and there shall they see me.

Luke 24:10-12

Now they were Mary Magdalene, and Joanna, and Mary the mother of James: and the other women with them told these things unto the apostles. And these words appeared in their sight as idle talk; and they disbelieved them. But Peter arose, and ran unto the tomb; and stooping and looking in, he seeth the linen cloths by themselves; and he departed to his home, wondering at that which was come to pass.

Interpretation

• The weeping Mary and the sad disciples looking into the tomb for their living Master, represent the forgetfulness of sense consciousness. Jesus plainly taught that He would rise from the dead, yet His disciples forgot this, and sought amongst the dead for the living. The church is looking into the tomb for the victorious Jesus while it teaches that He was crucified and He "died" on the cross. Through the quickening within of the Christ consciousness of life, we enter into life.

• The resurrection is the lifting up of the whole man—spirit, soul, and body—into the Christ consciousness. The resurrection lifts up all the faculties of mind until they conform to the absolute ideas of Divine Mind, and this renewal of the mind makes a complete transformation of the body so that the renewing of every function takes place daily in all who are conforming their lives to the regenerating Truth of Jesus Christ. The resurrection takes place here and now in all who conform their lives to the spiritual law under which it works.

• Death does not change man and bring him into the resurrection and eternal life. Death has no place in the Absolute. It is the result of sin, and has no uplifting power. Everyone who has reaped sin's wages must be restored to his place in the race, that he may have a body through which to work out his salvation under divine law.

• Old limited personal relationships do not continue in the resurrection. Those who are being raised into the Christ consciousness will gradually, as their growth in understanding makes it possible, let go all that is personal and selfish in their relationships and come into the larger love, the love universal, where all who do the will of God are fathers and mothers and sisters and brothers. The divine law is fulfilled by the love universal.

Mat. 28:11-15

Now while they were going, behold, some of the guard came into the city, and told unto the chief priests all the things that were come to pass. And when they were assembled with the elders, and had taken counsel, they gave much money unto the soldiers, saying, Say ye, His disciples came by night, and stole him away while we slept. And if this come to the governor's ears, we will persuade him, and rid him of care. So they took the money, and did as they were taught; and this saying was spread abroad among the Jews, and continueth until this day.

Interpretation

• The soldiers and the guards here represent forces within the consciousness that carry out the dictates of their superior, which in this case was the high priest intellectuality. These forces became frightened and returned unto the priest in authority. When intellectual thoughts are trapped they resort to falsehood and trickery to save themselves, which of course ends in defeat.

1208-1211.

Luke 24:13-35

And behold, two of them were going that very day to a village named Emmaus, which was threescore furlongs from Jerusalem. And they communed with each other of all these things which had happened. And it came to pass, while they communed and questioned together, that Jesus himself drew near, and went with them. But their eyes were holden that they should not know him. And he said unto them, What communications are these that ye have one with another, as ye walk? And they stood still, looking sad. And one of them, called Cleopas, answering said unto him, Dost thou alone sojourn in Jerusalem and not know the things which are come to pass there in these days? And he said unto them, What things? And they said unto him, The things concerning Jesus the Nazarene, who was a prophet mighty in deed and word before God and all the people: And how the chief priests and our rulers delivered him up to be condemned to death, and crucified him. But we hoped that it was he who should redeem Israel. Yea and besides all this, it is now the third day since these things came to pass. Moreover certain women of our company amazed us, having been early at the tomb; and when they found not his body, they came, saying, that they had also seen a vision of angels, who said that he was alive. And certain of them that were with us went to the tomb, and found it even so as the women had said: but him they saw not. And he said unto them, O foolish men, and slow of heart to believe in all that the prophets have spoken! Behooved it not the Christ to suffer these things, and to enter into his glory? And beginning from Moses and from all the prophets, he interpreted to them in all the scriptures the things concerning himself. And they drew nigh unto the village, whither they were going: and he made as though he would go further. And they constrained him, saying, Abide with us; for it is toward evening, and the day is now far spent. And he went in to abide with them.

And it came to pass, when he had sat down with them to meat, he took bread and blessed; and breaking it he gave to them. And their eyes were opened, and they knew him; and he vanished out of their sight. And they said one to another, Was not our heart burning within us, while he spoke to us in the way, while he opened to us the scriptures? And they rose up that very hour, and returned to Jerusalem, and found the eleven gathered together, and them that were with them, saying, The Lord is risen indeed, and hath appeared to Simon. And they rehearsed the things that happened in the way, and how he was known of them in the breaking of the bread.

1212-1222.

Interpretation

• These two converts of Jesus were on their way to Emmaus. The name Emmaus means "warm springs." Emmaus represents a place in consciousness where the healing, restoring life and love and Truth of Spirit spring up and flow freely through man's being.

• The two converts represent two states of mind not yet fully awakened. They could not understand complete body renewal. They still believed in the material consciousness, and when it was crossed out crucified , their hopes were shattered. This breaking up of the material must follow the consciousness of spiritual substance. The two believers were receptive and they were deeply interested. They were communing with each other concerning the experiences that had taken place, but they had not yet conceived of the body as spiritual substance. Jesus Christ, the ideal man, walked with them. He caused them to understand how, from Moses and all the prophets unto Jesus, one round after another of the ladder which extends from earth to heaven, from material to spiritual consciousness, had been climbed, until the very last one had been reached in the complete resurrection of the body into immortality.

• These two believers had walked and talked with Jesus. They had seen his works and had heard His teaching, but they had never affirmed as their own the truth that He had taught; they had not entered into the real understanding that comes through individual appropriation of spiritual substance and life—the real essence and meaning of the body and blood of Jesus Christ.

• These two followers of Jesus did not know the risen Lord until He made Himself known to them by blessing the bread and breaking it for them. Then their eyes were opened. The bread represented the pure spiritual substance of the resurrected body. By positive affirmations we must all appropriate life, substance, and Truth as ours individually, and as the very foundation and substance of our bodies. Then the blinded states of consciousness in us, represented by the two with whom Jesus walked to Emmaus, will be given sight; they will understand the resurrection and the renewal that are going on daily throughout our entire being—spirit, soul, and body—as we lay hold of the abiding, quickening life and substance of Spirit through faith and affirmation.

• Thousands in this day have found the law which Jesus demonstrated and the inner meaning of the Truth that He taught. They are working, praying, denying, affirming, concentrating, willing. They are in all ways building up the perfect body idea, transforming flesh corruptible into substance incorruptible; thus they are following Jesus in the regeneration. When they have renewed every organ and every part, both within and without, and have put away all evidences of old age, then the world-at-large will begin to accept their claims as true.

• The resurrection of Jesus is a great mystery, and to those who read the Bible in the letter and have no discernment of the power of Spirit to transform the body, it must remain a mystery. The question often is asked whether or not we believe that Jesus rose from the dead with the same body in which He walked the earth, and if so, what became of that body.

• In former times believers accepted it as a miracle and made no attempt to explain the law by which it was accomplished, but blind faith is not so popular in the church as it once was, and skeptics are more bold. The school of "higher criticism" is openly attacking Bible occurrences that it cannot account for under natural law. Thinking people are seeking a comprehensive explanation of the so-called miracles of the Bible. They wish to know how Jesus did His mighty works, including the resurrection of His body. The historical account makes clear that the body which had been crucified was the body which Jesus had after the resurrection.

• That Jesus knew how to restore life to dead organs is evidenced by His healing paralytics, blind people, and, in three cases, raising those who had died. He knew a way of restoring life which others living in His age did not know. He tried to explain it to His disciples and companions, but they did not understand. He told them that He would be crucified and that He would come to life again, but they seemed to have no comprehension of what He was saying. They thought He was telling them about the temple at Jerusalem, but He was talking of His body temple, which He could lay down and take up at will.

• It is not surprising that the very near friends of Jesus were filled with astonishment and fear, when they found that He was not in the tomb where they had laid Him. They could not understand that for years He had been training His soul to accomplish this very thing. But He had spent whole nights in prayer, and through the intensity of His devotions had made union with divine mind. This union was so full and so complete that His whole being was flooded with spiritual life, power, substance, and the wisdom to use them in divine order. In this manner He projected the divine body idea, and through it His mortal body was transformed into an immortal body. This was accomplished before the crucifixion, and Jesus knew that He had so strengthened His soul that it would restore His body, no matter how harshly the body might be used by destructive men.

• Jesus had obtained power on the three planes of consciousness: spiritual, psychical, and material. After His resurrection He held His body on the psychical and the astral planes for forty days, and then transmuted it to the spiritual, where it exists to this day as a body of thought and mind force. Having a body of thought, Jesus was able to quicken the bodies of people who attract His power by believing in Him; as a body of force, He energizes those who believe in His power.

Luke 24:36-45

And as they spoke these things, he himself stood in the midst of them and saith unto them, Peace be unto you. But they were terrified and affrighted, and supposed that they beheld a spirit. And he said unto them, Why are ye troubled? And wherefore do questionings arise in your heart? See my hands and my feet, that it is I myself: handle me, and see; for a spirit hath not flesh and bones, as ye behold me having. And when he had said this, he showed them his hands and his feet. And while they still disbelieved for joy, and wondered, he said unto them, Have ye here anything to eat? And they gave him a piece of broiled fish. And he took it, and ate before them. And he said unto them, These are my words which I spoke unto you, while I was yet with you, that all things must needs be fulfilled, which are written in the law of Moses, and the prophets, and the psalms, concerning me. Then opened he their mind, that they might understand the scriptures.

Interpretation

• Jesus stood before His disciples clothed in His body temple of pure spiritual substance.
• Evidence revealed the truths that man has power to demonstrate over death; to resurrect His body, transmute every cell and fiber from flesh into spiritual substance, which is eternal, deathless. Interpreted within the consciousness of man, the I AM here represented by the resurrected Jesus is endeavoring to reveal to man's spiritual faculties his disciples the resurrecting power of divine law. We perceive that step by step or by precept upon precept the indwelling I AM or Christ leads us from that which we know to be true into what seems at first a miracle. It is after this manner that we are unfolding the spiritual faculties of the immortal soul. "Handle me, and see; for a spirit hath not flesh and bones." "Have ye anything to eat? And they gave him a piece of broiled fish. And he took it, and ate before them."
• Our faculties open themselves to Spirit to the degree that they can see the outworking of the law, which is always governed by the orderly procedure of the principle of being.

Luke 24:46-49

and he said unto them, Thus it is written, that the Christ should suffer and rise again from the dead the third day; and that repentance and remission of sins should be preached in his name unto all the nations, beginning from Jerusalem. Ye are witnesses of these things. And behold, I send forth the promise of my Father upon you: but tarry ye in the city, until ye be clothed with power from on high.

Interpretation

• In race evolution it is observed that certain types clarify to their environment long after it has lost its usefulness.
• So in this very radical advance from the degenerate man to the regenerate Christ was a tremendous step in soul evolution. Those who understood anticipated the rebellion that would take place. The church especially was jealous of its privileges and resented any change or limitation of its power. Jesus saw all this, yet he realized it was his destiny to go through with it regardless of consequences which He did.
• He was crucified because of His ideals and demonstrations of the superman. He had gained the power over mortal man to rise above all limitations, and proved man was destined to be immortal and overcome death.

Mark 10:12-13

And after these things he was manifested in another form unto two of them, as they walked, on their way into the country. And they went away and told it unto the rest: neither believed they them.

Interpretation

Jesus was "manifested in another form unto two of them," who were walking into the country. They told of seeing Him, but again no one believed them. This reveals that the people still believed in the materiality of life, and their hopes were shattered when Jesus was crucified. They did not understand complete body renewal.

Mat. 28:16-17

But the eleven disciples went into Galilee, unto the mountain where Jesus had appointed them. And when they saw him, they worshiped him; but some doubted.

Mark 14b-18

and he upbraided them with their unbelief and hardness of heart, because they believed not them that had seen him after he was risen. And he said unto them, Go ye into all the world, and preach the gospel to the whole creation. He that believeth and is baptized shall be saved; but he that disbelieveth shall be condemned. And these signs shall accompany them that believe: in my name shall they cast out demons; they shall speak with new tongues; And they shall take up serpents, and if they drink any deadly thing, it shall in no wise hurt them; they shall lay hands on the sick, and they shall recover.

1235-123

Interpretation

• Later Jesus manifested Himself to the eleven, and He upbraided ther for disbelieving the accounts of His resurrection. He commissioned His followers to make disciples of all the nations.
• In order to make the world Christian, individuals must become Christian. The Christ Spirit must enter every one. Christ is knocking at the door of every heart, and He will enter when He is invited to come in. When a men become open and receptive to the Christ Truth, the Christ kingdom will be established in the earth.
• Jesus told His disciples to cast out demons in His name, to take up serpents and be unhurt, to lay hands on the sick and they would recover. Whenever the Truth is declared in the name of Jesus Christ, the demons of fear and disease are cast out.

123

Mat. 28:18b-20

All authority hath been given unto me in heaven and on earth. Go ye therefore, and make disciples of all the nations, baptizing them in the name o the Father and of the Son and of the Holy Spirit: teaching them to observe al things whatsoever I commanded you: and lo, I am with you always, even unt the end of the world.

(Note: This interpretation (1238-39) also appears in MYSTERIES OF JOHN, but was O.K.'d by Cora.)

1238-123

Interpretation

• Christianity began with Jesus Christ, was carried on by the apostles and the seventy whom Jesus sent out two by two, then by other persons as they came into understanding of Truth. This process of Christianizing will continue until the entire race is redeemed from error. Even so, as the truth i: taught to our faculties, our senses, and our thoughts, they in turn give light and life to the remaining thoughts and parts of our organisms which are still in darkness. In this way the entire man will become established in immortality—eternal life.
• This commission was given to them on a mountain in Galilee. A mountain always symbolizes a high place in consciousness, or spiritual elevation. When the spiritually awakened and spiritually taught faculties and thoughts assemble with the I AM in spiritual consciousness, they are sent throughout the entire man to the very outermost parts of body consciousness.

Luke 24: 50-51

And he led them out until they were ever against Bethany: and he lifted up his hands and blessed them. And it came to pass, while he blessed them, he parted from them, and was carried up into heaven.

Mark 16:19b

and sat down at the right hand of God.

Luke 24:52-53

And they worshipped him, and returned to Jerusalem with great joy: and were continually in the temple, blessing God.

Mark 16:20

And they went forth, and preached everywhere, the Lord working with them, and confirming the word by the signs that followed, Amen.

1242.

Interpretation

Metaphysically interpreted within ourselves, Jesus symbolized the indwelling Christ which withdraws to the super-consciousness Mind. Sitting at the right hand of God symbolizes the executive power of the indwelling Christ. From this high vantage point, it is enabled to work with the disciples man's faculties and aid them in all ways.

ABOUT THE AUTHOR ~ EDITOR

Rev. Toni G. Boehm, Ph.D., is an ordained Unity minister, nurse practitioner, author &/or editor of 12 books, a mystic, and master facilitator of energy.

It was through the teachings of Charles Fillmore that her life was transformed dramatically, and the path of mysticism and energy work opened for her.

Boehm is the recipient of the Charles Fillmore, life-time achievement award for visionary leadership.

Endnotes from Introduction by Rev. Toni G. Boehm, Ph.D.

NOTE: For ease these were inserted at the end of the Introduction

---

[i] Unity South East Region Annual Conference. October, 2009.

[ii] Unity Library Archives is located in the Education building on grounds at Unity Village, MO. It is one of the largest metaphysical libraries in the United States.

[iii] Weekly Unity...

[iv] Unity healing revival

[v] Beginners Healing Pamphlet

[vi] 1923 conference talk

[vii] UCC

[viii] Regeneration, March 1933 March 29, 1930

Made in the USA
Coppell, TX
14 November 2023

24224076R00134